APPROACHING
THE TREE

Interpreting 1 Nephi 8

Permissions. No portion of this book may be reproduced by any means or process without the formal written consent of the publisher. Direct all permissions requests to Permissions Manager, Neal A. Maxwell Institute for Religious Scholarship, Brigham Young University, Provo, UT 84602 or email: MIpermissions@byu.edu

The paper used in this publication meets the minimum requirements of the American National Standards for Information Sciences—Permanence of Paper for Printed Library Materials. ANSI Z39.48-19

ISBN: 978-0-8425-0059-3

Library of Congress Control Number: 2023945750

(CIP data on file)

Book and Cover Design: Kelly Nield, Hales Creative

Cover Art: J. Kirk Richards, *Pulling Up the Iron Rod*

Printed in the United States of America

APPROACHING
THE TREE

Interpreting 1 Nephi 8

EDITED BY

Benjamin Keogh | Joseph M. Spencer | Jennifer Champoux

2023

Contents

Joy Nevada, *Lehi's Dream*, digital chalk drawing, 2021.

Introduction

APPEARING EARLY AND OFTEN IN BOOK OF MORMON-INSPIRED ART, the tree at the centre of Lehi's dream, found in 1 Nephi 8, is perhaps the text's most famous image. In Latter-day Saint classrooms, illustrations of the dream's path, rod, tree, and building are routinely used to instruct rising generations. The static landscape and one-to-one-correlations of these chalk-board reproductions are perhaps a major reason why the shifting landscapes and undefined images of Lehi's dream appear to have a stable interpretation. Compared to encounters with other scriptural texts, the uniformity of the dream scene's interpretation can be jarring. And yet, as this work demonstrates, the dream has always spoken in a variety of ways to its readers who have produced interpretations in art and print. By situating ourselves in this rich tradition we aim to aid a deepening engagement with scripture. Texts, like events, require interpretation—and both texts and events can sustain multiple interpretations. When engaged together this variety forms a tapestry that gives one a greater view of the whole precisely because the green is not blue, and the blue is not red.

Consider, for example, the four narratives about Jesus that open the New Testament. Each begins in a different way. Where Matthew and Luke lead with distinct tellings of his birth, Mark dives straight into his baptism, disregarding his birth altogether. John reaches back to the very beginning in order to identify Jesus with the Word. There is also variety in each Gospel's conclusion. John finishes his narrative on the shore by the sea of Tiberias with Peter thrice declaring his love. Mark, originally, ended with three terrified women fleeing an empty tomb. Luke concludes with ascension at Bethany, while Matthew's final word is the great commission on a Galilean mountain. Further, between beginnings and endings, there is variance both in the stories told and in how those stories are used. For many, these differences require an explanation.

To this explanatory challenge, readers have risen. Some have suggested the intended audience of a particular Gospel can account for these differences. Others have found an explanation in the portrait of Jesus a particular Gospel aims at. Yet others have pointed to the time of writing or the interests and social location of the writers themselves. In the offered reasons, the variety of suggested explanations for differences between the Gospels has proliferated. To some, that scholars can work with the same texts and survey the same documents yet come to different conclusions is perplexing. This phenomenon is expertly unpacked by the German theologian Gerhard Lohfink. He suggests a thought experiment wherein one imagines the New Testament Gospels were never written. Instead, the entirety of Jesus' ministry is captured on camera and presented unedited. If the circumstances of this thought experiment prevailed, what we would have is unfiltered access to the ministry of Jesus. To this, Lohfink asks a penetrating question: if this was the case, what would we know? In response, he suggests we would have access to any number of historical details, what Peter's house looked like, what first-century Aramaic sounded like, and the detail of Sabbath worship in Capernaum. In addition, we'd have unfiltered access to every word of Jesus, and be witnesses to his miracles, seeing the sick healed, the lame walk, and the blind see. And of course, we would see Jesus himself. The sight of him—a near Eastern, first-century Jewish man—Lohfink suggests, would probably surprise us. While we'd have access to his every word, only a few specialists would be able to understand his Aramaic, and we would sense that he lived at a very different time and in a very different culture from ours in the twenty-first century.

With this established, Lohfink returns to his question: what would we know? And more particularly, "Would we know more than what the gospels already tell us?"[1] In one sense, as we have seen, the answer is clearly yes. In another, more important and fundamental sense, Lohfink suggests, the answer is no—and not only would we not know more, we would know much less. This is the case, Lohfink explains, because "if no interpretation is given to an external event it cannot tell us anything."[2] Bare facts, as the unedited life of Jesus in this thought experiment would be, Lohfink suggests, are not yet history. "History is interpreted event."[3] And in this scenario, with no Gospels, what we'd have is the life of Jesus as an uninterpreted event and therefore, Lohfink concludes, "we would know *nothing* of what really matters about Jesus."[4] For Lohfink, it is because the New Testament Gospel writers interpret the "bare facts" of the events of Jesus' life that Gospel readers can know what these events are supposed to convey: that Jesus is the Son of God, the Redeemer and Reconciler of the world. And yet, amongst the four Gospels, interpretative variation remains. Paula Fredriksen, for example, locates variation in the Gospel accounts in their theologies of Jesus. John's Jesus she terms "The Stranger from Heaven," Luke's "The Messiah of the Gentiles," Matthew's "The Christ of the Scriptures," and Mark's "The Secret Messiah."[5] In this way, she makes clear that what the respective Gospel writers want to convey about the meaning of the events of Jesus' life accounts for the difference in their presentation at least as much as the social and historical context of their writing. Or, from another perspective, one might say that the social and historical context of their writing influences the emphasis of their interpretation. For example, Matthew's focus on Jesus as "The Christ of the Scriptures" may be explained by his audience of Jewish Christians, as Luke's focus on "The Messiah of the Gentiles" is by his audience of Gentile Christians. What is true of the writing of scriptural texts is also true of the interpreting of scriptural texts. For example, Donald Baillie, a twentieth-century Scottish theologian, has observed that in our reading of the New Testament "we can only say that 'God was in Christ' in that great atoning sacrifice." That there "is in the New Testament no uniformity of conception as to *how* this sacrifice brings about reconciliation."[6] Thus while it is generally agreed that atonement aims at reconciliation and renewed relationship, there is no agreement as to the manner of its outworking. It is this that gives rise to the variety of accounts of atonement that attempt to explain how reconciliation is affected.[7] Each account is developed from scripture, and each has commendable things to contribute to an understanding of Christ's work. However, none has proved sufficient. Neither can they be entirely reconciled.

As has been hinted at, part of what lies behind the variety of theological explanations is, again, the diversity of scripture. While theological presuppositions may shape how one approaches atonement, so does the variety of images used in scripture to portray it. It is on this basis that Ben Pugh's aptly named *Pictures of Atonement: A New Testament Study* surveys six such New Testament images, showcasing pictorial language as that which is most often used by the writers of the New Testament in depicting atonement.[8] Ranging from diplomatic treaties and prophetic lawsuits to temple courts and slave markets, and from imperial victory processions to dying and rising deities, scripture provides many ways of imagining redemption through Jesus. And yet these images are themselves multivocal, with any particular image having the potential to provoke a variety of understandings. It is through this variety in scripture that a variety of accounts of Christian salvation emerge.

What then is one to make of the interpretive proliferation and multiplicity occasioned by scriptural texts? If one considers again the example of Matthew and Luke and the respective communities for which their Gospels were intended one can say at least these two things. First, that variety in the presentation of Jesus is necessary if all are to come to recognise him as God's Christ. And second, that variety in the presentation of Jesus is necessary if all are to properly understand what it means for him to be God's Christ. Matthew's audience may not have recognised a presentation of the Messiah of the Gentiles, and Luke's audience may not have understood a presentation of the Christ of the Jewish Scriptures, even as both are accurate depictions of who Jesus is. Similarly, to describe Jesus as the Messiah of the Gentiles is true, but not exhaustively so. Jesus is also the Christ of Jewish Scripture. Ultimately, recognition of him as one aids recognition of him as the other, and together they provide a more complete account of who Jesus is—even as there may be elements of their particular presentations that cannot be entirely reconciled.

In the case of atonement specifically, engaging with the proliferation of images and the multiplicity of accounts has a similar function. No one image, no one account can exhaustively express the totality of the meaning of Christ's work. When followed through, this thought suggests that images and accounts in their plurality—even when they cannot be entirely reconciled—allow God's purposes to be more fully displayed. In the case of scriptural variety more generally, it may be that scripture's variety and interpretative multiplicity provides a window into the expansiveness of God's relating, suggesting it is not one-size-fits-all.

Considering the benefits of the multiplicity of interpretative approaches to biblical images throws the general uniformity in the interpretation of Lehi's dream scene into sharp relief. Of course, these chalkboard correlations are not plucked from the air. Rather, their identifications are taken from Nephi's reporting of a prophetic vision of his own. There, Lehi's tree is identified with the tree of life, Lehi's rod of iron with the word of God, and Lehi's building with the pride of the world. Yet even as Nephi provides these interpretations, he subtly warns against taking too narrow a view. For example, by reporting that he saw not the tree of his father's dream but a tree *"like unto* the tree which my father had seen" (1 Ne. 11:8, emphasis added), Nephi subtly distinguishes his experience from his father's. As his vision continues, it may be Nephi learns an important justification for seeing his own tree: the tree, he discovers, "is the love of God" (1 Ne. 11:22). If God is a loving being, then God is a relational being. Love, as an emotion oriented towards others, requires the existence of others in order to be experienced or expressed. Love, that is, presupposes relationship, and one's relationships with others are as diverse as the others involved. Thus, while God's love sheds "itself abroad in the hearts of the children of men" (1 Ne. 11:22), each necessarily experiences that love uniquely. As with the trees of Nephi and Lehi, individual experiences of God's love are *like unto*, not the *same as*.

Associating the tree with Christ sharpens the point, as it suggests an encounter with the tree is an experience of redemption. Given the many ways in which we are disrelated and, therefore, the very particular ways we each require redemption, the redemptive experience must also be as individual as we are. It, too, will be *like unto*, but not the *same as* another's redemptive experience. This gets towards what Theodore Vial means when he describes religion, in its essence, as "an experience of the infinite" and theology as the "attempt to express this experience in as adequate a language as possible."[9] Yet for each, the experience and expression will vary. From this it follows that individual encounters with the texts of redemption—scripture both biblical and uniquely Latter-day Saint—will elicit a variety of experiences expressed in a variety of ways.

The present volume proceeds on this basis. Allowing Nephi's "like unto" to guide experiences with and expressions of Lehi's dream, it gathers a variety of essays and artworks focused on 1 Nephi 8. In its conception, the project takes inspiration from Rabbi Lawrence Kushner's remarkable book, *God Was in This Place & I, i Did Not Know*. Kushner's whole focus is on the twelve words the biblical patriarch Jacob speaks in Genesis 28:16 after waking from his famous dream of a ladder reaching to heaven. In conversation with the rabbinic commentators, Kushner provides seven different readings of Jacob's words. While these various readings cannot be entirely reconciled, each "is clearly supported by the text," and each "is coherent, self-contained, and convincing."[10] Each throws light upon the text. Here, with our focus on the text of 1 Nephi 8, we follow Kushner in providing original readings of a single text. These too are supported by the text, and are internally coherent and self-contained, while convincingly interpreting the text. As with Kushner's project, that any one particular reading convincingly makes sense of the text does not mean that any two of them can be entirely reconciled. However, again as with Kushner's project, each throws light upon the text. Or, to return to the metaphor of the tapestry, while one reading may weave in red thread, another may weave in blue, another in green, and another in purple, their differences add texture to the whole. For Kushner "the holy words" of scripture "are intimately related not only to what God means but even to who God is."[11] In this volume, therefore, we have asked our theological interpreters to conclude their essays with a reflection on the kind of God their reading reveals. Here, we follow in the wake of Terence Fretheim's challenging opening to his influential book, *The Suffering of God*: "It is not enough to say," Fretheim writes, "that one believes in God. What is important finally is the *kind* of God in whom one believes." This is so he suggests, and we concur, because those beliefs "have a powerful impact on the shape of the life of the believer."[12] All theology is ultimately practical, lived out in the arena of everyday lives. Here an adequate expression on the page is one that benefits the community in its attempts to live as Christians.

In a departure from the style of Kushner's project, we have added artistic engagements to literary and theological investigations. Alongside the writings of scholars whose work appears in the chapters making up this book, nine artists have contributed new work on Lehi's dream. Its presence here is a gift that demonstrates art's potency as a valid form of theological interpretation, raising the number of theological interactions with 1 Nephi 8 to sixteen. Further, hoping to place our project within a larger interpretive context, we have included two historical studies. The first surveys how Latter-day Saint scholars have read Lehi's dream in the past; the second, how Latter-day Saint artists have depicted the dream. Together they make clear that the kinds of readings set forth here, both verbal and visual, find their place in a long history of interactions with the sacred text.

Naturally, some might worry that in gathering so many readings we needlessly (and perhaps confusingly) multiply interpretations. Some might, that is, object that a text cannot be made to mean *just anything*. Their objection would be correct. And yet, that a text cannot mean anything at all does not preclude it from meaning multiple things. Texts require interpretation and in leaning into the variety of multiple interpretations we find a depth of meaning and real existential force. We, therefore, take the position asserted by many theorists of interpretation that while a text "will always be to some degree open-ended," its "never-changing words on the page provide constraints."[13] Rather than multiplying interpretations, then, we aim to take the text, and its circumscription, seriously. We are confident the Book of Mormon can sustain robust theological examination, and we trust that it has serious *things* to say about the experience of redemption.

In that spirit, the invitation we make through *Approaching the Tree* is to view Lehi's dream and the text of 1 Nephi 8 again and again. Repeatedly. How does it look through the eyes of imaginative artists—J. Kirk Richards, Rose Datoc Dall, Megan Knobloch Geilman, Sarah Winegar, Hildebrando de Melo, Caitlin Connolly, José de Faria, Annie Poon, and Kathleen Peterson? And how does it read under the gaze of theological interpreters? To explore with Benjamin Keogh what happens when Lehi is re-placed at the centre of the dream? To contemplate with Rosalynde Welch the effect of reading the dream's central images through the prism of Joseph Smith's cultural milieu? To consider with the Rev'd Dr. Andrew Teal what the dream's spiritual significance is when read in light of other Christian theological traditions? To wonder with Kimberly Matheson what the tree at the centre of the dream actually is? To investigate with Kylie Turley what is to be made of the dream's persistent doubling? To probe with Timothy Farrant what emerges when the dream's arboreal visual imagery is read in dialogue with the arboreal visual imagery in Augustine's *Confessions*? And to ask with Terryl Givens what the dream has to say about Zion-building? Further, how do Joseph Spencer and Jennifer Champoux's historical essays help to situate these new readings?[14]

As disciple-scholars our attempt here is the application of the tools of our trades to the task of discerning the richness and depth of Lehi's experience. In doing so we hope to contribute towards the recognition of the Book of Mormon as theologically robust and redemptively important. Having discovered the dream to be both rich and deep, what follows represents our best attempt at its adequate expression.

—Benjamin Keogh

PLATE 1. J. Kirk Richards, *Pulling Up the Iron Rod*, oil on panel, 14 × 16 inches (35 × 40 cm), 2020.

Artwork:

Pulling Up the Iron Rod

J. KIRK RICHARDS

NEPHI TELLS US THE IRON ROD FROM HIS FATHER'S DREAM IS A representation of the word of God. It's the word of God that leads to the tree of life and its fruit, the love of God. The more familiar I become with the experiences of life as they relate to God's word in written scripture, the more material the rod becomes. It is heavy. There is a weight to the word of God. The world has changed dramatically in the last twenty-five years. The first time I understood what email was, I was serving a mission in Italy. My grandmother passed away during the final months of my mission, and my parents sent an email to a branch member to notify me of her passing. Letters took weeks to travel to and from Europe, so these instant messages seemed miraculous. Today, I receive dozens of emails every day. I interact with thousands of people on social media with a few imprints of my finger on a hand-held sea of glass. Information is not only at the tips of our fingers, but constantly presenting itself to us even when we don't go looking for it. Do the words spoken by ancient prophets apply to us today? Do the words spoken by prophets thirty years ago apply to us today? I'm grateful for the ninth Article of Faith: God will yet reveal many great and important things pertaining to His kingdom. Another scripture says we will be given new things as quickly as we are able to receive them. It's hard work preparing as a group of people to receive change. I think about the hearts and minds that grew in preparation for the revelation restoring priesthood and temple blessings to Latter-day Saints of color.

The iron rod is weighty. As the world grows up around us—remaking itself into a new world as quickly as new generations replace the old—we are tasked with lifting the weight of the word of God. We must wrestle with the application of scripture to our present context. How do I live the two great commandments in 2023? When creating this painting, I also thought about the words of Elder Dieter F. Uchtdorf: "Lift where you stand." It's not enough to maintain where we stand. It's not enough to keep the status quo where we stand. This thought is echoed in the words of Christ himself, in the injunction to take up our cross and follow Him. Being a disciple means to lift the weight of wood, the weight of iron, the weight of words, the weight of others, and in turn be lifted by the charity of those pulling up the iron rod next to us.

PART I

Visioning the Dream

Wandering in Strange Roads:
Interpretations of Lehi's Dream

JOSEPH M. SPENCER

AMONG THE BEST-KNOWN AND MOST BELOVED CHAPTERS IN THE
Book of Mormon is 1 Nephi 8, containing the story of Lehi's dream about
a life-giving tree. Early in the account of Lehi's experience, however, is a puzzling moment noted less often than other, perhaps more salient features of the
dream. Lehi says that he "saw . . . a dark and dreary wilderness" (v. 4), but after
"a man . . . in a white robe" succeeds in getting him to follow (v. 5), he says this: "I
beheld *myself*, that *I* was in a dark and dreary waste" (v. 7).[1] It is not at all clear
what the text means by this reflexive construction, "I beheld myself." One possibility is that readers are meant to understand that Lehi had a divided experience as the dream unfolded—as if he was simultaneously inside and outside
of the dreamscape, sometimes seeing through the eyes of someone lost in the
dark and dreary waste and sometimes watching the drama (his own actions
included) only from a safe distance.[2]

This idea of a divided or reflexive visionary experience serves as a
nice emblem for the subject of this essay: the history of how scholars have

interpreted Lehi's dream. We, as readers of the Book of Mormon, have had our own visions of and dreams about what 1 Nephi 8 might mean. And just as Lehi's dream reflects back to him his own immediate anxieties and desires, the many ways we have read Lehi's dream reflect back to us the history of our collective anxieties and desires. In reviewing the history of how readers have interpreted this text, then, *we behold ourselves.* To study or to tell this history is a reflexive experience, something undertaken from within the confusing flux of interpretive history and yet also something striving for critical distance and neutrality.

A review of how various scholars have interpreted Lehi's dream, moreover, might provide a clear vision of what it means to interpret the text at the present moment, at the beginning of the third decade of the twenty-first century. The fact is that the authors whose work appears in this volume labor at a specific and significant moment in the history of Book of Mormon scholarship: the beginnings of what appears to be a new period in the study of this remarkable scripture. The purpose of this essay is to trace in broad outlines the historical backdrop to the present interpretive moment. What has made it possible or desirable for theological approaches to the Book of Mormon to assume a place of real influence on the interpretive landscape? Where the historical lens was once not only the dominant but also arguably the only one that scholars used to view the Book of Mormon, and where a literary angle came eventually to unsettle that dominance but never to usurp it completely, there is now emerging a real and promising interest in theological interpretation. Further, where there was once a strong impulse toward establishing fixed and determinate meanings for Book of Mormon texts, there is today general openness to the idea that these texts bear within themselves the potential for many right and productive readings. How did these developments occur, and what is the shape of their history?

It turns out that the history of the interpretation of Lehi's dream is interesting and rich, more varied in crucial ways than might be expected. It is in fact *so* interesting and rich that the subject requires much more than a single essay to recount it. Scholars have scrutinized the dream with academic tools, ecclesiastical leaders have drawn on its pathos for pastoral ends, artists have painted and sculpted and otherwise imagined various aspects of the dream, entrepreneurs have made trinkets and collectibles of its images, and lay readers have allowed the dream to absorb them as they search earnestly for divine direction. Others have studied parts of this history,[3] and, given the increasing interest in recent years in the Book of Mormon's reception history, there is reason to anticipate others will yet study other parts of this history. The present essay, however, analyzes just one dimension of the history of how readers have interpreted Lehi's dream. What follows considers only specifically *scholarly* attempts to read 1 Nephi 8.

Even within these necessary limits, however, there is still far too much in the history of interpretation that deserves attention and cannot receive it here. It would be useful to examine various interpretations of just this or that image from Lehi's dream—say, the iron rod or the man clothed in white, not to mention the tree itself. Sadly, even these details lie beyond the scope of this essay. It will be enough just to gain a broad sense of the history of *what interpretive angles* scholars have used as they have approached the task of reading 1 Nephi 8. What presuppositions should one bring to the text, and what should one be looking for in reading it? What kinds of methods might one mobilize in the task of interpretation, and what sensibilities should one cultivate in order to read the text productively? What follows will ask only about the history of how scholars have answered these questions, whether implicitly or explicitly. It will be enough, here, just to develop an understanding of the general contours of the field of Book of Mormon scholarship, with particular emphasis on how one reads Lehi's dream.

In what follows, then, the history of interpretation relatively naturally divides itself into three broad and somewhat overlapping periods. During the first period, lasting from the beginnings of serious scholarly interpretation of the Book of Mormon all the way into the 1980s, historical interpretations were not only dominant but more or less without any real competition. The second period, beginning in key ways in the late 1970s and stretching to the end of the first decade of the twenty-first century, witnessed the appearance of a self-consciously literary style of interpretation, which vied with dominant historical approaches as well as doctrinal styles of interpretation. (Because of the complexity of this second period in particular its treatment below divides into several parts.) Finally, the third and still-current period began at the outset of the new millennium when theological interpretation (informed by both historical and literary work) emerged as an interpretive force to be reckoned with.

THE HISTORICAL LEHI (CA. 1945–CA. 1985)

It was arguably not until the mid-1940s that a genuinely scholarly study of the Book of Mormon began to appear. Orson Pratt represented the most deeply intellectual approach to the text in the first generation of Latter-day Saints—an approach he had occasion to insert directly into the edition of the Book of Mormon he produced shortly before his death—but, for reasons quite beyond his control, he lacked academic training.[4] The publications of George Reynolds and Janne Sjodahl in the last decades of the nineteenth century, like those of B. H. Roberts in the first decades of the twentieth century, were more informed by academic scholarship than Pratt's had been, and there is no question that they contributed in crucial ways to the foundations of the field. Nonetheless, they still produced pre-professional work on the text, an impressive labor of love.[5] It was thus arguably only when Sidney Sperry's *Our Book of Mormon* appeared in 1947 that a fully scholarly field was first surveyed. And Sperry did not neglect Lehi's dream in that first substantial work of Book of Mormon studies, even if, on analysis, his treatment of the dream was largely conventional.[6]

A major aim of Sperry's book was—drawing on his training in biblical literature at the University of Chicago—to make preliminary efforts "toward discovering, describing, and appraising the various types of literature found in the Book of Mormon."[7] To that end, Sperry finds in Lehi's dream "a fine example" of "symbolic prophecy."[8] With an eye more to the historical reconstruction of literary genres than to an illuminating literary interpretation of the dream itself, Sperry provides only a sketch of its meaning. He cautions against pressing "the symbolism" of the dream "too far" and in fact claims that "the moral and religious applications of it are fairly obvious and certain."[9] What follows in his text, then, is a simple allegorical reading of the dream, taken to symbolize every individual's pursuit of God's love.

Soon after Sperry's book appeared,[10] two much more forceful, more strikingly influential, and more emphatically historical approaches to Lehi's dream appeared in print. The first came in a 1950 magazine article by Hugh Nibley. Hoping to show that 1 Nephi fits well into an ancient context, Nibley places Lehi's dream in a premodern Arabian setting. To secure such an interpretation, he found it necessary to clarify what he takes to be the substance of Lehi's dream—not to let the dream interpret itself, as Sperry had done shortly before him. Nibley thus argues that "the substance of Lehi's dream" directly reflects the travails of a trek through the Arabian desert.[11] The dark and dreary waste of Lehi's dream is the desert itself, and Lehi's wandering in the dark "is the standard nightmare of the Arab."[12] The famed large and spacious building well reflects "the great stone houses of the city" that desert travelers regarded with suspicion, just as the large and spacious field mirrors Arabic poetry's references to the open plain of the desert.[13] When Lehi "dreams of a river, it is a true desert river, a clear stream a few yards wide with its source but a hundred paces away . . . , or else a raging muddy wash, a *sail* of 'filthy water' that sweeps people away to their destruction."[14]

Nibley's interpretation of Lehi's dream was soon made available anew as part of his first book, *Lehi in the Desert and the World of the Jaredites*, published in 1952.[15] It was immediately influential, cited as early as 1953 in the first attempt at a scholarly commentary on the Book of Mormon (which never moved beyond a volume on 1 Nephi), written by Eldin Ricks.[16] Further, clearly signaling official interest in Nibley's work, the leadership of The Church of Jesus Christ of Latter-day Saints soon asked him to develop his approach to the Book of Mormon generally into an official manual of study for the priesthood quorums of the Church.[17] This appeared in 1957 and included further treatment of Lehi's dream along similar lines.[18] But something new appeared also in the 1957 volume. An explicit aim of Nibley's priesthood manual was, interestingly, to shift the attention of Book of Mormon hobbyists (those Nibley describes as "people calling themselves archaeologists") away from ancient America.[19] He explains in the opening paragraph of the manual, "We are going to consider the Book of Mormon as a possible product not of Ancient America (for that is totally beyond our competence) but of the Ancient East (which is only slightly less so)."[20] Where Nibley had at first been content simply to provide an ancient Arabian setting for Lehi's dream, he now apparently felt the need to contrast such a setting with another and specifically ancient American one.

What seems to have motivated Nibley's use of such a heavy methodological hand in an official Church manual was another historical approach to Lehi's dream which had just then arisen as a kind of rival to his own. In 1953, the first of what would be a long series of publications by Wells Jakeman appeared in which he attempted to connect Lehi's dream to a monumental stela found in Izapa, Chiapas, Mexico.[21] The stela in question (Izapa Stela 5) came to the attention of scholars only in the late 1930s. Jakeman, a professor at Brigham Young University (BYU) with training in archaeology, became aware of the stone monument a few years later and was soon publishing arguments that it might be a carved illustration of the dream from 1 Nephi 8. Sensation over a potential discovery of a Book of Mormon artifact spread quickly, and before long many Latter-day Saints were familiar with "the tree of life stone."[22] In his own initial publication on the subject, Jakeman provides a brief analysis of Lehi's dream into its "fixed elements" (symbolic objects from the dreamscape), its "characters" (the various human figures in the dream), and its "dynamic features" (the events reported in succession).[23] This he then employs in a point-by-point comparison between the dream account and the monumental stone. He finds "as many as thirteen and possibly twenty-five" significant features of the stela to correspond directly with the account of Lehi's dream and so insists that "the resemblance of this sculpture to the Book of Mormon account cannot be accidental or due to independent development; but is almost certainly the result of common origin or an historical connection between them."[24]

Apart from providing an analysis of Lehi's dream into depictable elements for comparison, Jakeman offers no substantial interpretation of the dream's meaning. Whereas for Nibley, historical work on the dream is interpretively illuminating, Jakeman assumed with Sperry that Lehi's dream is effectively self-interpreting, the kind of thing that can be defended as historical without any need for complicating interpretive questions. And Jakeman's explanation of the stela's connection to the Book of Mormon prompted not only excitement but also criticism—as much from within the believing community as from without. Among the earliest critics was Nibley himself. In an unpublished paper that circulated in the late 1950s, Nibley accused Jakeman of breaking with academic standards in his argument and the style of its publication.[25] What apparently spurred Nibley's writing of this direct critique was a pair of further publications by Jakeman, a pamphlet and a book. The pamphlet never directly mentions the Book of Mormon, although it concludes with a comparison between the stone and various ancient near eastern artifacts.[26] The book, however, published the same year and by the same publisher, addresses at length the alleged similarities between Izapa Stela 5 and "the 'Lehi account' of the tree of life."[27] Even in such an expanded form (perhaps especially in such an expanded form), Jakeman's arguments struck Nibley as historically tendentious and flimsy.

Despite criticisms, Jakeman's interpretation caught the imagination of many Latter-day Saints, especially of amateur researchers who hoped to gather concrete archaeological evidence for Nephites in ancient America. More careful than these amateur researchers was Garth Norman, another BYU archaeologist who worked in the 1960s and 1970s to increase the level of professionalism in interpreting the stone from Izapa. He provided readers with high-quality photographs of the stela and argued that many of his colleague's conclusions regarding the Book of Mormon "must be rendered invalid because of the inaccuracies in the Jakeman reproduction of Stela 5."[28] Norman would nonetheless later claim when writing for or to Latter-day Saints (rather than fellow archaeologists) that Jakeman was right in many ways. Stewart Brewer quotes from a letter Norman wrote to John Welch claiming that "Izapa Stela 5 *is* a portrayal of the vision of the Tree of Life in the Book of Mormon," although "it is much more" than that alone.[29] Because Norman was willing to publish his more careful opinion in the Church's official magazine,[30] Jakeman's general approach to the stone continued in popularity even among Latter-day Saint scholars into the 1980s.[31] It continues with amateur researchers and lay Latter-day Saints right into the present.[32]

Sperry, Nibley, and Jakeman all retreated from the world of Book of Mormon scholarship by the late 1960s—Sperry because he retired in 1971 from his university position, Nibley because he found a new intellectual pursuit after the Church's 1967 acquisition of the Egyptian papyri connected with the Book of Abraham, and Jakeman apparently also because he was approaching retirement. The shared impact of this triad of BYU scholars on the future shape of Book of Mormon studies for the next several decades was nonetheless deep. John Sorenson, for instance, recalled reading work by all three as a missionary and deciding to pursue Book of Mormon studies for exactly that reason: "What those men were doing with scripture studies, comparing them with external sources, using scholarly methods, seemed very much worth my doing."[33] Sorenson in fact became the first obvious heir to all three scholars, publishing on the Book of Mormon and biblical literature and Book of Mormon archaeology in the very years his mentors turned their attention in other directions.[34] Demonstrating an increase of professionalization over Jakeman, when Sorenson published his first full monograph on the Book of Mormon and ancient America, he said nothing of Izapa Stela 5.[35] A consequence of this increased care with archaeological evidence was, however, that the post-Jakeman (and post-Norman) generation of Book of Mormon archaeologists—despite their insistence on a strictly historical approach to the text—had little to say about Lehi's dream.

Another young Book of Mormon scholar deeply influenced especially by Hugh Nibley was in the making during the same years, however, and he would contribute in several ways to the study of 1 Nephi 8. John Welch created the Foundation for Ancient Research and Mormon Studies (FARMS) in the late 1970s. It was Welch's foundation that later published Sorenson's key work on the Book of Mormon's potential fit in a Mesoamerican context, but Welch's own interests lay closer to the Old World. Welch would not directly publish on Lehi's dream until the late 1990s,[36] and he would not serve as co-editor of a crucial collection of essays on the tree of life theme until well into the new millennium,[37] but under his guidance, FARMS would publish numerous studies pursuing Nibley-like work on the dream of the tree of life. Even as the second generation of historically focused Book of Mormon scholars was taking its rise, however, productively distinct approaches to the Book of Mormon—approaches less concerned about reconstructing history—were also taking their rise elsewhere in the academy.

THE LITERARY LEHI (CA. 1975–CA. 2010)

Beginnings (ca. 1975–ca. 1980)

Sidney Sperry's *Our Book of Mormon* in 1947 included a chapter titled "The Book of Mormon as Literature," and several other chapters of the book focused on the various literary genres discoverable in the book. Sperry's conclusion about the literary value of the book, however, was less than enthusiastic and deeply representative of the period. "Though the Book of Mormon has little sustained literary beauty," he wrote, "it is a great literature because of the unusual religious and historical truths which it sets forth with profound spiritual fervor."[38] Despite a kind of defeatism evident in Sperry's conclusion, several individuals with literary inclinations began to draw attention to the book's structures and styles in the late 1960s and early 1970s. John Welch, a full decade before he launched FARMS, published a famous and astonishingly influential essay on the use of chiastic literary structure in the Book of Mormon.[39] The same year Welch's essay appeared, the journal *Dialogue* published Robert Nichols's "Beowulf and Nephi: A Literary View of the Book of Mormon," which began to make good on Douglas Wilson's essay published a year earlier in the same journal: "Prospects for the Study of the Book of Mormon as a Work of American Literature."[40] 1972 then saw the publication of Robert Thomas's "A Literary Critic Looks at the Book of Mormon."[41] This flurry of literary attention, signaling coming changes in Book of Mormon studies, nonetheless offered little by way of interpreting Lehi's dream. Only Nichols even mentions the dream, and he does so only to suggest that the dream confirms a problematic pattern in Lehi's rhetorical delivery, one of expounding "deeply-felt emotions with the rhetorician's flourish of metaphor" that leaves hearers unsure of meaning.[42]

Just a few years later, however, the first serious literary treatment of Lehi's dream would appear, taking its cue especially from Wilson's suggestion that literary study of the book might be productively archetypal in orientation.[43] In "The Dark Way to the Tree: Typological Unity in the Book of Mormon," originally published in 1977, Bruce Jorgensen argues that the "figural unity" of the whole Book of Mormon lies in Lehi's dream.[44] What Jorgensen has in mind is the idea that Lehi's transformation "from dark and barest waste by means of the Word to a world fruitful and filled with light" is "enacted again and again in the Book of Mormon, at both the individual and communal levels."[45] He notes various individual stories of conversion in the Book of Mormon that follow the contours of Lehi's experience, but he climactically emphasizes the way that Jesus Christ's arrival among the children of Sariah and Lehi in 3 Nephi follows the pattern. Calling to his fallen children from within an impenetrable darkness, the Christ of 3 Nephi "lays open the core of the figural structure of the Book of Mormon, revealing" that "all of God's actions in his world—creation, conversion, covenant, redemption—are one act of transformation from dark, barren chaos, by the Word, to a world abounding in light and joy."[46] The experience of the people on the path in Lehi's dream is typical of many events, and especially of the most sacred events, according to the Book of Mormon.

The timing of Jorgensen's intervention was no accident. The year prior to the original appearance of his essay marked the founding of the Association for Mormon Letters (AML), which initially met alongside meetings of the Modern Language Association. And the first several years of AML's meetings featured several important papers analyzing the Book of Mormon as literature—papers by Richard Rust and Steven Walker, by Mark Thomas and Steven Sondrup, by George Tate and Clifton Jolley. Some of these are now classics,[47] while others became the foundations of later books that would serve as foundations for the literary study of the Book of Mormon—especially Thomas's *Digging in Cumorah* and Rust's *Feasting on the Word*. Both of these books feature discussions of Lehi's dream, Rust's more briefly and obviously influenced by Jorgensen's reading,[48] and Thomas's at greater length and in new directions. Although Thomas's book did not appear until 1999, the chapter on Lehi's dream had its origins in a 1979 AML paper.[49]

In that early essay, Thomas brings to the study of Lehi's dream questions of literary genre, arguing convincingly that the re-presentation of Lehi's dream in Nephi's subsequent vision "transforms it from a dream with apocalyptic overtones into a full apocalypse."[50] On its own, apart from the vision that interprets it as "historical allegory," Lehi's dream is rather constructed of symbols that "are archetypal. That is, they express a bundle of meanings that have deep roots in the consciousness of man as man."[51] Thomas thus emphasizes how Lehi's dream embodies a kind of "moral dualism," very much at odds with the way "many people today" see things.[52] In the later, more developed version of Thomas's interpretation, he argues that the water images of Lehi's dream illustrate this forcefully, since "the same fountain" of water is presented "as both good and evil," as somehow fusing "the depths of hell and the justice of God."[53] According to Thomas, what creates such a peculiar interpretive situation is the likelihood that "Lehi intended the river as an image of righteousness, but Nephi reinterpreted it later in his vision."[54] The dichotomy of the temporal and the spiritual—explicitly highlighted in 1 Nephi 15—serves to ground "a two-tiered method of interpretation." Lehi's own dream and its symbols "are universalized by the spiritual interpretation" native to Lehi's recounting of the experience, but the same sources are "allegorized by the temporal interpretation" of Nephi's dream.[55]

Retreat (ca. 1980–ca. 1995)

By the early 1980s, the future looked bright for literary research on the Book of Mormon—and perhaps for the literary study of Lehi's dream in particular. Various journals were publishing literary work on the Book of Mormon, AML was providing literary scholars with a context to present their research, and BYU's Religious Studies Center published a collection of essays that included literary work on the Book of Mormon by Jorgensen, Rust, and Tate. Further, Rust was working with "a non-Mormon colleague, John Seelye," to create "a handbook to the Book of Mormon as literature," and Jorgensen was planning to make his study of Lehi's dream "the core of a longer projected work."[56] These projected works did not materialize as planned, however,[57] and soon rising interest in the literary study would be sidelined by a renewal and intensification of interest in the historical dimension of the Book of Mormon. As already noted, the late-1970s flurry of literary attention received by Lehi's dream coincided historically with the rise of FARMS, and further events in the early 1980s gave the historically-driven projects of scholars associated with FARMS more public attention than they did to literary research. In many ways, in fact, these same events raised questions about whether there was any space at all for a literary study of the Book of Mormon among the faithful.

It would be too involved in this context even to list the events and changing pressures of the early 1980s that led to the developments just mentioned.[58] Particularly important among them, however, was one matter: a crisis in Latter-day Saint historiography occasioned by Mark Hofmann's forgeries, forgeries of documents that directly questioned the historical validity of the Book of Mormon. Before the forgeries were revealed as such, believing Latter-day Saints found themselves with increasing need for a reasoned defense of the antiquity of the Book of Mormon. The scholars associated with FARMS stepped in to fill the need of the moment. There emerged simultaneously an opposition group, counterpoised to FARMS, some of whose members advocated for acceptance of the Book of Mormon as inspired scripture but simultaneous rejection of the book's antiquity.[59] In an era of increased emphasis on the Book of Mormon's spiritual importance—all these events coincided with the presidency of Ezra Taft Benson, whose message regarding the Book of Mormon proved culturally transformative[60]—the position taken by FARMS's opponents was rejected by the majority as beyond the pale of orthodoxy. Not only was FARMS generally seen as fighting in defense of traditional faith, however, the literary approach to the Book of Mormon that had begun to emerge just a few years earlier could now look a little too like the emergent fringe claim that the Book of Mormon is inspired fiction.

It is therefore significant that literary approaches, despite the intensity of such work in the last years of the 1970s, largely retreated during the 1980s and then surfaced again only in the later 1990s, and primarily in collaboration with FARMS. (It is significant, for example, that the only substantial literary study of Lehi's dream during the 1980s was a master's thesis in the English department at BYU—Julie Adams Maddox's "Lehi's Vision of the Tree of Life: An Anagogic Interpretation.")[61] In the meanwhile, there emerged a new but somewhat fleeting genre of doctrinal scholarship on the Book of Mormon. This project, largely pursued by Religious Education faculty at BYU and unmistakably spurred by the emphasis placed on the Book of Mormon by President Benson, modeled itself on the late apostle Bruce R. McConkie's *Doctrinal New Testament Commentary*, published in the 1960s and 1970s.[62] This of course included publications on Lehi's dream. Because FARMS scholars largely gave their attention to other dimensions of the Book of Mormon[63] and literary interpreters retreated into the background during the 1980s, it was the doctrinal approach that dominated discussion of 1 Nephi 8 for much of the decade.

In 1987, for instance, Kent Jackson's "The Tree of Life and the Ministry of Christ" appeared. Jackson takes Nephi's vision in 1 Nephi 11–14 to be a kind of doctrinal expansion of Lehi's dream, a vision "of much more than the scene of the tree of life and the efforts of some to obtain its fruits." For Nephi, "that scene provided the setting and the backdrop for an even greater set of revelations"—especially regarding the condescension of God (as interpreted by McConkie).[64] Jackson's strikingly quick turn from Lehi's richly symbolic dream to Nephi's doctrinally expositional vision is illustrative of the style of interpretation of the 1980s. Susan Easton Black, however, followed in 1988 with a treatment of Lehi's dream that never swerves from its focus on that chapter alone. Her essay is largely a doctrinally-toned paraphrase of the dream account in 1 Nephi 8. Interesting and illustrative is her treatment of Sariah's place in the dream: "Sariah, [Lehi's] most beloved companion and mother of his family, was the first one he saw [when he looked for his family]. She had only the last, but surely the darkest and most dangerous, steps ahead to reach the tree. To Lehi's eyes, opened by God's mercy, the difference between life and death was clear and unmistakable. But Sariah, joined by Sam and Nephi, hesitated (v. 14). His wife and his children must obey the patriarch's lead to avoid the snares of Lucifer in the river of water. Would she be tempted to ignore his call and rely on her own wisdom?"[65] Here, Black imagines Sariah in a struggle with a subtle temptation toward individualism, at odds with the Church's strong emphasis on roles defined by family life.

The definitive entry in the list of doctrinal studies of Lehi's dream came, however, in the 1987 first volume of Joseph McConkie and Robert Millet's *Doctrinal Commentary on the Book of Mormon*. For McConkie (son of Bruce R. McConkie) and Millet, the dream—like so much of the Book of Mormon—is an occasion for teaching doctrine. On Lehi's alternating description of his experience as "a dream" or "a vision" (v. 2), they comment: "Lehi's inspired dreams were indeed visions; the mind and will of the Lord was made known to him during the hours of sleep."[66] On Lehi's desire to share the tree's fruit with his family (see v. 12), they say this: "As the spirit without the body cannot have a fulness of joy, so the man without the woman is incomplete, as are the parents without the children. The sweetest joys in all existence are manifest in righteous family living."[67] Throughout their commentary on the dream, McConkie and Millet draw out potential connections with other passages of scripture, particularly those where imagery similar to that of Lehi's dream appears. Perhaps the most provocative such connection they make—it is certainly the one that has appeared the most often in other doctrinal and devotional studies of Lehi's dream—is between the dream's "vivid description of four main groups of people" and the New Testament's parable of the sower, with its four categories of receptivity to the Kingdom of God.[68]

Despite its powerful cultural force during the 1980s, doctrinal exposition of Lehi's dream—which would continue in a less dominant way into the twenty-first century—worried some observers for what they saw as characteristic weaknesses of the genre. A review of McConkie and Millet's commentary by Louis Midgley, for instance, described it as "a series of didactic discourses, little sermons, or homilies prompted by phrases in the Book of Mormon, which may have little or nothing to do with the meaning of the passage or even the phrase which functioned as the trigger."[69] Midgley in fact offered far harsher criticisms than that just cited in his review—motivated at least in part by the ways he saw McConkie and Millet as casting aspersions on the sort of approach to the text that he and other historically-minded scholars represented. Indeed, that such a negative critique of the doctrinal approach came from a FARMS scholar in a FARMS publication at the end of the 1980s is perhaps telling. The upsets of the early 1980s had resulted in a proliferation of competing approaches to the Book of Mormon's interpretation, and there were accordingly difficult questions to ask about how scholarly study of the book might proceed. Midgley's critique heralded what would soon be a kind of reclaiming of Lehi's dream (and the rest of the Book of Mormon) for the historical enterprise, always with a polemical apologetic edge. Thus, in the early 1990s, when FARMS had established its bona fides and also created several venues for publishing more strictly historical research on the Book of Mormon, the dream of the tree of life became the principal purview of the historical enterprise again for a time.

That FARMS scholars saw their work on the Book of Mormon as continuing Hugh Nibley's earlier historical work is clear from the fact that FARMS published in 1993 four volumes of transcripts of Book of Mormon lectures delivered by Nibley between 1988 and 1990 at Brigham Young University. The transcripts included a lecture on Lehi's dream, which found Nibley exploring new comparative and historical connections that might place the dream in a temple context (a major theme of his research and reflection at that point in his life). Nibley thus discusses "a statement in the *Midrash*" about a rod of iron that once led up the sacred, zigzagging road to Jerusalem's first temple. "There was a railing that went up, and you could follow it. It was iron, and it rusted away in time. It was replaced with a wood railing. They had to cling to the iron rod to get up to the temple so they wouldn't slip and fall on the rocks."[70] This kind of reading of the dream, related to students in 1988 but published only in 1993, heralded the work of FARMS scholars on the dream during the 1990s.

For instance, in the second volume of the *Journal of Book of Mormon Studies*, both issues of which appeared in the same year of 1993, there appeared three distinct articles on Lehi's dream. Picking up a theme of interest to Nibley himself, Kevin Christensen's essay "'Nigh unto Death'" connects Lehi's dream to Raymond Moody's research on near-death experience. He writes, "Lehi's account of the iron rod, and many people being lost in the mists of darkness, and falling into the filthy river echoes many of the medieval 'Test Bridge' accounts" in Carol Zaleski's comparative study of near-death experience accounts.[71] Jeanette Miller, exhibiting a Nibley-like penchant for ancient texts and citing other FARMS scholars' work, argues in another essay that the tree of Lehi's dream is a feature of ancient temple worship and therefore a figure for Jesus Christ. For example, she points to scholarship that connects "the tree and the temple" with "the sacral meal" and points out that Christ in John 6 "declared himself to be the Bread of Life."[72] In yet another essay from the *Journal of Book of Mormon Studies* in 1993, Corbin Volluz combines interest in the temple with interest in afterlife experiences to provide a multifaceted reading of Lehi's dream. Volluz essentially argues that the dream must have interpretations "various and sundry"; "from the simple scenario of the tree of life . . . spring interpretations involving the history of the world from the advent of the Savior to the last days, the destiny of the wicked and the righteous in the hereafter, and the strategy of what we must do as individuals during this mortal phase of our existence to assure us of attaining eternal life."[73]

Reemergence (ca. 1995–ca. 2010)

The flurry of FARMS publications on Lehi's dream in 1993—tracing a short trajectory toward a kind of interpretive eclecticism—was quickly over. And the latter half of the 1990s witnessed the reemergence, largely under FARMS's protection, of literary work on the dream originally begun in the late 1970s. This literary reemergence arguably began with the sudden appearance of a new literary critic with deep interests in the Book of Mormon, albeit one who did not publish anything on Lehi's dream at the time: Alan Goff. As early as the late-1980s, he was publishing literary work on the Book of Mormon in FARMS journals, including an essay in the very first issue of the *Journal of Book of Mormon Studies* in 1992.[74] Soon, though, more established literary readers of the Book of Mormon were publishing with the FARMS imprint. Richard Rust's long-projected literary study of the Book of Mormon appeared in 1997, co-published by FARMS and Deseret Book, with a few (but relatively brief) analyses of Lehi's dream.[75] In 1996, Marilyn Arnold published "Unlocking the Sacred Text" in a FARMS collection,[76] but also a full book of literary interpretation of the Book of Mormon with a different publisher. In the latter, she addressed her attention to Lehi's dream and especially to Nephi's subsequent and dependent vision. For Arnold, Lehi's dream is born out of his "justifiable anxiety about his less-than-valiant sons, Laman and Lemuel," but its depth is largely obscured by the fact that we receive an account of it only "secondhand," through Nephi's telling.[77] "Where the account attributed to Lehi simply sketches out the basic components of Lehi's dream," she writes, "Nephi's reconstruction of his own experience is grandiose, full of fire and wonder." In part, though, this is because "Lehi apparently did not ask to know the interpretation of his own magnificent vision."[78]

Mark Thomas's full book on literary study of the Book of Mormon, *Digging in Cumorah*, also finally appeared in 1999, building on his late-1970s work on Lehi's dream as apocalyptic literature. Thomas, however, published this volume with Signature Books, often FARMS's sworn rival throughout the 1980s and 90s. Scholars associated with Signature Books often accused FARMS scholars of doctoring data in defense of traditional Latter-day Saint claims, while scholars associated with FARMS often accused Signature Books authors of lacking the professional training relevant to their efforts at critiquing traditional Latter-day Saint claims. It had, moreover, been Signature Books who had put into print the first systematic argument that the Book of Mormon should be received as inspired fiction. Because this appeared in 1993 (in a book that in fact spurred the publication of a whole—and particularly large—issue of FARMS's *Review of Books on the Book of Mormon*),[79] it arguably set the tone for the reemergence of literary approaches to the Book of Mormon in the late 1990s. That Thomas elected to publish his study with Signature signaled to many readers that he had taken a side in a debate over what it might mean to read the Book of Mormon literarily. Nonetheless, Thomas himself attempts in his book to establish a kind of middle-ground position, fusing a hermeneutics of obedience with a hermeneutics of suspicion. He states explicitly in the introduction to *Digging in Cumorah* that he has little to say to the debate of the previous decade; his intention is to lay "the foundation for a new tradition in Book of Mormon studies."[80]

The published response to Thomas's book marked a key moment in the development of the literary approach to the Book of Mormon. Two reviews of the book appeared side by side in the *FARMS Review of Books* in 2000. First comes Alan Goff's, tellingly titled "Scratching the Surface of Book of Mormon Narratives," which runs to more than thirty pages. It opens in a strongly polemical spirit: "Thomas's book seriously underestimates the complexity of the scripture—whether for ideological reasons or just because of the writer's incapacities as a literary critic isn't clear yet."[81] Goff takes Thomas's book to be a historicizing reading that pegs the Book of Mormon to the nineteenth century, but one that is thinly disguised as a literary interpretation. Immediately following Goff's response, one finds another by Grant Hardy, titled "Speaking So That All May Be Edified." Countering Goff's critique to some extent, Hardy insists that "it is important to view [Thomas's] work in proper perspective. . . . I take at face value his insistence that his desire is to build faith."[82] Where Goff sees Thomas's literary angle betraying a latent positivism and his actual readings an ineptness in interpretation, Hardy sees a project of great promise that does not entirely succeed in its ambitious aims. For Hardy, though, Thomas "is moving in the right direction."[83]

These strongly contrasting reviews of *Digging in Cumorah*, published at the dawn of a new century, were jointly prescient. Next to Hardy's ironic response, Goff's seems overly defensive, more interested in rekindling the fire of a fading controversy than in working together for a better and fully literary reading of the Book of Mormon. And, although perhaps no one could have known it at the time, Hardy was poised to become not only a key literary interpreter of the Book of Mormon but also arguably the most recognizable interpreter of the Book of Mormon at all over the following decade. And significantly, Hardy would forcefully remove the literary approach from the site of the debate between critics and apologists. In 2003, the University of Illinois Press published his *Reader's Edition* of the Book of Mormon, an edition deliberately organized to invite—if not in fact to provoke—literary interpretation of the book. And then, in 2010, Oxford University Press published *Understanding the Book of Mormon: A Reader's Guide*, a companion of sorts to the *Reader's Edition*. Hardy's method is narratological, interested especially in discerning authorial and editorial intent. And his aim is explicitly to create a style of Book of Mormon study accessible as much to those outside as to those inside the faith.

Understanding the Book of Mormon has little to say about Lehi's dream,[84] but Hardy published only a year later a rich study of Lehi's dream and its relationship to Nephi's subsequent vision. Hardy's point in his study is less to interpret the details of the dream than to trace the "different meanings" Lehi and Nephi find in their respective versions of the vision.[85] What for Lehi is "apparently" a dream with an "obvious" point (an expression of his deep concern for his family) is for Nephi a complex allegory for which an angel is needed "to provide the key interpretive identifications."[86] This is a point others before Hardy had noted, of course, but for him, what matters in this contrast is the way the contrast between Lehi's more affective and Nephi's more intellectual experiences of the same dream or vision lead to dramatically different practical relationships within the family. The dream spurs Lehi to preach to his oldest sons; he "has not given up on them." Nephi, by contrast, proves "judgmental" in his attempt to discuss the dream with his brothers.[87] Hardy summarizes his conclusions: "Lehi was concerned about how the building might entice people away from the tree; Nephi apparently worries that the tree might attract people from the building who are not worthy to eat of its fruit."[88] For Hardy, then, the key to Lehi's experience of the dream is that it drove him to preach to his sons "with all the feeling of a tender parent" (v. 37).

By 2010, Hardy had become the clear leader of a literary revival in Book of Mormon studies, but he was of course only one of many literary interpreters during the first decade of the twenty-first century. Thanks in large part to the fact that the 2011 Sidney B. Sperry Symposium at BYU took as its focus Lehi's dream and Nephi's subsequent vision, a goodly handful of literary interpretations of Lehi's dream appeared at the end of that decade. Hardy's own full essay on the dream was delivered at the symposium, but instructive literary studies came also from Daniel Belnap, Jared Halverson, Heather Hardy, Jared Parker, and especially Amy Easton-Flake and Charles Swift. Belnap, although he presents his study explicitly as deploying a "sociological/cultural" approach to the text, revives Bruce Jorgensen's literary study from the late 1970s.[89] Belnap, however, dramatically expands Jorgensen's brief suggestion that Lehi's dream provides a cultural narrative for the later account of Christ's visit to the New World.[90] Halverson, for his part, might be seen as reviving Mark Thomas's treatment of the dream in terms of apocalyptic literature, discerning genre and probing comparison with the Book of Revelation much further.[91] Heather Hardy explores how "Nephi's editing initially de-emphasizes the unity of Lehi's discourse" that extends from 1 Nephi 8 into 1 Nephi 10, suggesting that the point is to distinguish between the individual plan of salvation (embodied in the dream of 1 Nephi 8) and the global plan of human redemption (lectured on in 1 Nephi 10).[92] For his part, Parker explores the way that Nephi returns literarily to Lehi's dream and its imagery late in his record.[93]

Standing out in the collection of the symposium's talks as a particularly probing literary study is Amy Easton-Flake's "Lehi's Dream as a Template for Understanding Each Act of Nephi's Vision." Easton-Flake divides Nephi's vision in 1 Nephi 11–14 into four acts and then shows how each of Lehi's dream elements finds its peculiar place in these several acts of the longer vision-ary drama. Moving far beyond the obvious connections—moments where Nephi's angelic guide mentions or explains images from Lehi's dream—she reveals a complex literary web of allusions to and expansions of Lehi's dream in Nephi's vision. Exemplary is her treatment of the great and spacious building from Lehi's dream. It appears explicitly in 1 Nephi 11, but Easton-Flake points out how "the angel emphasizes that both general and (multiple) specific inter-pretations exist" for the symbol, directly noting its equation with "the world and the wisdom thereof" but also the gathering of "the house of Israel . . . to fight against the twelve apostles."[94] The same image appears more subtly, then, in the second act of Nephi's vision, garnering "a new historical interpretation in the New World: Nephites and Lamanites 'gathered together to battle, one against another' (1 Nephi 12:2)."[95] The third act then provides yet another "new symbol" with "striking similarities to the great and spacious building," namely the famed great and abominable church; Easton-Flake argues that the similar-ities are strong enough to make the church "a historical analogue of the build-ing."[96] This reemerges later in the same third act of the vision, when "the mother Gentiles" become "another iteration of the great and spacious building," another "historical analogue to the symbolic opposition between the inhabitants of the great and spacious building and the individuals at the tree."[97] Finally, in the fourth act, the building reappears once more as the great and abominable church gathers to fight against the Lamb of God, "just as the great and spacious building has 'gathered together' (1 Nephi 11:35) multitudes to fight against the Twelve Apostles of the Lamb, the Nephites, the Saints of God, and the Gentiles in America."[98]

Charles Swift's contribution to the same symposium is actually just one of several studies he published over the course of the first decade or so of the twenty-first century. All of these publications, it seems, grew out of his 2003 doctoral dissertation, "'I Have Dreamed a Dream.'" In that dissertation, Swift aimed to bring to the Book of Mormon a typological or even archetypal reading focused on what he calls "literature's experiential nature."[99] He divides Lehi's dream account into twenty specific scenes that strike the reader as distinct vignettes in a dream-like experience.[100] He then pursues a point-by-point analysis of each image in the dream, archetypally—reminiscent of the archetypal study from the mid-1980s by Julie Maddox Adams. A good example of Swift's interpretive style lies in his analysis of the man robed in white from Lehi's dream. "After the darkness of the wilderness at the beginning of the vision, we now have a contrast in the whiteness of the man's robe, representing 'an elemental opposition of dark and light,'" Swift writes.[101] White, he points out, drawing from archetypal literature, signals not only purity but also "timelessness."[102] He surveys passages of scriptures in which robes—and particularly white robes—appear, and then he sets forth an argument that "the man in the white robe is John the Revelator," but also simultaneously "a type": "John, but . . . more than John."[103] Finally, he explores the way in which the figure in white serves as a potentially exemplary teacher, a figure who "did not even do so much as take [Lehi] to the tree of life," but rather "helped Lehi get to a point, as a student, where he could do what he needed to do in order to learn."[104]

That literary interpretations began again to dominate discussion of Lehi's dream in the first decade of the twenty-first century by no means implies that all other approaches disappeared suddenly. Historical concerns generally dominate in Brant Gardner's 2007 multi-faceted commentary, and this is especially true in his treatment of Lehi's vision, where he interacts at length with earlier scholars' theses regarding Izapa Stela 5.[105] A 2002 summary of research on possible Arabian connections with 1 Nephi written by Kent Brown includes a Nibley-like sketch of the dream's appropriateness to the Arabian setting.[106] One essay from the 2011 Sidney B. Sperry Symposium—written by Dana Pike—takes up a strictly historical angle in illuminating the way that ancient Israelites understood dreams.[107] Further, doctrinal studies of Lehi's dream were also part of the Sidney B. Sperry Symposium from 2011,[108] and doctrinal commentaries in the tradition of McConkie and Millet appeared in the first decade or so of the twenty-first century too.[109] Despite the existence of these other contenders, it was clear by the end of the first decade of the twenty-first century that the literary study of Lehi's dream had arrived and even assumed a privileged position. Yet, although literary interpretations came to a kind of prominence as Book of

Mormon studies entered a new era in a new century, they quickly came to share the stage with another emergent approach to the text.

THE THEOLOGICAL LEHI (CA. 2000–THE PRESENT)

Grant Hardy's *Understanding the Book of Mormon* was unmistakably a breakthrough book in 2010, a serious study of the Book of Mormon published by a non-Latter-day Saint press for a broader academic audience. What cleared the space it came to occupy, however, was another key study of the Book of Mormon that the same press published in 2002: Terryl Givens's *By the Hand of Mormon*. Where Hardy would take up a narratological perspective on the text—and therefore invest in a serious way in the text of the Book of Mormon itself—Givens offered to the world a study of how various readers have responded to the Book of Mormon from its first appearance to the end of the twentieth century. The result is an approach arguably less focused on the text of the Book of Mormon itself, but nonetheless an approach with a deep theological sensibility. For Givens, the reason to talk about the Book of Mormon to the larger academic world is to make room for a serious assessment of the Restoration's theological contribution. Somewhat ironically, the core of Givens's argument in *By the Hand of Mormon* is that the Book of Mormon actually has little to *say* that is of lasting theological value; its theological provocation lies rather in what it *does*, in its very existence. In Givens's own words, "the history of the Book of Mormon's place in Mormonism and American religion generally has always been more connected to its status as *signifier* than *signified*, or its role as sacred sign rather than its function as persuasive theology."[110] The Book of Mormon brings believers into a religion where the compelling theology is to be received through direct prophetic revelation, rather than providing them with a compelling theology within its own pages.

Where Hardy's book would mark a culminating endpoint for a period in which literary interpretation of the Book of Mormon struggled to establish itself, Givens's book was arguably an inaugurating gesture, the beginning of a new era for the Book of Mormon and its interpretation. Givens forcefully asked the question of what the Book of Mormon might have to do with theology, while influentially insisting that theological questions matter most. As it turned out, there were other theologically minded scholars emerging at that very moment, eager to respond to the call Givens was issuing. Only a year after the appearance of Givens's book, a group of Latter-day Saint philosophers and theologians gathered to organize the Society for Mormon Philosophy and Theology, an institution to host annual conferences beginning in 2004 and publish a printed journal (*Element*) beginning in 2005. Similarly minded Latter-day Saint scholars created the Association for Mormon Scholars in the Humanities shortly thereafter, holding its first annual conference in 2007. In 2008, moreover, the Mormon Theology Seminar (recently renamed the Latter-day Saint Theology Seminar) sponsored the first of its many seminars on scriptural theology. By the end of the decade, it was clear that theology would be a major focus of Latter-day Saint intellectual life in the twenty-first century.

Although much of this emergent theological work had its focus on the Book of Mormon—especially the specifically scriptural seminars hosted by the Mormon Theology Seminar[111]—little of it gave its attention directly to Lehi's dream in 1 Nephi 8.[112] In fact, the most explicitly theological investigation of Lehi's dream to appear in the first decade of the twenty-first century was penned by Terryl Givens, in a brief study that suggestively moderated his earlier position (that the Book of Mormon has relatively little to say theologically in its own right).[113] In his 2009 *The Book of Mormon: A Very Short Introduction*, he provides a sketch of a reading that finds in Lehi's dream (and Nephi's expansion of it afterwards) "five themes" that "constitute the backbone" of the Book of Mormon theologically: "personal revelation, Christ, varieties of Zion, new configurations of scripture, and the centrality of family."[114] Several of these themes are more at home in Nephi's apocalyptic expansion of Lehi's simpler and less apocalyptic dream, but Givens roots two of them directly in literary features of Lehi's dream account itself. The Zion theme Givens ties to "Lehi's unusual emphasis on the temporal and geographical details of his present vision"—his references to "a dark and dreary wilderness," to "the space of many hours," to "a spacious field," and so forth.[115] As for the centrality of family, Givens points out that "Lehi's vision of the Tree of Life is framed at both ends and marked internally by his parental preoccupation," as readers of the dream often note.[116] For Givens, these are themes that reach out from Lehi's dream into the rest of the Book of Mormon, giving theological shape to the whole volume.

A more systematically theological interpretation of Lehi's dream would appear in my own study of 1 Nephi, published in 2020. Taking Nephi's expansive vision in 1 Nephi 10–14 as the key to understanding Lehi's dream in 1 Nephi 8, I argued that the dream divides into two halves—a first half focused on Lehi's and Sariah's sons, and a second half focused on somewhat mysterious multitudes. In the first half, there is "no talk of iron rods, narrow paths, dark mists, or strange buildings." Thus, "the whole family of Lehi apparently has ready access" to the life-giving tree, while the later multitudes have a more complex pathway to the tree and its deliverance. Because "what marks the break between the easier experience of Lehi's family and the more difficult experience of the multitudes" is "the moment when Laman and Lemuel 'would not come . . . and partake of the fruit,'" it seems apparent that the multitudes consist of the distant descendants of Laman and Lemuel.[117] Thus, although "we're accustomed to thinking that the second half of Lehi's dream is about all human beings striving to find Christ," it turns out that "we're meant to see it as a representation of the difficulties faced at specific points in history by specific peoples. . . . Latter-day Lamanites must hold the iron rod (the Book of Mormon) and follow the path (the gospel of Jesus Christ) as they avoid the dangers of the great and spacious building (the Gentiles' great and abominable church)."[118]

What makes this interpretation theological? The answer is that it functions as part of a larger and thoroughly systematic exposition of the Book of Mormon's covenant theology. The Book of Mormon, on this reading, has a consistent but complexly deployed theological conception of how God intervenes in the world to redeem humankind. He creates a people with a responsibility for the whole world but then watches as they betray his purposes, and so he redeems them by grace in a way that wakes up all the world to his truth.[119] The Lamanite part of this story is told in Nephi's vision and likened to patterns in Isaiah's prophecies but allegorically encoded in Lehi's dream. Naturally, this is not the only way one might understand the theological implications of the relationship between Lehi's dream and Nephi's vision. In another representative of emerging theological interest in the Book of Mormon, Bradley Kramer finds in Nephi's expansive vision the result of an experiential and contemplative approach to the dream. That is, Kramer argues that Nephi himself models a certain theological approach to Lehi's dream that might be emulated by latter-day readers, a way of reading scripture that proves to be akin to that of rabbinical Judaism. Readers need to learn to ask, like Nephi, about the varied layers of the dream's meaning.[120]

Although relatively few directly or sustainedly theological readings of Lehi's dream have yet been offered in the context of the increasingly apparent theological turn in Latter-day Saint intellectual culture, it is clear that the theological climate is having its effects on other, more traditional approaches to 1 Nephi 8, which continue to appear in print. A good example can be found in *Lehi's Dream*, a doctrinal and pastoral reflection on the dream authored by Robert Millet. Although he interprets the dream in recognizable ways, Millet offers in his short book-length study a pastorally rich and genuinely affecting engagement with each sequence of the dream account. Of the iron rod, Millet writes, "And what is this anchor, this Godsend that enables us to pass safely through the tsunamis of the soul? Nephi explains simply that it is 'the word of

God' (1 Nephi 11:25)."[121] Writing on the great and spacious building, he says, "hubris knows no boundaries or class distinctions, and high-mindedness has no age restrictions. One thing all the residents have in common, however, is their obsession with the best and the finest, the flashiest and the most expensive."[122] Here a doctrinal scholar seems to work from a more strictly theological sensibility, at the very least a deeper predilection for pastoral theology.

Another example of an increased theological sensitivity in work that is not directly or unreservedly theological is Matthew Scott Stenson's 2012 article, "Lehi's Dream and Nephi's Vision." Tapping into the larger literature on whether and how Lehi's dream (and Nephi's vision) might be placed within the genre of apocalyptic literature, Stenson nonetheless goes further than his predecessors by clarifying the theological consequences that follow from such a genre assignment. He provides theologically toned reflections on the disorienting nature of the dream's symbols, on the strong sense of dualism that operates in the dream, and on the "conceptual and doctrinal basis" the genre provides for Nephi's larger theological project.[123] Another important example is David Calabro's 2017 article, "Lehi's Dream and the Garden of Eden." Calabro's study is in many ways a familiar example of historical research, attempting to find a place in the ancient world for Lehi's dream. Expanding beyond the findings of earlier scholars (for example, those publishing in the first issues of the *Journal of Book of Mormon Studies* in the early 1990s), Calabro concludes that "the setting of Lehi's dream represents a conception of the garden of Eden generally consistent with Genesis 2–3 but varying in some significant matters of detail."[124] Those matters of detail lead Calabro to conclude that "the Book of Mormon presupposes an alternate version of the Genesis account, perhaps a version from the brass plates" that has other traces in ancient traditions.[125] For Calabro, significantly, this suggests a different theological schema for Book of Mormon authors, figures familiar with a different set of foundational stories that might affect their theological assumptions and conclusions. (Mirroring Calabro's approach—Lehi's dream is "a partial correction of the Eden story"— despite offering a briefer treatment is Michael Austin's interpretation in *Buried Treasures*.)[126]

A much more peculiar theological inflection of earlier and more strictly historical approaches to Lehi's dream has appeared in what has arguably become a whole school of interpretation. This particular theological approach has its roots in historical research on Nephi's vision undertaken by Daniel Peterson and developed by other historically-minded scholars.[127] Peterson argued at the end of the 1990s that Nephi's references to both the tree of life and the virgin in 1 Nephi 11 might allude to controversial Israelite worship of the Canaanite goddess Asherah. Apparently apprehensive about how his argument might be appropriated, Peterson published his earliest and longest treatment of the subject with a disclaimer: "So that there will be no mistake about my position, let me briefly speak rather more personally: This essay should not be misinterpreted as a brief for theological or ecclesiological innovation within The Church of Jesus Christ of Latter-day Saints."[128] Perhaps because the disclaimer did not appear in the more accessible piece published a few years later, Peterson's research has been used by many among rising feminist interpreters of the Book of Mormon to elaborate the Latter-day Saint theological notion of a Heavenly Mother.

For the latter sort of interpreter, the association in the ancient Near East between Asherah and tree imagery provides a connection between Lehi's dream and the worship of a female divinity. Thanks especially to the writings of Margaret Barker, a revisionist biblical scholar with a startlingly unique picture of ancient Israel, such interpreters feel they have ample grounding to argue for a restoration of the divine feminine to the Book of Mormon.[129] This has spurred a flurry of what should be called sublimationist feminist readings of the Book of Mormon—that is, feminist readings that give less time to analyzing how female human beings fare in the book than to looking for traces of the divine feminine.[130] Sublimationist readings of the Book of Mormon have been available in certain forms since at least the 1990s,[131] but they have only recently claimed to be on serious scholarly footing. At the end of the second decade of the twenty-first century, few such interpretations have appeared in peer-reviewed publications, but there is evidence of increasingly widespread popular interest in this approach, evidenced in poetry and visual art.[132]

Also simultaneously historical and theological is increased interest in placing the Book of Mormon's notion of the tree of life in conversation with a variety of tree-of-life traditions spread throughout the world's various religions and cultures. Hugh Nibley pointed out already in the mid-twentieth century that "many hundreds of books and articles have been written on the Tree of Life as a symbol and a cult-object."[133] Unpacking that passing claim, John Welch and Donald Parry organized a symposium in 2006 on the subject, bringing together a host of scholars to talk about the importance of tree-of-life imagery across the whole of the ancient world. They summarize in their introduction to the symposium's published proceedings: "It is found among the Assyrians, Babylonians, and others of the Levant (greater Eastern Mediterranean area); various groups in Egypt, sub-Saharan Africa, and Greece; the Aborigines and Warramunga of Australia; the Coorgs and Khasiyas of India; and several other Asian religions (especially Buddhism, Taoism, and Hinduism). Furthermore, sacred trees serve to characterize North American native religions, including the Kwakiutl of the Pacific, the Karok in the Northwest, and the Seneca of the Northeast, as well as the Haida, the Salish, the Kiowa, the Zuni, the Navaho, the Mandan, the Lakota, and the Oglala Sious. South American and Mesoamerican sacred tree mythologies are also prominent and include the Uyurucares of Bolivia, the Maya, the Aztecs, and the Warao."[134]

Comparative study of Lehi's dream along such lines, while certainly historical in a crucial way, helps in other ways to shift the conversation about 1 Nephi 8 into the theological register. This is particularly evident in Welch and Parry's decision to include Jaime Lara's "The Tree of Life in the Catholic Religious and Liturgical Imagination" in their collection of essays. Lara asks readers to reflect on differences between Protestant and Catholic ways of reflecting on the divine and so invites them "to ask and answer the correlative question, How do Latter-day Saints imagine religiously?"[135] With such a gesture, and with deep attention to the ways in which distinct world traditions communicate through their shared interest in the symbol of a life-giving tree, the historical begins to give way to the theological. This finds further corroboration in the fact that it is this incredibly widespread interest in sacred and life-giving trees that serves to explain the particular popularity of Lehi's dream as a subject of artistic depiction among Latter-day Saints outside of the United States and Europe.[136]

A distinctively theological era in the interpretation of the Book of Mormon quite generally—and of course, in particular of Lehi's dream—has thus begun in earnest. Yet, although strictly theological interpretations of the dream have only just begun to appear in the first decades of the twenty-first century, the essays that follow in the present volume add in a striking way to the furthering of the new interpretive interest. If the Book of Mormon is rather generally revealing itself to be a source for rich and sustained theological reflection, then the theological interpretation of Lehi's dream must become a load-bearing wall in the edifice that is now being built. The scholars who bring their theological training and interests to bear on the interpretation of the dream in the following pages show just how much theological weight Lehi's dream can hold. If the essays in this volume are any indication, then, there is every reason to believe that the tree of Lehi's dream will yet yield rich and varied kinds of theological fruit.

The Thing
Which I Have Seen:
A History of Lehi's Dream in Visual Art

JENNIFER CHAMPOUX

LEHI'S DREAM—WHICH HE ALSO APPROPRIATELY CALLS A VISION—WAS a profoundly sight-based experience. In the 38 verses that make up 1 Nephi 8, the idea or act of seeing or being seen is mentioned 33 times. The language used to describe this visionary experience includes the phrases "I have seen," "I saw," "I beheld," "I looked," and "I cast my eyes." Additionally, the dangers of the obstruction of sight are highlighted in these verses, including Lehi's initial harrowing journey through "darkness" and later a "mist of darkness" that obscures the path, causing some people to lose their way. Visual perception is at the heart of Lehi's encounter. And yet, Lehi's dream is related to us through words, not pictures. The tree, river, building, and other elements are images, or mental pictures, that exist only in the mind of Lehi. His verbal description of these elements was recorded by his son Nephi, removing them a further step from Lehi's original vision. Moreover, these elements are only known to us now through Joseph Smith's much later translation of Nephi's writing. Artistic portrayals of the dream are then images of images—not replicas of a known object

Approaching the Tree: Interpreting 1 Nephi 8

27

but, rather, creative expressions of a fundamentally unviewable idea. This is what makes Lehi's dream art so challenging and also so full of possibility.

When you think about Lehi's dream as recounted in 1 Nephi 8, what images spring to mind? A tall leafy tree with white fruit? An iron rod next to a river? Do you imagine a large rectangular building with Italianate arched windows and balconies, or a building that looks more like an ancient Near Eastern ziggurat? If there are people, do they look happy or anxious? Do you know who they are? Are you one of them? Is it dark or daylight? In answering these questions perhaps, whether you realize it or not, you have a certain artist's rendering of the scene in mind. Paintings, drawings, sculpture, and other artworks based on Lehi's dream heavily influence how we picture the prophet's dream in our mind's eye. Moreover, the visual arts influence how we *understand* the dream. As historian Richard Bushman has noted, artists are "theologians of depiction."[1] Artists make decisions about what to include and what to leave out, and how to approach the scene. These decisions can affect the way members of The Church of Jesus Christ of Latter-day Saints think about moments in history or passages of scripture, like Lehi's dream.

Today, images of Lehi's dream are ubiquitous, accounting for about 7 percent of all visual art based on Book of Mormon content. This is by far the most artistic attention given to any one topic from the Book of Mormon.[2] But for the first 45 years after the Book of Mormon was published, there were no depictions of Lehi's dream. And for the first 150 years after the Book of Mormon was published, there were about 25. There are over 250 known Lehi's dream images today, and almost all of them are from only the past 40 years. Much (but not all) of that imagery follows somewhat traditional patterns of portraying Lehi's dream that were established by the earliest artists. There are a number of themes and approaches that are not well represented in the existing artwork, such as images that: (1) consider the order of events as Lehi relates them (rather than condensing them into one scene), (2) think about the implications of and possibilities in "visionary" scripture, (3) highlight the familial focus of Lehi's retelling of the dream, (4) assess the role of women in the dream, (5) give attention to Lehi's journey in the dark wilderness before arriving at the tree, and (6) include Christ in the scene.

Why is this the case? This chapter seeks to trace the development of approaches to portraying Lehi's dream and considers what may have led artists to consistently return to the same patterns. This chapter will thus create a narrative of how Lehi's dream art developed, which will in turn expose some of the conflicts and opportunities in portraying 1 Nephi 8. Furthermore, Lehi's dream imagery is demonstrative of larger issues in Latter-day Saint visual art. This case study reveals the potential of images to affect interpretation of scripture, the role of the institutional Church in determining image saturation and preference among Church members, and patterns of image use within the Latter-day Saint tradition. As there is quite a bit of overlap in the themes, a general overview of trends in the development of Lehi's dream art will be presented first, followed by a discussion of patterns and possibilities raised by the historical record, and then a contextualization of Lehi's dream art within the larger scope of changes within Latter-day Saint art. The historical record will be covered in three time periods: 1830–1979, 1980–1999, and 2000–2019.

For purposes of this survey, the art can generally be divided into four broad categories based on how it depicts the scene: panoramic, symbolic, universal, or Lehi-focused. The panoramic images try to illustrate all aspects of the dream, creating a map-like terrain filled with a river, a mist, a narrow path, a rod of iron, a spacious building, and a fruited tree. Often the panoramic images include crowds of people. On the other hand, artists who use the symbolic approach concentrate on one element and use it to represent the whole dream. A painting of a solitary tree is an example of this approach. A third standard approach is to personalize or universalize Lehi's experience. In this case, the image no longer seeks to represent Lehi or precisely what he recounted, but instead applies symbols or themes from the dream to other people. In some cases, there is a single figure before a tree, or in other cases latter-day families or groups of people are depicted in the familiar dreamscape. Finally, the fourth approach emphasizes Lehi and sometimes also his family, often showing them standing near the tree or with fruit, but without many other elements.

EARLY DEVELOPMENT OF LEHI'S DREAM ART (1830–1979)

One of the remarkable things about Book of Mormon art is how little there was of it until quite recently. In fact, the first recorded illustration of a Book of Mormon scene was in 1872 (42 years after the publication of the Book of Mormon) with a painting of the baptism of Limhi. The artist, George Ottinger, wrote in his journal that he had just completed "the first Picture ever painted from a subject suggested by the Book of Mormon."[3] Two years later, in 1874, Lehi's dream was also one of the very first scenes from the Book of Mormon to be visualized in art, although not by a member of The Church of Jesus Christ of Latter-day Saints. David Hyrum Smith, son of Joseph Smith Jr. and a leader in the Reorganized Church of Jesus Christ of Latter Day Saints (now renamed Community of Christ), painted Lehi being led to a tree by an angel (Fig. 1).[4]

FIG. 1. David Hyrum Smith, *Lehi's Dream*, c. 1875, Courtesy of Community of Christ Archives, International Headquarters, Independence, MO.

Lehi wears a belted brown robe and sandals, and his long white beard shows his age. The angel appears more youthful, with brown hair and a clean-shaven face. The angel wears a white robe, and his bare feet float several inches above the ground. While the angel looks ahead, Lehi looks back towards the other figures, holding up a fruited branch of the tree in one hand as if to offer it to them. Lehi's left hand firmly grasps the iron rod that winds around the tree. To the left, a dark river recedes into mist, where several people are swallowed up in cracks in the earth. Above them, a corner of a large building is filled with people. Smith's panoramic image compresses the dream to capture the many symbols that appear over the course of 1 Nephi 8.

It was 75 years later that Lehi's dream was first visually depicted by a member of The Church of Jesus Christ of Latter-day Saints with Minerva Teichert's, *The House of the World* (Fig. 2). Teichert included the various elements such as a tree, white fruit, iron rod, river, and large building, but she concentrated on Lehi and his family, who are pushed up to the front of the picture plane. In fact, the image uniquely centers on Sariah, in a red and gold robe, who grasps the

The Thing Which I Have Seen: A History of Lehi's Dream in Visual Art

rod and kneels while pointing to the tree with her other hand. John Welch and Doris Dant have read Sariah's pose as indicating her desperate pleading with Laman and Lemuel, who can be seen rowing a boat towards the entrance of the building.[5] Lehi wears eastern dress and stands firmly by the tree, holding out fruit to his family as they approach. Their other sons, also in exotic eastern dress, shuffle in line behind Sariah, holding to the rod.

FIG. 2. Minerva Teichert (1888–1976), *The House of the World*, 1949–1951, oil on masonite, 36 × 48 inches. Brigham Young University Museum of Art 1969.

A few years later, Avon W. Smith Oakeson painted another panoramic dream image in her 1955 *The Tree of Life* (Fig. 3). The building is emphasized by its central placement, large size, and bright light. The mist of darkness surrounds the building, and a river of water divides it from a narrow path with an iron rod. The tree stands in contrast to the building but is smaller. Many figures in various attitudes crowd the building, the field outside of it, and the path to the tree, but only a few figures are stopped at the tree. The painting conveys a strong sense of movement. The design of the image draws the viewer's eye in a zig-zag motion starting with the building, then down the misty landscape to

FIG. 3. Avon W. Smith Oakeson, *The Tree of Life*, 1955, oil on canvas, © Intellectual Reserve, Inc.

the crowds of people, forward and across the canvas along the iron rod until it rests on the tree and then continues to the right again as figures move off into rocky paths. Two larger figures stand before the tree, both with white hair, white beards, and white robes. One wears a red mantle and one a blue mantle, and both point to the tree. It's unclear who these figures represent but given their clothing and appearance they may be Heavenly Father and Jesus Christ (often shown in Christian art with a red mantle). Perhaps Lehi and his family are the figures kneeling around the tree. This painting appears in the Church's *Come, Follow Me: Learning and Teaching Resources 2020* printed and online manuals.

Lehi's dream was portrayed again in 1975 with Franz Johansen's bronze sculpture *The Iron Rod* (Fig. 4). Rather than trying to recreate what Lehi may have seen, Johansen focused just on the iron rod and one individual's effort to cling to it, representing the spiritual longing of all people. The difficulty of the task is apparent in the boy's body, which sags down as if falling. His legs even break through the lower border of the sculpture. His gaze, focused on the rod, does not allow him to see the heavenly figure approaching. Christ floats effortlessly toward the boy—his toes pointed down and his drapery fluttering—and holds his arms outstretched in a reminder of his crucifixion but also in a gesture of aid. His fingers barely extend from beneath the veil separating him from the mortal boy. Vertical and horizontal movement are perfectly balanced, culminating in the potential energy of the empty space between the boy's hand slipping off the rod and the reaching hand of divinity. Richard Oman, former curator at the Museum of Church History and Art[6] explained, "The viewer must, by imagination, continue the boy's and the heavenly being's reaching until they touch. This interaction emotionally engages the viewer in the creation of the sculpture and especially in the spiritual yearning of the youth."[7] Johansen's piece was the first to universalize themes and symbols from Lehi's dream.

FIG. 4. Franz Johansen, *The Iron Rod*, 1975, cast bronze, 252 × 213 × 16 cm, © Intellectual Reserve, Inc.

In the late 1970s, Jerry Thompson created a few illustrations of Lehi's dream for the Church's *Book of Mormon Stories* publication. They still appear in the Primary manual, the Gospel Art Book, and in the *Come, Follow Me: Book of Mormon Learning and Teaching Resources 2020* manual. Thompson's *Lehi's Dream* (Fig. 5) sticks with the panoramic approach but positions viewers as if they are moving forward toward the tree, drawing them into the scene. Individuals and families in biblical dress move along the rod. Dark mists cover

the very front of the picture plane, but in the background the bright light of the tree beckons at the end of the iron rod and lights the path to it. The river of water runs in a chasm separating the tree from a large building teeming with people. Of the many figures in the image, only four face the viewer, and they stand beneath the tree welcoming others. They may represent Lehi (in the belted robe and long shawl), Sariah, Nephi, and Sam, who are described in 1 Nephi 8 as partaking of the fruit. Two other figures turn away from the tree and wave to others in the building, likely Laman and Lemuel, who refused to eat the fruit. The painting is a very literal and panoramic rendering of the scripture passage.

These five artworks are among the handful of known finished images created of Lehi's dream in the 150 years from the Book of Mormon's printing in 1830 up until 1979. Apart from Johansen's sculpture, they are all panoramic, and they all seem to include Lehi, his family, and several narrative elements. Their purpose appears to be largely didactic, helping Church members visualize the various elements of Lehi's dream. The paucity of Lehi's dream art in this period is not surprising, given that in the first 100 years of the Church, there were not many religious scenes at all, either based on scriptural or historical scenes. Early Latter-day Saint artists focused instead on landscapes. With a few exceptions, art was not employed for religious education until the mid- to late-twentieth century.

It is perhaps surprising, though, that Lehi's dream was not included in most of the Book of Mormon illustrated series during this period, including George Reynolds' 1888 series for *The Story of the Book of Mormon*, C. C. A. Christensen's 1891 series for the Deseret Sunday School Union, and Arnold Friberg's 1952–55 series commissioned by Primary general president Adele Cannon Howells. In fact, the Deseret Sunday School Union did consider Lehi's dream as one of the scenes. In 1890, George Q. Cannon, then General Superintendent of the Deseret Sunday School Union, issued a call for art illustrating Nephi's life in twelve scenes, including "Lehi's vision of the iron rod, etc., I Nephi, chapter viii."[8] For unknown reasons, this scene and another one listed (the death of Laban) did not end up in the final illustrations.

Similarly, Friberg seems to have considered Lehi's dream for his famed Book of Mormon series. He sketched at least 40 different Book of Mormon scenes in the early 1950s, of which only 12 were fully realized as paintings for the commission from Howells. The series was limited to 12 because Howells originally intended to print one per issue in *The Children's Friend* monthly magazine during its 50th anniversary year.[9] Friberg, Howells, President David O. McKay, the First Presidency, and members of the Quorum of the Twelve worked together to select the final 12 scenes based on their "doctrinal and historical importance," their ability to "inspire the young with heroic views of the great religious leaders," and their "artistic possibilities."[10] Although Lehi's dream was not selected for the series, Friberg did sketch a compositional study of *Lehi's Vision of the Tree of Life* (Fig. 6) as well as two related studies of Lehi standing before the tree, and a pastel sketch of *Nephi and His Wife Hold to the Iron Rod* (Fig. 7). This largely unknown pastel is distinct for its tender portrayal of Nephi and his wife supporting each other as they cling to the rod, with Lehi

FIG. 6. Arnold Friberg, *Lehi's Vision of the Tree of Life*, graphite on paper, 8½ × 10¾ inches, c. 1950, Anthony's Fine Art and Antiques.

to the left encouraging them. Friberg's larger compositional study (Fig. 6) for Lehi's dream also included both Nephi and his wife holding to the rod. Lehi, standing before a towering tree, calls to them with open arms. The outline of the spacious building appears in the background, and two figures walking away from Lehi are seen in the lower right, along with perhaps another figure lost in the mists of darkness. Despite the inclusion of these elements, Friberg's composition focuses on characters rather than on landscape, highlighting the strong figure of Lehi beckoning to his family.

POPULARIZATION OF LEHI'S DREAM ART (1980–1999)

The 1980s and 1990s saw an explosion of new images about Lehi's dream. As Table 1 illustrates, that upwards trend has held constant since then.[11] The dramatic increase in Lehi's dream art production in the 1980s and 1990s was symptomatic of a more large-scale increase in religious art production and use by the Church. BYU professor Anthony Sweat explains that images of early Church history, such as Joseph Smith's first vision, were not used in the first one hundred years of the Church's existence. He suggests this may have been

Table 1. Number of Lehi's dream artworks by decade.

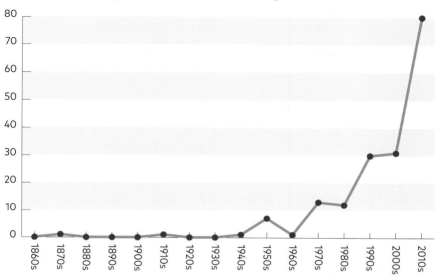

FIG. 7. Arnold Friberg, *Nephi and His Wife Hold to the Iron Rod*, pastel on paper, 16¾ × 21¾ inches, c. 1950, Anthony's Fine Art and Antiques.

due in part to Protestant iconoclastic tendencies and financial constraints in the early days of the Church, but mainly to the lack of official discourse on the events. Sweat argues that "the single most salient cultural reason is that the First Vision simply was not emphasized by the early Restored Church as a focal point for its historical or theological narrative," and that more discourse on the First Vision led to more art about it.[12] To some extent, this logic holds true for Lehi's dream images. References to Lehi's dream in General Conference talks were made more frequently in the 2010s than any other prior decade and were made frequently since the 1980s. Those decades of the 1980s through 2010s also saw a sizable output of Lehi's dream art. Yet, Lehi's dream and the tree of life have been referenced heavily in other decades too, including the 1850s, the 1930s, the 1940s, and the 1960s, without an accompanying uptick in art production.[13] While the impact of rhetoric on particular topics may be a factor in the increased production and use of religious art on those topics, to say it is the defining factor overlooks more global trends, including the rise in didactic use of art by the Church in the second half of the twentieth century.

In his 1992 article on Lehi's dream art, Oman noted the shift at that time in Latter-day Saint art away from American western landscapes and pioneer figures and towards scenes inspired by the scriptures.[14] At the same time, the Museum of Church History and Art was encouraging artistic production with commissions and with the establishment of the International Art Competition in 1988. Church publications such as the *Ensign* and *Liahona* also began publishing more art images at this time. The popularization of Lehi's dream art in the 1980s and 1990s is another example of this larger pattern for Latter-day Saint religious art, and it seems to have less to do with increased rhetoric about the dream than it does with an increased desire for religious art of all kinds.

In the 1980s, most images kept to the panoramic approach. Steven Neal's massive *Lehi's Dream—Tree of Life* (Fig. 8), for example, depicts a sprawling landscape with mountain ranges in the background, rivers spilling forward, rocky cliffs in front of the building, and a grassy field under the tree. Light and dark are used to represent good and evil, with rays of light streaming from heaven onto the glowing tree on the left, and gray storm clouds swirling over the building on the right. Neal's approach is also somewhat universalizing, in that he included figures and architecture from various cultures as well as a portrait of himself and his wife and daughter in the foreground. But he also included the narrative detail of Lehi dozing and dreaming in the lower left. Neal's painting was the Grand Prize Winner of the First International Art Competition held in 1988 and is one of only two images based on Lehi's dream

FIG. 8. Steven Neal, *Lehi's Dream—Tree of Life*, 1984–1987, 48 × 96 inches, used with permission of the artist.

sold in the Church History Museum store. It is featured in the *Come, Follow Me: Book of Mormon Learning and Teaching Resources 2020* manual.

Robin Luch Griego's stained glass *Lehi's Vision of the Tree of Life* (Fig. 9) is another of the most frequently reproduced images on the theme from the 1980s. Lehi offers white fruit from the tree to Sariah. They stand under the tree, which is the focus of the image. Other elements such as an iron rod, a straight and narrow path, a river, and a mist are also included, making it a sort of panorama. This image was featured on the cover of the *Ensign* magazine in June 1996.

Greg Olsen's *Tree of Life* (Fig. 10) is another good example of the panoramic approach in this era, and the piece remains popular today. Following the pattern established by artists such as Oakeson, Thompson, and Neal, Olsen situated the tree and rod on the left, with people moving from the foreground to the background along a straight path. A river and chasm divide this scene from the tall building on the right. Mist covers the ground on both sides, and the tree glows with light. Yet, in a break with tradition, rather than focusing on Lehi or others enjoying the fruit, Olsen foregrounds three "lost" figures that have turned their backs on the tree and are seeking to cross the chasm to join the people in the building. Reproductions of Olsen's painting are among three images about Lehi's dream to be sold by Deseret Book.[15]

Quite different from the other images of the time, John Benthin's *The Iron Rod* (Fig. 11) from 1989 was the first image to simplify Lehi's dream to one symbolic element without any figures. A dark and slightly diagonal line

FIG. 9. Robin Luch Griego, *Vision of the Tree of Life*, 1983, glass and lead, 59 × 47½ inches, © Intellectual Reserve, Inc.

cuts horizontally across the entire canvas. There is neither ground line nor landscape. Only the abstract area of light on the right might be interpreted as a heavenly figure, but otherwise the rod floats in empty space. The artist explained, "I want to help the viewer co-create with me by exploring the

The Thing Which I Have Seen: A History of Lehi's Dream in Visual Art

FIG. 10. Greg Olsen, *The Tree of Life*, 1989, used with permission of the artist, www.GregOlsen.com.

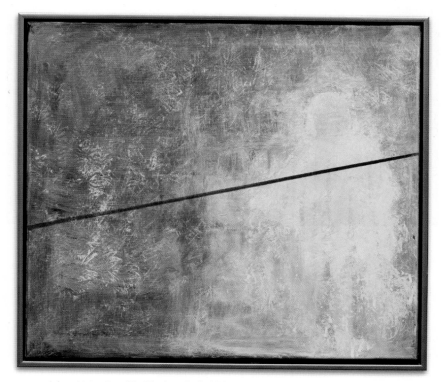

FIG. 11. Johan Helge Benthin, *The Iron Rod*, 1989, oil on canvas, 27 × 31 inches, © Intellectual Reserve, Inc.

painting more with his emotions than with his intellect."[16] This was a decided departure from the didactic, panoramic images. Rather than trying to draw a road map of the dreamscape, Benthin's work attempts to be a medium through which the viewer can seek spiritual insights in an open-ended way.

Kurt Sjokvist from Sweden was one of the first artists to use a three-dimensional approach in his carved wood *Lehi's Dream of the Tree of Life* (Fig. 12). The scene appears atop a globe, with a tree on one side and a building on

FIG. 13. Kazuto Uota, *Tree of Life*, 1990, tempera and plaster on board, 139 × 138 cm, © Intellectual Reserve, Inc.

the other. Figures circle the globe and follow a path upwards and between these two projecting elements. Although the carved globe approach is new, it maintains the map-like feel of earlier panoramic depictions.

Kazuto Uota's 1990 *Tree of Life* (Fig. 13) was the first artwork to focus solely on the tree, and it has become the most widely reproduced image of the tree of life in Latter-day Saint art.[17] Next to Neal's painting, it is the only other image based on Lehi's dream sold in the Church History Museum store. The golden-brown leaves and white fruit stand out against a dark monochromatic background. The artist's Japanese heritage influenced his approach to this piece. Richard Oman explained that the Japanese tea ceremony's "ritual journey, purification, and humility have parallels with Lehi's vision of commitment, humility, cooperation, and faith."[18] As guests at the tea ceremony are provided with a simple floral arrangement or branch to look at, so "Uota presents the tree of life with its glowing fruit as an object for contemplation."[19] In contrast to the panoramic images that show movement and urge a kind of active inspection and decoding by the viewer, Uota's image encourages a quiet introspection. His image of a solitary tree would inspire many similar tree images by Latter-day Saint artists over the years.

FIG. 14. Marwan Nahle, *1 Nephi 8:5–6 [He . . . Bade Me Follow Him]*, 1995, © Intellectual Reserve, Inc.

FIG. 15. Marcus Vincent, *The Tree of Life*, 1998, oil on linen, 34 × 36 inches, © Intellectual Reserve, Inc.

The 1990s also saw the first images to focus more particularly on Lehi, beginning with a piece by Marwan Nahlé of Lebanon. His abstract *1 Nephi 8:5–6 [He . . . Bade Me Follow Him]* (Fig. 14) depicts the beginning of Lehi's dream, when he followed a heavenly messenger through "a dark and dreary waste" (v. 7) before arriving at the tree. Two small figures are swallowed up in a vast and foreboding red and black landscape. This is one of the very few pieces that depict Lehi's journey before arriving at the tree.

More familiar to most Church members is Marcus Vincent's *The Tree of Life* (Fig. 15), that shows the prophet alone under a tree holding a piece of fruit he has just tasted. He wears priestly robes, closes his eyes, and raises his hands in a gesture of prayer. The blank background highlights the figure of Lehi. The image appears in the *Come, Follow Me: Book of Mormon Learning and Teaching Resources 2020* manual.

FIG. 16. Miguel Romero, *Sweeter Than All Sweetness*, 1999, hammered copper, 20 × 20 × 1 inches, © Intellectual Reserve, Inc.

In 1995 the Church issued "The Family: A Proclamation to the World," which stated the family is "ordained of God" and "central to the Creator's plan for the eternal destiny of His children."[20] Perhaps because of this emphasis, some artists began to show Lehi with his family during this time. In 1999, Miguel Romero entered *Sweeter Than All Sweetness* (Fig. 16) in the Church's Fifth International Art Competition. This piece has a strong focus on family, highlighting just this moment when Lehi's family gathers to taste the fruit, and leaving out the many other narrative details and symbolic elements. Romero's piece is also included in the *Come, Follow Me: Book of Mormon Learning and Teaching Resources 2020* manual.

The 1980s and 1990s witnessed the beginnings of an increase in religiously themed artistic production by Latter-day Saint artists. Characters and stories from scripture, including Lehi's dream, became popular subjects. Much of this art was narrative and figurative in style, focusing on telling the story and relaying a moralizing message. For Lehi's dream, the panoramic approach remained popular because it fit this instructive model so well, compressing many elements of the dream into one scene. During the 1990s, the volume of new artworks based on Lehi's dream increased dramatically. Critical interest in Lehi's dream art also spiked in the 1990s, during which time the Museum of Church History and Art commissioned artworks and held an exhibition on the theme, and several articles reviewing Lehi's dream art appeared in the *Ensign* and *Liahona* as well as in *BYU Studies Quarterly*.[21] At the same time, the Museum's curator, Richard Oman, made a concerted effort to facilitate and collect Latter-day Saint art produced outside the United States. As part of that effort, images of Lehi's dream were specifically encouraged because of their universal appeal (tree of life symbolism being common in many cultures), the rarity of previous works on the subject (allowing for greater freedom of visual expression not beholden to precedent), and the thought that American Latter-day Saints would be more accepting of a range of international styles if the subject matter was identifiable and relatable.[22] Oman hoped to "stylistically empower non-Western artists" by encouraging them to create art informed by their own culture, artistic heritage, lived experience, and individual reading of scripture.[23]

Exemplary of this approach is Tammy Garcia's, *Lehi's Vision of the Tree of Life* (Fig. 17). Garcia is an award-winning Santa Clara Pueblo sculptor and ceramic artist from New Mexico. In this redware clay piece, she combines traditional Pueblo techniques and geometric style with Latter-day Saint iconography. The pot shows Lehi led by a messenger to the tree with white fruit. Other artists such as Wang Xiu, David Bolarinwa, Joseph Banda, Jorge Cocco Santángelo, and Leta Keith similarly began to portray Lehi's dream using a variety of native techniques, cultural symbols, and materials. They also began depicting a diversity of figures and landscapes, showing Lehi's dream as if it took place in areas like Taiwan, Nigeria, Malawi, Argentina, or a Navajo reservation.

In the 1990s, artists from various countries began to bring their own styles, materials, and traditions to Lehi's dream art, and some artists experimented with different compositions or points of emphasis in Lehi's dream. This trend would influence the trajectory of Lehi's dream art, particularly as international artists introduced more symbolic or universalizing approaches to the scene.

LEHI'S DREAM AS SYMBOL (2000–2019)

After the turn of the century, there was substantial increase in the percentage of pieces that used symbolic or universalizing approaches (see Table 2). In 2004, the *Ensign* published a compilation of images based on 1 Nephi 8, the majority of which focused on the tree in the symbolic approach.[24] The first truly

Table 2. Number of Lehi's dream artworks in each category, by decade.

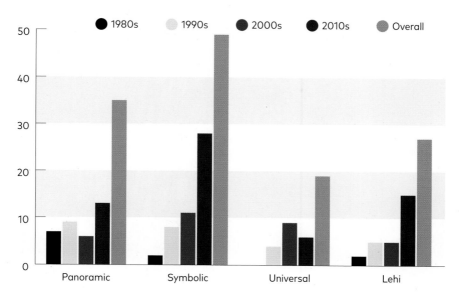

universalizing Lehi's dream art appeared in the 2000s. Sarah Merkley's *Heed Them Not (1 Nephi 8:34)* (Fig. 18) was featured in the *Ensign* in a review of pieces from the Church's Seventh International Art Competition.[25] It shows a woman sitting among the gnarled roots of the tree of life and holding a glowing piece of white fruit. She looks over her shoulder, perhaps in response to people jeering and looking down on her from a balcony of the spacious building. The building rises dramatically out of the mist, and the foreshortening of the Gothic architecture makes it even more imposing. Although the anonymous woman wears a kind of antique toga, she looks modern and thus appears to represent a timeless "everywoman." Her search for the fruit of the tree in spite of the world's mocking is depicted as a universal theme to which all people can relate. It encourages individuals to imagine themselves in Lehi's dream.

Similarly, in 2005 J. Kirk Richards was commissioned by a Latter-day Saint family to paint them at the tree of life (Fig. 19). A father, mother, and five children hold hands and gaze up to a large tree with white fruit. The tree is at the center of the image and there are no other symbols or narrative details from Lehi's dream. This modern family now takes the place of Lehi and his family in approaching the tree of life. The painting was later included in the *Ensign* as an

FIG. 18. Sarah Merkley, *Heed Them Not (1 Nephi 8:34)*, 2006, oil painting, 25.5 × 39.5 inches, used with permission of the artist.

FIG. 19. J. Kirk Richards, *Tree of Life*, 2005, private collection, used with permission of the artist.

illustration in Elder Daniel L. Johnson's "Hold Fast to the Rod" article about studying the scriptures regularly.[26]

Although the symbolic and universal approaches gained popularity in the early 2000s, the panoramic approach continued to be pervasive as well. Jon McNaughton painted his version of the tree of life in 2007 (Fig. 20), in a scene that echoes earlier panoramic images like Olsen's. In the center of the image, a tree springs forth from a barren, mountainous landscape. The tree is backlit by a rising sun and surrounded by a blue sky and yellow and pink clouds. A

FIG. 20. Jon McNaughton, *Tree of Life*, 2007, used with permission of the artist.

stream of water springs forward from the tree. The iron rod and a line of small figures cuts diagonally across the canvas, which creates even greater emphasis on the tree. The mist catches in the rocky foreground, where figures wander. A large building sits to the left, its slanting walls and flat roof reminiscent of Mesoamerican temples. It is perhaps not surprising that McNaughton kept with the traditional panoramic approach, as many of his paintings are typically heavily didactic and often political, and the panoramic approach allows for a straightforward moralizing portrayal of the scene.

The past decade saw a large increase in the number of Lehi's dream images using the symbolic approach, making it the most popular method today (see Tables 1 and 2).[27] Symbolic images most often focus on the tree. For example, Timothy Little's *Tree of Life* (Fig. 21), a three-dimensional mixed media sculpture using rebar, bike chains, and marbles, is symbolic. Little's sculpture was purchased by the Church History Museum in the Ninth International Art Competition in 2012.

The symbolic approach requires viewers to already know the associated scripture and narrative. Symbolic images do not seek to recount a story so much as they seek to bring certain abstract themes and moral lessons to mind. An artwork focused on the tree of life, for instance, does not visualize Lehi's experience or emotions for the viewer, but rather presents the tree as a symbol of God's love and of mankind's search for eternal life. Describing the power of symbols, Alonzo Gaskill wrote, "Once we have attached a specific meaning to a given symbol, any future encounter of that symbol will bring a resurgence of thoughts or feelings associated with the assigned meaning."[28] Although the

FIG. 21. Timothy Little, *Tree of Life*, 2011, mixed media (twisted rebar, bike chains, bike gears, marbles), © Intellectual Reserve, Inc.

many Latter-day Saint artworks of solitary trees differ in their use of color or light or style or media, they all employ the same symbol, which elicits the same response from the viewer.

One image that does use the tree symbol in a rather different way is Nick Stephens's 2012 *Desirable Above All Other Fruit* (Fig. 22). Instead of depicting a solitary tree, Stephens put the tree in context with other symbols, including a circumscribed square and nine windows. In this painting, a small branch of an olive tree appears within a circle, set within a square. The circumscribed square or, conversely, the squared circle, is a symbol used extensively in Latter-day Saint temple decoration, including the Salt Lake Temple. It may have reference to the union of heaven, represented by the curving circle (drawn with a

FIG. 22. Nick Stephens, *Desirable Above All Other Fruit*, 2012, oil painting, © Intellectual Reserve, Inc.

compass), and earth, represented by the square and its associations with creation and building.[29] Putting a representation of the tree of life within this symbol is unique to this artwork and adds a layer of meaning. Furthermore, Stephens created a new symbol for the spacious building, showing it not as an actual looming building, but as nine windows suspended in the air, representing the building's fragility and lack of foundation.

In the 2010s, even in images that we might classify as universalizing, symbols are prevalent. For instance, Justin Wheatley's *The Man, The Tree, The Rod, And The Words of Strangers And Friends* (Fig. 23) uses the familiar pathway with an iron rod leading from the foreground back to the tree, but the path is now made even more precarious as it is surrounded by a drop-off and

FIG. 23. Justin Wheatley, *The Man, The Tree, The Rod, And The Words of Strangers And Friends*, 2016, acrylic and photo transfer on cradled wood panel, used with permission of the artist.

Approaching the Tree: Interpreting 1 Nephi 8

55

cavernous space. An anonymous man walks alone towards the tree, holding the rod. A monochrome building encompasses the tableau and fills the entire background, its identical windows repeating rhythmically and seemingly infinitesimally. By universalizing the image and condensing it down to the symbols of rod, tree, and building, the artist provides a fresh perspective on the story. As scholar Joseph M. Spencer describes,

> The suffocating and monotonously designed building surrounds the scene, rather than standing simply at a distance to one side, and one has the impression that it's supposed to wrap around behind the viewer as well. In fact, it seems likely the viewer's meant to assume that she's looking out on this from a corner window in the great and spacious building. The solitude of the figure in the scene therefore provokes sympathy even as the viewer's meant to recognize that her role is to mock. This is a remarkable image of what it is to seek out Christ in a starkly modern world.[30]

During the 2010s, panoramic images largely followed established patterns in Lehi's dream art, with the notable exception of an imaginative *Lehi's Vision* by Casey Jex Smith.[31] Smith combined Lehi's dream with fantasy figures from role-playing games such as Dungeons and Dragons. The viewer may recognize symbols such as the iron rod, river, tall building, and tree, but Smith has rearranged everything, added new elements, and included mythical creatures and strange figures so that the scene looks more like a Hieronymous Bosch painting. The image encourages viewers to look closely and to reconsider traditional depictions of Lehi's dream. Yet there is also an undeniable element of whimsy and cheekiness to the piece, which calls attention to the artist and privileges his own interpretation of the dream.

Finally, several images of Lehi and his family by the tree appeared in the 2010s. Artist James C. Christensen produced several images that were included in the book *Lehi's Dream*, written by scholar Robert L. Millet and published by Deseret Book in 2011. In *Lehi Beckons His Family* (Fig. 24), Christensen imagines Lehi standing under the tree of life, already having tasted the fruit and now calling to his family to join him. Lehi faces away from the viewer and towards three figures (Sariah, Nephi, and Sam) approaching from the background, beside a dark river. A starlit sky covers the scene. There is no rod, no mist, no building, and no theatrics. No crowds are jeering, no one is being swallowed up in the earth, and no one is trying to scramble away from the tree. The mood is quiet and intimate. Lehi's family looks small and helpless in the landscape, their figures reflected and distorted in the river, but Lehi's tall posture and welcoming gesture are reassuring.

FIG. 24. James C. Christensen, *Lehi Beckons His Family*, 2011, The Cris and Janae Baird Collection.

The early twenty-first century thus witnessed several major changes in Lehi's dream art, including a new emphasis on symbolic elements and new approaches that highlight the individual viewer's personal experience with the dream. Additionally, as part of this interest in individual experience with the dream, new types of media have been brought to bear on 1 Nephi 8 in recent years, including John Moeller's *Tree of Life* 24-channel sound installation as well as an augmented reality (AR) mobile app designed for the Church to help its members experience Lehi's dream.[32] Over the past two decades, many artists shifted away from the panoramic approach, opting instead for more symbolic or universalizing pieces. For a scripture passage that has been visualized so many times, this shift to symbolism may be due to artists experimenting or seeking to do something new that sets their art apart from what has come before. But it is also likely the direct result of the Church's efforts since the 1990s to include a greater proportion of international artists in its art exhibits, collections, and publications. Oman believes the panoramic method represents a more traditional Western approach since it emphasizes narrative and landscape, and many non-Western cultures do not have a tradition of naturalistic landscape painting. For some non-Western cultures, symbolism and abstraction *are* the traditional approaches, and Oman encouraged artists to bring this heritage to bear on Lehi's dream.[33] As non-Western techniques and styles became more accepted and more prevalent in Church collections and publications, more varied approaches to portraying Lehi's dream developed among all artists.

TENSIONS AND POSSIBILITIES FOR LEHI'S DREAM ART

In reviewing Lehi's dream art, patterns become clear. Interest in tree of life art grew in the 1990s, under the guidance of curators at the Museum of Church History and Art, and has continued since then. Although certain approaches were popular during particular decades, overall, the panoramic and symbolic approaches are used the most often to visualize Lehi's dream. However, there has been a slow and steady shift towards more symbolic representations of the dream. It should be noted that some images defy easy categorization or use a combination of approaches, and there can be quite a range of styles within each approach.

Although Lehi's dream was one of the earliest Book of Mormon scenes visualized, and now appears to be the most frequently depicted Book of Mormon scene, it only appears in a few of the major series of Book of Mormon paintings. Teichert included Lehi's dream in her Book of Mormon series in 1949–51, with no known prior model to look to. Most of Teichert's works, including her Book of Mormon paintings, did not become well-known until the late 1990s, which is perhaps why her composition focusing on Sariah was not emulated by later artists. For largely unknown reasons, Friberg's sketch of Lehi's dream did not make the cut for his final painting series in 1952–55 series. With its familial focus and central inclusion of a woman, one wonders how the development of Lehi's dream art might have been different if this sketch had been fully realized as part of Friberg's series. Lehi's dream was also not included in the two earliest Book of Mormon series led by Reynolds in 1888 and Christensen in 1891, nor in Walter Rane's 2003 series of nineteen Book of Mormon scenes. One possible reason for this is that dream depictions may feel out of place within a series of historical narrative events, perhaps detracting from an aura of historicity. Another possibility is that artists such as Friberg may have felt that other scenes from the Book of Mormon would better fit their commissioned project of inspiring LDS youth with dramatic scenes of heroic ancient characters. For Walter Rane and perhaps for other artists, the compositional challenges presented by trying to fit the sequence of events in the dream into one canvas has been a deterrent.[34]

This survey of Lehi's dream art reveals several inherent tensions as well as several possibilities for new directions. First, there are many map-like images of everything Lehi recounted, but condensing the dream into one landscape can be problematic. In Lehi's retelling, the various groups of people do not overlap, but rather appear in separate moments within the dream. Moreover, not all symbolic elements of the dream appear at the same time. Some things only become visible or noticeable further into the dream. As Charles Swift points out, "Lehi is standing next to the tree of life but does not see the river until he is looking for his family, even though the river is next to the tree by which he is standing."[35] The panoramic approach, while having its own uses, is divorced from the scriptures, in a sense, because the very idea of a panoramic approach is not how Lehi described his dream. Because the overwhelming proportion of Lehi's dream art falls into the panoramic category, Church members tend to view art that does not express how Lehi experienced it.

Rather than depicting the dream as one moment teeming with people and symbols, could depicting the dream as a *series* of moments open new avenues of understanding? There is only one such artwork, *The Tree of Life (El Arbol de la Vida)* (Fig. 25), done by Jeronimo Lozano in 1995. Using the format of a *retablo* from his native Peru, Lozano created a comic-book-like diorama illustrating Lehi's experience in separate scenes including his journey, his arrival at the tree, the joining of his family, and the addition of the iron rod, multitudes of people, and a spacious building.

Lehi's dream offers distinctive opportunities for visual depiction, especially because it is a recounting of an interior vision and not an external event. This allows artists to use the increasingly popular universalizing approach, putting an anonymous figure or a particular family in place of Lehi. This approach is not something seen in most images based on scripture narratives. For example, we don't see universalized depictions of Nephi building a ship or Joseph Smith's First Vision, because these things happened in the external world to particular individuals. Lehi's journey, the tree, the building, and the iron rod, on the other hand, are, by definition, imaginary, and so the possibilities for depiction are manifold. Panoramic images try to capture the dream's physical appearance, but that is not the same as capturing its essence or feeling. The dream was, after all, a reality of the mind and not a reality of the material world. The visionary nature of the scene also presents unique challenges to artists because there are so many ways to picture the scene and work out the sometimes confusing or contradictory details. As Swift observes:

FIG. 25. Jeronimo Lozano, *The Tree of Life (El Arbol de la Vida)*, 1995, painted plaster paste on wood, 122 × 96 × 18 cm, © Intellectual Reserve, Inc.

It should be remembered, though, that visionary literature is "heavily symbolic but rarely pictorial." The symbols are meant to convey images of meaning, not necessarily pictures. . . . When we attempt to picture Lehi's vision of the tree of life, we quickly become confused about where things are supposed to be and what they should look like. How many bodies of water are there? Which body of water runs alongside what other element of the vision? How does the building hover in the air? Is the path straight, or does it meander as we would imagine the river doing? What makes a path "forbidden," and how is it marked or portrayed so that people know it is forbidden? Or does Lehi simply know intuitively of the forbidden nature of these paths? Though Lehi's vision is full of imagery that we can see in our minds, we can conclude that the purpose of the vision is not chiefly pictorial. We can imagine what we need to imagine, but if we try to be too precise, we lose the sweeping grandeur of the vision and are caught up in details that cannot be worked out.[36]

Another possibility for artistic exploration is the familial focus of the dream. There are many images of a symbolic tree, but there are few images that emphasize Lehi's expressed concern for his family. Yet, some scholars believe this fatherly concern is at the heart of the entire dream. Spencer describes how the dream is divided into two halves, hinging on the point at which Laman and Lemuel refuse to eat the fruit. This point marks the change in landscape and the addition of crowds of people.[37] Only a small percentage of images emphasize Lehi's (or Sariah's) tenderness towards family at the tree—Christensen's and Teichert's among them. There is, however, a more general sense of relationality between figures in many of the artworks of Lehi's dream. Of the four common approaches to the dream, the universal and symbolic are least likely or least able to communicate this theme of relationality, though.

The inclusion of women in Lehi's dream artworks presents distinctive possibilities. Lehi's dream is one of the few Book of Mormon passages to mention a woman by name. Thus, Sariah appears in a number of Lehi's dream images—although never with such force as in Teichert's rendition. Other anonymous women sometimes appear as peripheral figures in the panoramic images or in universalizing images such as the one by Merkley. Yet, there may be additional ways to explore how women can factor into visual depictions of the dream. Additionally, a growing scholarly attention to imagery of the divine feminine and to Asherah's iconographical connections with sacred trees may provide inspiration for new artistic directions.

Lehi's long journey in the "dark and dreary waste" before arriving at the tree has hardly been explored in the visual arts. In addition to the works by Nahlé and Lozano discussed above, one of the only other known images that deal with Lehi's journey is one by Christensen for Millet's book on Lehi. But the journey is no mere preamble and is described by Lehi as taking "many hours in darkness" (v. 8). It is only after this long blind march that Lehi prays for mercy and is finally granted access to the tree whose fruit filled his "soul with exceedingly great joy" (v. 12). As Swift explains, the narrative here presents two unexpected outcomes that are not well represented in the visual arts: first, Lehi finds himself in a "dark and dreary wilderness" and is guided away from it only to find another "dark and dreary waste" and, second, it is in this waste that the brilliant tree of life is found.[38]

Moreover, the entire experience of the journey and the tasting of the fruit is, for Lehi, a very physical one. In Rosalynde Welch's reading, "The experience is visceral, grounded in an existential force that acts on both Lehi and the reader from outside the mental operations of explanation or comprehension. It is the taste of the fruit, not its analysis, that beckons from the page."[39] It seems that there was something necessary about Lehi's long journey. His long walk required physical exertion and maybe even resulted in exhaustion. His description of the landscape as being dark and dreary as well as his ultimate cry to the Lord for mercy indicates that his journey stimulated his senses and made him acutely aware of his mortality. In the dark he felt the terrain through his feet. Perhaps he listened attentively for sounds or noticed smells. He probably became thirsty and hungry. It was in this state of heightened awareness that Lehi was finally brought to the tree and tasted the fruit. How might this aspect of Lehi's experience be portrayed in art?

Finally, although Lehi's dream points to Christ—especially as the vision is later expanded and explained by Nephi—only a handful of artists have included Christ in their depictions. Kathleen Peterson's *The Dream* (Fig. 26) places Christ at the very center of the image; his body straight like a tree trunk and his arms stretched out like branches in the tree of life that blooms behind him. His pose and his connection to the tree also call to mind the wooden cross on which he died to atone for the sins of mankind, adding a poignant meaning to the tree of life. To his right, Nephi, Lehi, Sariah, and Sam approach the tree. Nephi carries brass plates, Lehi carries the Liahona, and Sariah and Sam have their arms raised in prayer or thanksgiving. On the other side of Christ and the tree, Laman and Lemuel turn their backs and walk away, their arms folded in front. Peterson incorporates many symbolic elements from the dream including the white fruit, the river (represented by stylized blue swirls below Christ),

the narrow path, a mist of darkness, and the large building (reminiscent of Brunelleschi's Florentine Duomo). In the lower register of the scene, twelve men walk in a line with arms raised in the prayer gesture, a grouping not seen in other Lehi's dream images. The men likely represent the scattered twelve tribes of Israel, now gathered through Christ's redemptive power. Peterson also adds the additional elements of lightning bolts, trumpeting angels, the brass plates, and the Liahona, putting these symbols in dialogue with each other and with the more standard Lehi's dream symbols in inventive ways. In Peterson's rendering, Lehi's dream becomes not just a single moment but instead a united conglomeration of symbols representing Christ's triumph, love, and redemption.

LEHI'S DREAM ART IN CONTEXT WITH LATTER-DAY SAINT RELIGIOUS ART

What does this survey of Lehi's dream art tell us about Latter-day Saint religious art in general? How are depictions of Lehi's dream similar to other Latter-day Saint images, and how are they different? Several broad issues in religious art can be highlighted with this study of Lehi's dream depictions. First, religious art can both broaden and limit understanding and application of scripture. Second, the Church's commissioning and use of particular images and artists heavily influences the popularity of images among Church members and influences the approach of subsequent artworks. Finally, the spike in popularity of Lehi's dream images parallels a similar spike in popularity of other Latter-day Saint religious images.

Images affect the way scripture passages are understood. Latter-day Saint images of the New Testament sisters Mary and Martha, for example, although varied in style, almost universally show Mary as passive and heroic and Martha as active and foolish. This pattern maintains a traditional interpretation that began with Catholic thinkers and artists. Yet, there may be alternative interpretations to this scripture, perhaps even uniquely Latter-day Saint understandings that could be visualized.[40] Similarly, while visualizing Lehi's dream may help Church members think about it and remember it, sometimes even inspiring new lines of interpretation, the art also may prevent them from seeing the scene in alternative ways, especially when the art tends to follow the same patterns. Sometimes the parallels between Lehi's dream artworks are the result of an artist making an intentional reference to an earlier image. Other times, an artist's vision may be unwittingly influenced by prior images of the scene, especially those they have seen repeatedly, such as the ones commonly used in Church publications. This may explain why a number of the Lehi's dream artworks in the 1990s echo the panoramic compositions of artists in the 1980s. Likewise, symbolic images of the tree of life continue to largely follow patterns established early on.

Certain images of Lehi's dream have appeared frequently in Church media, and they tend to follow the panoramic or symbolic approaches. Uota's tree has appeared in the most places, including magazines, online exhibitions, and the

Museum store. Other commonly used depictions include Oakeson's painting, Thompson's painting, Griego's stained glass, Neal's massive painting, Sjokvist's carved globe, Vincent's Lehi painting, Johansen's sculpture, and Benthin's abstract painting. Out of the 23 images of Lehi's dream included in the Church History Museum's online exhibit "The Vision of the Tree of Life," 52 percent employ the panoramic approach, 22 percent the symbolic approach, 9 percent the universalizing method, and 17 percent the Lehi/family approach.[41] Looking more broadly at all artworks surveyed for this essay, the panoramic and symbolic approaches are also the two most popular approaches across the board from all Lehi's dream images in all time periods. This appears to be correlated to the type of artwork used in Church media. Among the panoramic images, many tend to be influenced by each other and it seems difficult for artists to break away from those sorts of traditional depictions.

The Church History Museum plays an important role in determining which images Church members are most familiar with, as its collection is often the source of images for Church media and exhibitions. Lehi's dream images owned by the Church History Museum are skewed towards the panoramic and symbolic approaches, with more than 50 percent of them falling in the panoramic category. The Church History Museum led the charge in production and acquisition of Lehi's dream images in the 1980s and 1990s—it owns almost all the known images of the scene from both decades. However, after the 1990s there was a substantial drop-off in the numbers of Lehi's dream artworks entering the Church History Museum collection. The stark decline in the collection of Lehi's dream images by the Museum since the turn of the century means that newer approaches—particularly those using a universal or Lehi-focused approach—are not as well represented in the collection and therefore not as well known by Church members generally.

CONCLUSIONS

With the dramatic increase in Latter-day Saint religious art since the 1980s, coinciding with the current wave of Latter-day Saint religious studies and textual analysis, it remains to be seen if Lehi's dream art in the 2020s will reflect varied and evolving interpretations or will adhere to traditional approaches. Already, certain artists have tackled the scene in inventive ways. Casey Jex Smith's fanciful panoramic drawing, for example, is nothing like the earlier theatrical panoramic paintings. And James C. Christensen's scene of Lehi under the tree calling to his family (Fig. 24) has a pathos not found in other portrayals of

Lehi under the tree. Kathleen Peterson's image with Christ (Fig. 26) is thought provoking and exceptional—not only aesthetically, but also theologically.

Yet, the panoramic and the symbolic approaches have been fortified by their repeated and almost exclusive use in Church media. The repetitive use of the same approaches in Lehi's dream art, or any religious art, can hinder the development of varied interpretations in both the discourse and the art. When Lehi's dream is always approached the same way in the art, interpretive images can become confused with fact. Encouragement of varied approaches in the visual arts, on the other hand, leaves room for alternative readings.

One of the purposes of art is to provide new perspectives. Just as individuals return again and again to the scriptures to mine further insights, so artists can return again and again to the same scriptures and come away with a multitude of visual renderings. We don't expect to exhaust all meaning from the scriptures after reading them only once. Neither should we expect our religious art to ever exhaust all meaning from the scriptures. As the naturalist Nan Shepherd wrote about her lifetime of observations in Scotland's Cairngorms mountain range, "I knew when I had looked for a long time that I had hardly begun to see."[42] She described moments when a revelatory flash of landscape caused her to realize "the truth that our habitual vision of things is not necessarily right: it is only one of an infinite number, and to glimpse an unfamiliar one, even for a moment, unmakes us, but steadies us again."[43] Making religious art, like reading scripture, is a creative and living act that can continue indefinitely and in myriad ways. Art can't make us taste the fruit from Lehi's dream; it can only give us that unfamiliar glimpse that inspires us to seek the fruit for ourselves. In that sense, perhaps the most successful religious art is that which sends us running back to scripture to engage with it again.

ADDENDUM ON NEW ART

The artists involved in this book project engaged deeply with the scriptural text as well as with the scholarly essays included here, creating a rich and rewarding dialogue. As a collection, these new works represent a variety of perspectives and styles that both complement and oppose each other, troubling our traditional representations of Lehi's dream and opening up new visual possibilities.

J. Kirk Richards is a Utah painter and sculptor. His art tends towards religious themes, and his subdued, earthy palette and sketch-like, layered style enhances the mystic, spiritual effect of his works. In *Pulling Up the Iron Rod* (Plate 1), a man and two women appear before a brilliantly lit tree. The three backlit figures appear to be part of a group that extends beyond the picture plane, each of them leaning forward to not just grasp but also to lift the iron rod. The figures do not necessarily represent specific characters from 1 Nephi 8, allowing the viewer to perhaps picture himself or herself as one of them. The image symbolizes each person's need to lift, wrestle with, and interpret the word of God. At the same time, there is a sense that everyone's effort contributes to the rest of the group, as they all lift together.

Rose Datoc Dall is a Filipina American who grew up in Virginia and now lives in Utah. Her religious art revisits scriptural moments from new perspectives, often incorporating Dall's own experiences as a mother. In *A Father's Plea* (Plate 2), Dall gives the observer a worm's eye view, looking up from the ground towards Lehi and the tree. Lehi stands with his arms outstretched, calling to his sons, and holding out the fruit. On either side of Lehi, filling the left and right thirds of the canvas, we see the lower limbs of his sons Laman and Lemuel walking away. By removing all details from the dream except the tree, the image focuses on Lehi's desire for his sons to partake of the fruit and his sadness when they refuse. The cool blue tones and dark shadows contribute to the mood of coldness and grief. The arched panel and gold leaf are reminiscent of medieval and Renaissance altarpieces, which were used to facilitate contemplation by worshippers. The intensely familial aspects of Lehi's dream have not historically been portrayed in images of the scene, but Dall suggests this moment deserves our deepest consideration.

Megan Knobloch Geilman is a Utah artist known for her mixed media digital compositions that reference famous works of art but imbue them with Latter-day Saint themes. In *Adaptations of Desire* (Plate 3), Geilman echoes the composition of Salvador Dalí's *The Accommodations of Desire* in visualizing Lehi's dream. By drawing on this iconic surrealist work, Geilman taps into the visionary and subconscious aspects of Lehi's experience, which have generally been overlooked in Lehi's dream art. Like Dalí's painting, Geilman's photograph is rendered in sharp detail, making the fantastical landscape appear even more jarring. Geilman's composition asks the viewer to carefully investigate and ponder to arrive at a deeper meaning. Rather than trying to depict what Lehi may have seen, Geilman uses symbolism to suggest broader themes contained within 1 Nephi 8—figs as the fruit and a reference to Matthew 24's description of the kingdom of God, a moth as a reference to Matthew 6:20 and a reminder of worldly decay and the passage of time, a clear stone like the brother of Jared describes, a replica of Joseph Smith's brown seer stone, and a lion as the ancient mother goddess Asherah, who in certain iconographies is linked to the tree of life.

Sarah Winegar works in her home state of Utah, specializing in relief printing and woodcuts. Her art often explores the human form and human relationships. *Rod of Hands and Feet* (Plate 4) depicts a series of women in various activities, including tending babies, passing food, and reaching out to others. Each woman has a halo, and each woman shows concern for someone else. The style is reminiscent of medieval Christian art, but also suggests the work of early twentieth-century German expressionists like Käthe Kollwitz, who explored the human form and female experience through woodcuts. The engraving technique and monochromatic printing ink create a graphic effect that emphasizes the repeated shapes and lines of the figures. The emphasis is not on one individual, but rather on the chain of human, and especially female, relationships. Moreover, this rod of flesh is circular and infinite, rather than straight and linear. This artwork thus encourages the viewer to consider the role of women in Lehi's dream and in the work of God.

Hildebrando de Melo is an abstract artist from Angola whose work deals with spiritual and political themes. His art often involves the viewer as a co-creator, and his *Tree of Life "LDS"* series (Plate 5) is no exception. By making the work a series of three images, de Melo encourages the viewer to engage and look closely, finding similarities and differences as the eye moves between the three canvases. The sketchy lines of the branches and gear-like markings of paint on the trunks indicate de Melo's desire to have viewers participate in finishing the image in their minds. Whereas de Melo's artworks typically avoid a clear focal point or even a definite spatial orientation, this triptych employs a more representational approach. Yet de Melo does maintain his non-narrative style here, as the trees each stand on their own without additional figures or symbolism. The drooping, angular branches punctuated with splotches of bright colors are reminiscent of Alexander Calder's hanging mobiles, giving the entire work a sense of movement and of precarious but precise balance. These themes of change, becoming, and transformation add a symbolic richness to a visualization of Lehi's dream, with its themes of choice and conversion.

Caitlin Connolly, from Utah, often explores women's experiences, human struggle and choice, and relationships in her drawings and paintings. Connolly's drawing, *Lehi's Dream* (Plate 6), captures both the undertones of loss and grief as well as the promise of compassion and community in 1 Nephi 8. At the center of the image, Lehi and Sariah are both crying and catching their tears, weeping for those who will not join them in eating the fruit. Lehi tenderly supports Sariah with one arm around her, beneath a halo that covers them both. Crowds of figures fill the space around them, and the tree of life is visible in one corner.

The drawing medium imparts a roughness and rawness to the image and indicates that the work of salvation and building relationships is yet unfinished.

José de Faria works in his native Portugal, employing a naïve surrealist style for his large paintings. De Faria's artwork tends toward geometric and symbolic abstraction, but for his *Lehi's Dream* (Plate 7) he takes a more figurative approach. Lehi is in the lower right and is the only figure with closed eyes, possibly to indicate his dream state. The spacious building leans dangerously over the scene and smoke from its chimney erupts in swirls of yellow, red, blue, purple, and white, the colors layered, combined, and three-dimensional. The zig-zagging mark of the brushstroke adds to the frenzy and chaos. The same impasto is used on Laman and Lemuel's robes, but in other areas, such as the trees, the paint is applied so thinly that the canvas peeks through. The figures crowding along the foreground are suggested almost impressionistically with dabs of color. De Faria creates a new symbol for the tree of life, shaping it like a mandorla (an elongated, pointed-oval frame around an icon, typically found surrounding the figure of Christ in traditional Christian art) around the white fruit. Throughout, de Faria plays with space, perspective, and proportion by using a variety of figure sizes, bold contrasting colors, patterning, and stippling. Taken together, these elements create a sense of ambiguity, which plays into the visionary aspect of the scripture and perhaps also Lehi's own discomfort during the dream.

Annie Poon is based in New York and works in a variety of media, including drawing and animation. Her work often explores psychological themes from both her own experiences and those of scriptural figures. In *The Dark and Dreary Waste* (Plate 8), Poon investigates Lehi's sensory experience as he was led through a dark wilderness in his dream before reaching the tree of life. It's a part of the dream that is rarely talked about and has only been visualized by a few other artists. Here, Lehi confronts the horror of the absence of God's light. His eyes strain, his mouth opens in surprise, his robe seems too big for his scrawny body, his hands are raised in fear and perhaps also prayer. 1 Nephi 8 recounts that Lehi "traveled for the space of many hours" in a "dark and dreary waste" before finally praying to God for mercy. It was only then that the tree of life was revealed to Lehi. In Poon's image, Lehi is still walking, his senses heightened as he feels his way through the darkness. He doesn't yet know the destination or whether he will make it there. His response is visceral and recalls the wrestle with darkness that Joseph Smith had before seeing a vision of God.

Kathleen Peterson works in Utah and her paintings draw on both her Western Latter-day Saint heritage as well as styles and techniques she has picked up from her international studies and travels. *A Father and Two Sons*

(Plate 9) employs her striking style and narrative approach to consider the relationship between Lehi and his sons Laman and Lemuel. Peterson emphasizes the psychological interplay of the three men's gazes as well as the contrast of Lehi's open and embracing hands with Laman and Lemuel's closed and inward-facing hands. The scene is dynamic as it urges the viewer's gaze to bounce around between the faces and hands. There is a flatness to the image—created by the compressed space, lack of shadows, heavy outline of figures, and graphic patterning—that calls attention to the materiality of the painted medium as a type of devotional object.

These nine artworks visualize 1 Nephi 8 in novel ways: some emphasize the parental concern of Lehi, others explore what "visionary" scripture might look like, one focuses on Lehi's journey in the dark wilderness, and many include women as central characters. These artworks also suggest possibilities for continued exploration. Perhaps as an indication of the powerful effect of traditional illustrations of Lehi's dream, even the abstract artists on this project opted for a more figurative style to depict Lehi's dream. What might a truly abstract visualization of 1 Nephi 8 look like and would it function the same way for the viewer? What other aspects of this scripture have been overlooked or downplayed? How might Lehi's dream be visualized in ways that are more inclusive for all of God's children in a global church? What visual connections might be made between Lehi's dream and other art or other scriptures? As artist James C. Christensen observed, "When we read Lehi's dream in the scriptures, each of us can conjure up our own vision of what it looked like. And maybe, if you look at some of the paintings and say, 'I never thought of it that way, but this works and helps me understand things in a different way,' that makes me happy."[44] The new artworks featured in this volume model these kinds of thoughtful, creative, and exploratory visions that provide different lenses through which to consider scripture and give us new ways to see the unseeable.

PART II

*Re-visioning
the Dream*

PLATE 2. Rose Datoc Dall, *A Father's Plea*, oil and metal leaf on panel, 43 × 23.5 × 3 inches, 2020.

Artwork:

A Father's Plea

ROSE DATOC DALL

IN THIS DEPICTION OF LEHI'S DREAM, LEHI IS PLEADING TO HIS SONS Laman and Lemuel to partake of the fruit of the tree of life, which is the love of God. However, they unfortunately "would not come . . . and partake of the fruit" (v. 8).[1] Lehi "exceedingly feared for Laman and Lemuel; yea, he feared lest they should be cast off from the presence of the Lord. And he did exhort them then with all the feeling of a tender parent, that they would hearken to his words, that perhaps the Lord would be merciful to them, and not cast them off" (vv. 36–37). I chose to focus on Lehi's expression of concern and earnestness. This dream gave him great foreboding, and I chose to portray not only the anxiety for his sons but the love he has for them, as any parent would have for wayward children.

Lehi and His Dream:
A Relational Reading

BENJAMIN KEOGH

IMAGINE A READER ENCOUNTERING THE BOOK OF MORMON FOR THE FIRST time. Not only has she never read the book, she's never read anything about the book. Hers is a totally fresh encounter. Imagine this same reader, taken by the dream experienced by Lehi and recorded in 1 Nephi 8, putting aside the book for a moment and, before reading any further, turning to commentaries produced about the book to learn more. Turning to some commentary's chapter on Lehi's dream, she might be surprised to read the title: "The Vision of the Tree of Life." Her surprise is born of her own experience. Unlike the commentator, she has not yet read past chapter 8. She has not yet encountered Nephi's vision. The more experienced reader might say her surprise is born of her own *in*experience—once she has read further she will have a greater view of the whole and her surprise will give way to a more complete understanding. This is undoubtedly the case. At the same time, however, it may also be true that her surprise allows new questions to arise and new insights to emerge that shine a greater light on the whole.

If we were to probe why our reader might be surprised at the title she finds in the commentary—"The Vision of the Tree of Life"—we might note at least these four things. First, the use of the definite article "the" functions to universalise Lehi's very personal experience. Not only does "The Vision . . ." connote something different to "Lehi's Vision . . ." each suggests its own interpretive possibilities. Second, such a title decides that what transpired was a vision. Lehi himself seemed much less sure, initially introducing it as "a dream" (v. 2). Third, it centres an interpretation of the dream's central symbol that is not found in the report of the dream itself. Instead, the "tree of life" is only found later: once in Nephi's report of his own vision (1 Ne. 11:25), and three times in Nephi's exchange with his brothers as he interprets his father's dream (1 Ne. 15:22, 28, 36). Our imagined reader, having only read to chapter 8, will not yet have encountered those words in the book. Fourth, emphasis on the *tree* may risk eclipsing Lehi's stronger emphasis on the tree's *fruit*, thereby obscuring the range of experiences partaking of the fruit elicits in the dream itself. Taken together, we might say our imagined reader's surprise may be summed up in the way this way of talking about Lehi's dream unintentionally displaces Lehi in relation to his dream.

With this in view, the aim of this essay is to read Lehi's dream with our imagined reader, before and apart—to whatever extent that is possible—from what comes later. Read this way, new insights into the dream do emerge. These include a dream that (1) while transcending Lehi, is primarily about Lehi; (2) centres the primacy of relation, and in particular, the negative effects of disrelation for both humans and God; and (3) reveals God's desire for right relation with and amongst humanity.

In what follows, a close reading of the text of 1 Nephi 8 will be offered, beginning with the material introducing the dream, then of the dream itself—split into three scenes—before concluding with a reflection on the kind of God the reading reveals. This reflection suggests God is inherently personal, absolutely relational, and ultimately capable of righting all relations.

INTRODUCING THE DREAM—VV. 1–4

As the narrative of his record unfolds, Nephi's recounting of his father's dream immediately follows the return of Lehi's sons to the wilderness camp with the family of Ishmael. The dream itself has two introductions. First, Nephi sets the scene for its telling, before Lehi provides his own introductory context. Both are instructive.

Nephi's Scene Setting—vv. 1–2

Between the rebellion and reconciliation in the desert that concludes chapter 7 and the dream that comprises the bulk of chapter 8, Nephi inserts a small sentence informing readers "that we had gathered together all manner of seeds of every kind" (v. 1). Why? How might this function as a transition between the two episodes? And how might it set up a reading of the dream? When one considers that chapters 6 to 9 were originally one complete chapter, these questions are all the more relevant.

As a transition, it may have two related functions. First, Nephi's identification of the gathering group as "we" underscores the sincerity of the repentance, forgiveness, and offerings that concluded the previous scene (1 Ne. 7:21–22). The reconciled families of both Lehi (including Zoram) and Ishmael are now united in a single purpose: gathering. Second, this united gathering together is reminiscent of the initial departure of Lehi's family from Jerusalem. There the family left and travelled together without any hint of the division that was soon to beset them (1 Ne. 2:4–5). This is important to keep in view because, as we shall see, in the dream's initial sequences other pivotal moments in the narrative thus far are revisited and recast. As a transition, then, it both marks a moment of right relation between previously disrelated parties and emphasises the textual unity of what has come before with what is coming next. In doing so it not only identifies relation as the dream's central theme, it provides an interpretive clue that links the dream's interpretation with Lehi's lived experience.

If this is so, what might it contribute to a reading of the dream? Here, identifying the gatherers as "we" emphasises the wholeness of the families, while the use of "all" and repetition of "every" in relation to seeds discloses the diversity of the gathered seeds—and of the gatherers. Indeed, the two go together. Gathering "all manner of seeds of every kind" not only requires a diversity of gatherers but that those gatherers form a community in which their differences are accentuated and utilised in service of the whole. It is because of the diversity of "every" person gathering that together they gathered "all manner of seeds." And yet seeds, regardless of their number and variety, are not provisions. Rather, they provide possibility and potential. The more seeds one has, the greater the possibilities, meaning their gathering seeds of "every kind" provides for "every kind" of provisional possibility. Further, the fact of their gathering preserves these possibilities. These seeds will not dry out in the sun or be foraged by animals. Together, these suggest the kind of community God is leading them into the wilderness to be. The survival and flourishing of the community, that is, not only depends upon the flourishing of the gathered seeds but of the gathered people. Thus, the use of "all" and repetition of "every" underscores the need for the collective to be both diverse and united, suggesting both the universal *and* relational nature of God's community.

Yet the collective is undercut in Nephi's next comment. After the description of *all* gathering, Nephi reports, "my father tarried" (v. 2). This hints at a tension that permeates the dream: the impact of individuals on the whole, and of one individual in particular: Lehi. Although open to interpretation, the use of the past tense "we had gathered" (v. 1), and the introduction of tarrying with "And it came to pass" (v. 2)—which usually indicates successive actions (see for example, vv. 4, 5, and 6)—suggests this tarrying occurred after the seeds were gathered. While it may be impossible to know why they remained once they were ready to go, it seems clear they did so because of Lehi, and that to some degree his dream was a response to his tarrying.

Lehi's Introduction—vv. 2–4

With these brief comments on gathering and tarrying, Nephi turns to the words of his father. In the first of these, Lehi introduces his dream by way of a contrasting parallel: because of the dream he (1) feels an emotion, (2) because of two sons, (3) for a particular reason. That is, Lehi frames the experience of his dream as the cause of certain different emotions, related to his various sons. This is outlined in the following table:

Lehi's Contrasting Parallel

V. 3

Emotion	Joy
Because of two sons	Nephi and Sam
For this reason	They and many of their seed will be saved

V. 4

Emotion	Fear
Because of two sons	Laman and Lemuel
For this reason	They and many of their seed will not be saved

Outlined in the above table is the interpretation of the dream that commonly accompanies the chalk drawings displayed and discussed in the introduction. The dream causes joy for Lehi over Nephi and Sam because it tells him they and many of their seed will be saved. At the same time, it elicits fear in Lehi over Laman and Lemuel because it tells him they and many of their seed will not be saved.

However, upon closer inspection it becomes clear the parallel is inexact and that our initial interpretations have been too hastily drawn. First, it is not clear whether Lehi *does* rejoice over Nephi and Sam. Rather, he states that because of the dream he has "*reason* to rejoice" (v. 3, emphasis mine). That is, for Lehi, the dream seems to provide grounds for rejoicing because of Nephi, Sam, and many of their seed. These grounds do not necessitate rejoicing and, in fact, may not even be present. It may also be that grounds for other emotions are also present. Further, the grounds enumerated—Nephi and Sam's salvation, and that of their seed—are likewise less assured than they may initially appear: Lehi has "reason to suppose" (v. 3) it. Thus, while the dream is not an assurance to Lehi that Nephi, Sam, and their seed will be saved, he does come away believing it provides him with grounds to believe in that possibility.

This suggests that if rejoicing does occur for Lehi because of Nephi, Sam, and their seed, it is not experienced viscerally. Rather, it emerges through his reasoned reflection. By contrast in relation to Laman and Lemuel, the dream causes Lehi a visceral reaction: exceeding fear (v. 4). Use of a superlative here suggests the felt fear is much greater than any potential rejoicing. Ultimately, the dream produces fear, not joy. For Lehi, it begins and ends in darkness.

The following table redraws the parallel.

Lehi's Contrasting Parallel Re-examined

V. 3

Potential emotion	Joy
Because of two sons	Nephi and Sam
For this reason	There are grounds to believe in the possibility of salvation for them and their seed

V. 4

Actual Felt Emotion	Exceeding fear
Because of two sons	Laman and Lemuel
For this reason	Telling of the dream

Redrawing the parallel reveals two other things worth noting. First, Lehi does not talk of "rejoicing over" or "fearing for," but rejoicing and fear "because of"

(vv. 3–4). These emotions it seems, despite their initial appearances, are more about Lehi than they are about his sons. This, combined with the parallel suggests a division *in Lehi* in relation to his sons. While the opening chapters of the Book of Mormon document a growing divide in his sons' beliefs and outlook, the introduction to his dream documents Lehi's internalisation of that division. He not only views them differently, he *feels* differently towards them. The second centres on Lehi's use of "seed." That it is used only in relation to Nephi and Sam does two things. First, it reminds the reader of verse 1. There, "we" gathered "all" and "every." Here, although it appears two families are listening (reading the "we" of verse 1, as equivalent to the "us" of verse 2), Lehi makes it clear he is talking to a specific subset of one family. After further dividing the subset, "seed" is mentioned in relation to only one side of the divide, and it is not "all" or "every," but "many" (v. 3). The universality hinted at in verse 1 has been vastly curtailed by verse 3, and it has been curtailed, it seems, by Lehi. Second, it suggests the chalk drawing interpretations are too hasty. Rather than Lehi's fear being ascribed to the opposite cause of his joy—salvation or not—the cause of his fear is to be found in his telling of the dream. It is this, the explanation of that cause, that motivates Lehi's telling.

SCENE I: DARK AND DREARY—VV. 4–8

As the dream's audience is constricted, so too is the dream. Nephi is clear that he has truncated its ending, while its beginning—"For behold, methought I saw" (v. 4)—gives a feeling of the action beginning *in medias res*. It is also fuzzy: Lehi *thinks* he sees "a dark and dreary wilderness" (v. 4). This wilderness, whatever it is, is an observation, not a present location. As the dream begins, Lehi appears to be in nowhere space, observing. He is joined there by a man in a white robe and invited to move (vv. 5–6). Lehi follows and beholds himself (v. 7). That is, Lehi both moves and does not move. He is both presently located in "a dark and dreary waste" (v. 7) *and* apart from it, where he continues to observe from nowhere space. He is now both participant and observer, involved and aloof. Following the man in the white robe produces—or exposes—a division in Lehi. However one approaches the dream, each way in is through a divided whole.

Here, too, the resonances are familiar. Both the dream and the narrative seem to begin somewhere apart from where Lehi is located. Jerusalem is the book's first named place and the scene of its initial action: preaching prophets. Yet for Lehi, Jerusalem was not a present location. This is true both physically: not only is his house "at Jerusalem" (1 Ne. 1:7) as opposed to in Jerusalem, the text makes clear he had "dwelt" there "all his days" (1 Ne. 1:4); and figuratively: hearing the prophets moved him to prayer, not protest (1 Ne. 1:4–5). Like the distinction between "at" and "in," however, the separation of Lehi and place in the dream and the narrative is both clear and fuzzy. Issues with Lehi's vision cause much of that fuzziness. This is readily apparent in the dream as he reports his own uncertainty: "methought I saw" (v. 4). Narratively, the issue is revealed much more subtly. While there is a distinction between Lehi and Jerusalem, the need for and response to his prayer suggests it is one of degree. He, too, needed the prophets' call to repentance (1 Ne. 1:4)—the "Wherefore" (1 Ne. 1:5) connecting his prayer to that call, and his "quak[ing] and tremble[ing]" (1 Ne. 1:6) a sign it was required.[1] The cause of his tremors: "the things which he saw" (1 Ne. 1:6). Lehi's prayer for redemption opened his eyes to the reality of his situation. Before, he thought he saw and prayed. After he had truly seen, he trembled.

In the dream there was a similar awakening as "methought I saw" (v. 4), gave way to "I saw" (v. 5). What he saw was "a man" who "came and stood before [him]" (v. 5). Here, resonance gives way to textual connection. After returning from the prayer that opened his eyes, Lehi "cast himself upon his bed" (1 Ne. 1:8) and saw more, including "One descending out of the midst of heaven" (1 Ne. 1:9), who "came and stood before [him]" (1 Ne. 1:11). This phrasal repetition connects the two apparitions, although notably, the dreamed iteration lacked the "luster" (1 Ne. 1:9) of the first. In both cases Lehi is invited to move: in the first instance into the life of a preaching prophet (1 Ne. 2:1); in the second, into "a dark and dreary waste" (v. 7). In both cases moving initiated Lehi into a difficult experience: in the dream, Lehi travelled for hours in darkness; previously his preaching incited mockery, threats on his life, and precipitated an escape to the wilderness. Both required deliverance through God's mercy.

Together, this works to create at least some association between the dream's dark and dreary wilderness and Jerusalem. There, rejection of the prophets already marked it as somewhat of a spiritual wilderness, while the Babylonians were about to carry its inhabitants into the actual wilderness, leaving the city itself, in the words of the prophets, "destroyed" (1 Ne. 1:4). In introducing his dream, Lehi makes one further association: "Laman and Lemuel, I fear exceedingly because of you; for behold, methought I saw in my dream, a dark and dreary wilderness" (v. 4). While, as has been suggested, the dream in its entirety relays the reason for Lehi's fear because of Laman and Lemuel, the most immediate expression of that fear is a wilderness. Linking the wilderness with both Jerusalem and Laman and Lemuel suggests Lehi fears they are headed for the same outcome: destruction.

As we shall see, however, destruction does not appear in the final reckoning to be an ultimate possibility. In a similarly subversive way the dream, which is soon to be populated by multitudes, is not primarily disclosing to Lehi something about others but, instead, about himself. This begins to reveal itself most fully with his prayer for mercy. If the decision to follow the man in the white robe exposed a division within Lehi, then his prayer for mercy is not only a plea for deliverance, it is also a decision in favour of the division's resolution. In response, deliverance comes. But in keeping with the tenor of things, it is not the deliverance one expects. Regardless, it is the deliverance Lehi repeatedly receives. In response to his first prayer of repentance Lehi was delivered into the stark reality of his own sinful situation, quaking and trembling as a result of what he saw; from the threats on his life in Jerusalem he was delivered into the wilderness, where he learned the stark reality of division amongst his family; and now, from the dream's dark and dreary waste, Lehi is not only delivered to a fruit tree but to the reality of his own internalisation of that division within his family.

Lehi's removal from difficult and dangerous situations, it appears, does not constitute mercy's complete expression. Rather, that is communicated through revealing the situation from which deliverance is most required. Situations which cannot be resolved by removal. Instead, their resolution requires reconciliation, the provision of which requires Lehi's active participation, not his withdrawal.

SCENE 2: TREE AND FRUIT—VV. 9–20

Lehi's prayer exemplifies the consequential nature of his participation: it is *after* he prays that the scene changes and he beholds a field and a tree with desirable fruit. Perhaps the familiarity of readers with the dream's contours blinds them slightly to its lack of inevitability. What would have happened for instance, if Lehi didn't follow the man who stood before him? Or didn't pray for mercy? Or didn't eat the fruit? In other words, the actions Lehi takes are fundamental to the dream's progression. The implication: this holds in his waking life as well.

What Lehi does initially is narrow the focus of his beholding, from the field (v. 9), to the tree (v. 10), to the fruit (v. 11). Where once the "seeds of fruit of every kind" (v. 1) were in view, one kind of fruit now dominates. This fruit, he observes, is "desirable to make one happy" (v. 10), and it becomes Lehi's primary interest. Later, Nephi will call the tree—which Lehi only mentions in relation to its fruit, or as a locator of his position—*not* the fruit, "precious above all" (1 Ne. 11:9). One wonders at the discrepancy. Is there something

Lehi's focus on the fruit causes him to miss about the tree? And, is there something Nephi's focus on the tree causes him to miss about the fruit? Further, what might the respective focuses say about their originators? While fruit as the outcome of the process may make one happy, it is the process that both produces the fruit and determines its quality. The process is, to use Nephi's language, "precious." To neglect it is to lessen the desirability of the fruit. It may be that Lehi's hyper-focus on the fruit hints towards a concern with outcomes at the expense of processes. Or, when applied to his sons, that too great a focus on their desirable or undesirable actions (the fruit) might cause him to miss something about the preciousness of their beings (the tree).

While later elements of the dream support this suggestion, Lehi's first response upon encountering the tree was to partake of the desirable fruit. In doing so, he got more than he bargained for. The fruit, once tasted, surpassed its perceived desirability for happiness, causing instead "exceedingly great joy" (v. 12). Its whiteness and sweetness outstripped any previously experienced (v. 11), while anticipation of its impact on "one" (v. 10) overflowed into concern for others (v. 12). For Lehi, it was a redemptive experience. As with his experience at the tree, Lehi's previous encounter with one standing before him (1 Ne. 1:9–10) filled his soul with joy (1 Ne. 1:15) and turned him to others (1 Ne. 1:18–19), having himself experienced the Messiah's merciful redemption. Desiring his family to experience the same, Lehi began to look for them. Yet, curiously, it was a looking almost entirely bereft of movement, involving only the casting of his eyes (v. 13). That Lehi had to look for his family means he did not know where they were; that he did so without moving suggests he was confident they were somewhere in sight. It may also indicate a looking without involvement. Either way, it works to demonstrate that there are things in plain sight Lehi is not seeing, perhaps because they have not been sufficiently cared for. Once again, there are issues with his vision.

This continues throughout his looking as Lehi is distracted from the purpose of his search by the first (new) thing he sees. Upon seeing the river, the object of his search changes from "discover[ing his] family, to "behold[ing] from whence [the river] came" (vv. 13–14). This second search is more complicated. Lehi is not only looking for the river's source but the source of the river's appearance. Where once there was a field and a tree with fruit, there is now a field, a tree with fruit, *and* a river. Lehi follows its course and soon discovers its head and with it part of his family, "Sariah, and Sam, and Nephi" standing "as if they knew not whither they should go" (v. 14). Not only does the presence of the river make their journey more perilous, this "not knowing" suggests the effect of encountering the tree is not universal. In contrast to his own anticipation of a positive experience, Lehi's wife and two of his sons were apprehensive, even as he stood by the tree.

Here again, there are resonances. This is not the first time Sariah, Sam, and Nephi did not know. Upon departing into and setting up camp in the wilderness, Nephi reported that in response to his cries the Lord "did visit me, and did soften my heart that I did believe all the words which had been spoken by my father," causing Nephi "not to rebel against him" (1 Ne. 2:16). The implication is clear: for Nephi belief was not inevitable. Similarly, Sam's journey from not to knowing was influenced by Nephi's intervention (1 Ne. 2:17), while Sariah's crossed into a complaint against "a visionary man" (1 Ne. 5:2). Only once her sons had returned with the plates was she "comforted" and could affirm that she now knew "of a surety that the Lord hath commanded [her] husband" (1 Ne. 5:7–8). In the dream, intervention came from Lehi as he beckoned and called "with a loud voice" (v. 15). Lehi's initial desire was for his family to "partake [of the fruit] also" (v. 12), which makes his call to "come unto *me*, and partake of the fruit" (v. 15) surprising, as it introduces a further step between his family and the fruit. A step that, as their response exemplifies, places their partaking in decidedly relational terms: "they did come unto [Lehi] and partake of the fruit also" (v. 16). Strangely, in contrast to Lehi whose partaking heightened his senses in multiple ways, nothing is recorded about the experience of Sariah, Sam, and Nephi with the fruit. Instead, they drop out of the narrative.

After Sariah, Sam, and Nephi partake of the fruit, Lehi's attention (re)turns to Laman and Lemuel. Having partaken of the fruit himself, Lehi "began to be desirous that [his] family should partake of it also" (v. 12). Once three of them had, Lehi "was desirous that Laman and Lemuel should come and partake of the fruit also" (v. 17). Again there is ambiguity as the "was" that (re)introduces Lehi's desire in relation to Laman and Lemuel does not clearly express a settled function. It may, for example, indicate the continuation of Lehi's desire for his family to partake of the fruit: three of them had and Lehi "was [still] desirous that Laman and Lemuel should . . . also." Or it may suggest an intensification of desire: Lehi "*began* to be desirous that [his] family should partake of [the fruit]," and once three of them had, that bud flowered and he now "*was* desirous" for Laman and Lemuel to do likewise. Or it may imply the desire's cessation: the beginnings of Lehi's desire for his family to partake were so thoroughly satisfied that after three of them did he could only admit that he "was [previously] desirous that Laman and Lemuel should . . . also."

While any of these options may be more or less likely, reading further does not resolve the issue. Initially, the language is the same: Lehi describes himself as "desirous" that they should "partake" (v. 12; v. 17), before enacting that desire by "cast[ing his] eyes" (v. 13; v. 17). Together these suggest *at least* a continuation of desire. The similarities, however, do not continue. In the first instance, Lehi casts his eyes to "discover" (v. 13), in the second to "see" (v. 17). In the first, looking to "discover" Sariah, Sam, and Nephi, Lehi "beheld" them (vv. 13–14), in the second, looking to "see" Laman and Lemuel, Lehi "saw" them (v. 17–18). Three things in the text suggest the distinction is meaningful.

First, and recapitulating some of what has gone before, Lehi reports that his initial search for his family was interrupted as he "beheld a river" (v. 13). Having looked to discover one thing—his family—he beheld another: a river. This interruption to his search diverted his attention: now his interest was "to behold from whence [the river] came" (v. 14). Embarking on this search Lehi "saw" the river's head, and "beheld his family" (v. 14). Again, the thing Lehi beheld was not the object of his search. This progression of Lehi's search, and in particular the proximity of his "seeing" the river's head and "beholding" his family, suggests there is in the dream a distinction between beholding and seeing.

Second, upon "beholding" Sariah, Sam, and Nephi, Lehi discerned something about them: they were standing "as if they knew not whither they should go" (v. 14); upon "seeing" Laman and Lemuel there was no such discerning. Considering the chapter holistically this trend holds, until, interestingly, Lehi fails to behold his oldest sons. Before then Lehi sees three things and, in each instance, provides a straightforward description of what he saw. For example, "I saw a man, and he was dressed in a white robe" (v. 5). However, previous to the appearance of Laman and Lemuel when Lehi beholds, he also discerns. For example, after beholding himself "in a dark and dreary waste" Lehi discerned that deliverance required the Lord's mercy (v. 7). Similarly, after beholding the tree Lehi discerned that its fruit was "desirable to make one happy" (v. 10). This suggests that the difference between beholding and seeing is one of intensity or attention. Or, that it is Lehi's heightened attention in beholding that allows him to discern beyond the plain descriptiveness of sight.

Third, the discernment that results from Lehi's beholding moves him to action, while when he reports that he "saw" something Lehi remains motionless. For example, when Lehi discerned that escape from the dark and dreary waste required the Lord's mercy, he began to pray (v. 7). Similarly, when Lehi discerned that the fruit on the tree was desirable for happiness, he went "forth and part[ook] . . . thereof" (v. 11). Or, again, when he discerned that Sariah, Sam, and Nephi "knew not whither they should go," Lehi "beckoned unto them" and called "with a loud voice" (vv. 14–15). In contrast, when he "saw a man . . . in a white robe," Lehi remained motionless until that man "stood before [him], spake unto [him], and bade [Lehi] follow him" (vv. 5–6). Likewise, after Lehi "saw" Laman and Lemuel, he observed that they "would not come" (v. 18) without any mention of movement on his part. This suggests that beholding was an involved process that moved Lehi from sight to discernment to action, whilst seeing was a relatively disengaged process in which Lehi did nothing more than observe.

Together these suggest if not a cessation of desire, at least its diminution. If this is so, one naturally asks why? One answer may be that it is this point in the dream that reveals to Lehi just how far he has internalised the division between his sons. Perhaps the activity of his beholding, beckoning, and calling in relation to Sariah, Sam, and Nephi is an indication of his expectation of a positive response, and his passivity toward Laman and Lemuel an expression of their expected negative response. If this is the case, there are two consequences. First, the dramatic shifts about to occur in the dreamscape are due to this internalised division. If mercy is being delivered into the reality of the situation from which deliverance is truly needed, Lehi is about to get a heavy dose of reality. Second, it is this reality, the recognition of division and its consequence, that is the root cause of Lehi's fear. From this perspective the dream, it seems, is less about the tree and more about Lehi and his relationships.

As previously noted, Lehi's calling to Sariah, Sam, and Nephi extended beyond his initial desire and placed their partaking in decidedly relational terms. That is, they didn't just partake of the fruit; rather, "they did *come unto [Lehi]* and partake of the fruit also" (v. 16). Here it is possible to read "also" as "likewise," referring to their partaking of the fruit as Lehi did in verse 12. The intervening narrative, however, provides an alternative explanation. The extension of an invitation beyond his initial desire is occasioned by Lehi's beholding that "they knew not whither they should go" (v. 14). Crucially, Lehi does not use "whether" here. This is not a binary choice between coming to the tree or not. Rather, it expresses their confusion in the face of multiple options. There were, it seems, many ways they could go. For the narrative of the dream, this has two effects. First, it introduces the possibility of moving away from the tree. Previously, all the movement in the dream had been toward the tree. Now, there are other options. Second, and following from the first, having taken up a position by the tree, choosing an option other than the tree meant choosing an option other than Lehi. Framed this way, movement again becomes a binary choice. However, it was not between coming to the tree or not, but between affirming a relationship with Lehi or not. It is in this context that Lehi beckoned and called "unto them with a loud voice that they should *come unto me, and partake of the fruit*" (v. 15). Preservation of the relationship had become the primary concern. It is also in this context that "they did *come unto [Lehi]* and partake of the fruit *also*" (v. 16). That is, they chose relationship with Lehi and, as a byproduct of that choice, shared in the fruit of the tree by which he stood. If this is so, Laman and Lemuel's not partaking is also relational and, likewise, derivatively so: they did not partake because they did not come to Lehi. To the perilousness of the river, Lehi added the complication of his person.

Laman and Lemuel do not move, and two things happen simultaneously. First, Lehi beheld without discerning. From this point on, his beholding and seeing are equivalent: both consisting of direct observation. If seeing clearly required an additional step of discernment, there are, again, problems with Lehi's sight. Second, the dream scene's configuration began to change at a rapid pace. Extending "along the bank of the river" appeared "a rod of iron" (v. 19), and then "a strait and narrow path" (v. 20). The rod seems to run from the head of the river to the tree, while the path leads both to the tree and beyond the river's head to "a large and spacious field, as if it had been a world" (v. 20). The same path leads to the tree *and* the field. This doubling of the path's direction has a number of implications. First, as befitting the not knowing of Sariah, Sam, and Nephi, it suggests the head of the river is an in-between space. It is not the tree, but it is also not the field, its "as if" containing all the possibilities of a world. Second, Laman and Lemuel, by remaining in that in-between space, have not yet made a decision. The path's appearance, extending in both directions, is a concrete indication that they could have moved towards Lehi or away from him. Instead, they remained entirely static, as if struck by indecision, appearing and disappearing from the dream's narrative without a single movement. Third, this same extension suggests Lehi too can move. Rather than lamenting that Laman and Lemuel "would not come unto [him]" (v. 18), Lehi could have gone to them. Relationships, like the path, are bi-directional. Instead, having been full of movement to this point, in this interaction Lehi is almost as static as Laman and Lemuel, doing no more than casting his eyes.

Thus, in response to his prayer for mercy, Lehi had three consequential encounters at the tree, including contrasting experiences with the sons he had divided when introducing the dream. As with his deliverance from the crowd at Jerusalem, deliverance from the dark and dreary waste exposed Lehi to the reality of the division between his sons. This time, however, it was a division he had imbibed. Further, with active participation required for its resolution, remaining motionless laid bare his withdrawal. Mercifully, Lehi is learning a hard lesson.

From here, the pace of the dream picks up and its scope explodes. Where once there was Lehi alone there are now "numberless concourses of people" (v. 21). The dream's progression from Lehi to Lehi and his wife and children suggests that this latest development populated the scene with Lehi's posterity—both the seed of Nephi and Sam mentioned by Lehi in the dream's introduction and the seed of Laman and of Lemuel that are not. The implication: what Lehi is about to witness is the inevitable consequence of the current division between his sons for his descendants. The dream's revelations are becoming prophetic.

The description, "numberless concourses of people" is suggestive. The primary distinction is not the number of people, but the number of concourses. It is not an innumerable number of people (although it *may* be that too) but an innumerable number of *meetings between people*; not (only) people in all their variety, but people in all their relationships. These relations both brought people together and divided people into camps. What was observed, then, was not one mass of people, but people divided into discernable masses. Lehi continued, "many of whom were pressing forward, that they might obtain the path which led to the tree by which I stood" (v. 21), and the suggestive descriptions multiply. The first thing to note is that we are now dealing with "many," not "all." As suddenly as they appear in the narrative, a portion drops out again. Confirmation, if any was needed, of division. Those that remained, "were pressing forward." Given that the scene opened with a view of people in relationship, the suggestion is that their pressing forward is likewise in relationship or, perhaps, because of their relationships. Indeed "pressing" has connotations of urging with force and of squeezing or constraining. This gives the sense that the "pressing forward" was not entirely agentic, that the movement of travel was in some sense swept along, that not only was it movement in relationship, but that those relationships somehow caused the movement. This is a new thing in the dream's narrative. Until then, all of the dream's interactions had been with Lehi. These are the first to interact amongst themselves.

That the movement was in the direction of the path is significant. At a basic level, it means they were not yet on the path. Occurring in undefined space, these pressing interactions were aimed at the path. Yet, they were not aimed there necessarily. Some had already chosen a different course. Why then this press for the path? While no reason is offered, there is perhaps an indication. Lehi describes the path as leading "to the tree by which I stood" (v. 21). Curiously, while there is only one tree mentioned in the dream, this is the third time in quick succession that Lehi identified it in relation to himself (vv. 19,

20, 21). Further, in his previous breath, he had described the path as leading both to the tree *and* to the field. Now, it is described as leading only to the tree. Together these work to solidify Lehi's relation to the tree. The path was pressed for because it led to the tree (regardless of its potential for leading to the field), and the tree was important because it aligned one with Lehi.

As the instigator of their departure from the old world and the founder of their colony in the new, ties to Lehi were equally important for both sides of his divided posterity. This is true regardless of the personal feelings of his immediate progeny. Identification with Lehi was a source of legitimacy. It may be for this reason that the pressing toward the path is described as an effort to "obtain the path" (v. 21). The verb "obtain" can be used transitively or intransitively and its meaning varies according to its use. As a transitive verb, the sense is one of gaining or acquiring possession of a thing. In the writing of Nephi, every use, whether in reference to records (1 Ne. 3:19) or property (1 Ne. 3:25), land (1 Ne. 7:13) or food (1 Ne. 16:17), is transitive, indicating one's gaining possession of a thing. And yet to talk of gaining possession of a path sounds a little unusual. What might be behind it? It may be that possession of the path gave one a certain degree of control over access to the path's destination. Alignment with Lehi depended upon possessing the path—hence the pressing of competing masses to obtain it.

Read this way, possessing the path equates to control of the narrative. If one could establish one's alignment with Lehi, one could not only regulate the stories included in the founding narrative but crucially, their interpretation. There is then, a certain irony to the narrative shifting as soon as the path is commenced in. First, those who did not participate in the press for the path are fully excised as "many," (v. 21) become "they" (v. 22); second, the tree loses its identification with Lehi (v. 22); and third, "there arose a mist of darkness" so "great" that all who "commenced in the path did lose their way, that they wandered off and were lost" (v. 23). The potential expressed with Sariah, Sam, and Nephi for movement in a direction other than the tree is realised here and these "many" who commenced in the path find themselves back at the dream's beginning, wandering in darkness. Further, the path, commenced in but never obtained, is not mentioned again. If identification with Lehi was what was sought, it was never found, and if these represent Lehi's posterity, it is a devastating blow: all "wandered off" and all "were lost."

With no time to dwell on the loss, the scene shifts again, quickly cycling through four more groups. Two of these used the rod of iron and made it to the tree; the other two are associated with a strange building. The first of each pair is described in Lehi's words, and the second in Nephi's as he truncates his father's telling of the dream. A brief comment on each. The first of these "others" (v. 24), by which it seems is meant "distinct from the numberless concourses" and not "outside Lehi's posterity," grasp "hold of the end of the rod of iron" and "clinging" to it move "through the mist of darkness" (v. 24) to reach the tree. Where once the way to the tree was obstacle free, now approaching the tree is only possible by wrapping oneself around an iron rod. This difference in ease of access is mirrored by the different reactions to partaking of the fruit. While both these and Lehi immediately began to "cast their eyes about" (v. 25; cf v. 13 for Lehi), they did so for dramatically different reasons: Lehi, in search of his family, having been "filled . . . with exceedingly great joy" (v. 12), these "as if they were ashamed" (v. 25). On this, two observations: first, and most basically, the response to partaking of the fruit was not universal. In fact, of the four sets of people who do partake, only Lehi is reported as having a positive experience. Second, the "as if" suggests they were not yet ashamed, rather they were casting their eyes around as one would if one was ashamed. After Lehi's partaking of the fruit, his turn to others was immediate and relational. He looked for his family, people with whom he was in relation, in an effort to strengthen that relation by sharing with them what he'd found to be "desirable above all other fruit" (v. 12). For these others, partaking of the fruit also brought a turn to others, but it was others with whom they did not have a relationship, and it was in expectation of a negative response. Their turn to others, while immediate, was *dis*-relational.[2]

The casting of their eyes by this group at the tree brought the next group into the scene as "a great and spacious building" materialised, standing "in the air" and "filled with people" (vv. 26–27). These people are described as "old and young," "male and female," and "their manner of dress" as "exceedingly fine" (v. 27). This last detail is perhaps particularly significant. If these groups that populate the dream after the standoff with Laman and Lemuel are Lehi's posterity, it is these expensively dressed souls in the building we have the best chance of identifying. Throughout the Book of Mormon, it is only Nephites (see, for example, Jacob 2:13; Alma 1:32; 4:6; 5:53; 31:28; Hel. 13:28),[3] and latter-day "followers" of Christ (see Morm. 8:36–37) who are described as expensively appareled. This is particularly surprising given those in the building are depicted as "in the attitude of mocking and pointing their fingers towards those . . . partaking of the fruit" (v. 27). The descriptive "in the attitude of" suggests Lehi's comments are less about particular actions of mocking and pointing, and more about a disposition, a way of being in or of viewing the world. That is, their relational posture is one of mocking and pointing. The disrelational turn of the partaking "others" was met by the anti-relational stance of the building's finely attired inhabitants.

From here attention returns to those at the tree. Previously described as having partaken of the fruit, they are now described as having "tasted of the fruit," and with that tasting "they were ashamed because of those that were scoffing at them" (v. 28). Having encountered the scoffers, their shame has been actualised. Again there is a new form of interaction as different groups interact with each other. The dream then, depicts (1) a widening progression of interaction from between Lehi and other(s), to amongst one group, to between different groups; and (2) an increasing pattern of disrelation from the disengaged interaction between Lehi and Laman and Lemuel, to pressing interactions in numberless concourses, to scoffing by one group at another. Curiously, the fruit tasters are described as shamed "because of" the scoffers and not "by" the scoffers. That is, the scoffers are not described as the agents or instruments of the tasters' shame, rather the tasters are shamed because there are scoffers. Instead of relating to the tree on its own terms, they cast their eyes. In doing so they looked to others to define their relationship with the tree. Encountering others who related to the tree negatively they appropriated a negative relationship. Because there were scoffers, the tasters were ashamed, and because they were ashamed "they fell away into forbidden paths and were lost" (v. 28). Following Lehi's encounter with Laman and Lemuel, three representations of his posterity appeared on the dream's stage: two were completely lost and the third scoffed at those partaking of the desirable fruit on the tree.

The loss of this second group to forbidden paths marks the end of Nephi's reporting of Lehi's words. Nephi himself, "to be short in writing" (v. 30) summarised the dream's end. A first set of "other multitudes" pressed forward with the aid of the rod and partook of the fruit (v. 30), while another felt their way toward the building (v. 31). In the attempt, many of this second set of "other multitudes" were "drowned in the depths," and others, "wandering in strange roads" were "lost from [Lehi's] view" (v. 32). It is here, in Nephi's summary, that we are told what it means to be lost in the dream. Two of the first three groups were described as "lost" (vv. 23, 28), without any indication as to what that meant in the context of the dream. Now it is made clear that to be lost in the dream is to be outside Lehi's sight—to be, in some sense, outside the bonds of relationship with Lehi. Others, although entering the building and "point[ing] the finger of scorn" (v. 33) at those "partaking of the fruit" were nevertheless still within sight and therefore within relational bonds, albeit disrelationally. If, as has been suggested, the various groups encountered in the dream do represent Lehi's posterity, then the dream is a nightmare. The appearance of others in the dream was a response to Lehi's desire to share with his family an experience of "exceedingly great joy" (v. 12) and enter into a more fulfilling relationship. By its end, the vast majority are in a state of disrelation.

It may be for this reason that Lehi concludes the account as he does by returning to Laman and Lemuel "not partak[ing] of the fruit" (v. 35). It was here that things began to unravel. So, after relaying the dream Lehi exhorts them—Laman and Lemuel—"with all the feeling of a tender parent" (v. 37). Indeed, compared with his silence toward them in the dream, Lehi's exhorting, preaching, prophesying, and bidding at its completion are a deafening contrast. Having entered the dream in darkness, Lehi exited it in fear. In between, and in response to his dreamed prayer for mercy, Lehi experienced the reality of the extent to which he had internalised the real-life division between his sons and the inevitable consequences of that division for his posterity. In response to the revelation of things as they really were, Lehi immediately set about putting them right.

WHAT KIND OF GOD

It is in the nature of this merciful response that the question of the kind of God that emerges from this reading of the dream may begin to be engaged. God, it is revealed, is utterly and unflinchingly merciful. Yet this mercy is of an unexpected and difficult kind. Rather than removing hard situations, God's mercy delivers one into their full reality. In this instance, it revealed the reality of Lehi's relationships. Delivered from darkness, Lehi's encounter with the tree turned him to his family in a manner that exposed him to the reality of his own internalisation of his family's divisions. The dream, primarily, is about Lehi. The principal expression of this disrelation is found in the difference in his interactions with his sons. It is here that Lehi's internalising of their division is disclosed. While painful, this is necessary if true deliverance is to be found. There is no way around it. Anything else is insufficient. Redemption requires the righting of all relations and the healing of all souls. Crucially, this disclosure was made to Lehi. As an expression of God's mercy, it is intimately personal. God, then, this reading suggests, is an inherently personal being.

Personality, of course, entails relationship. But relations can be realised in right and wrong ways. This is as true of relations between God and humans as it is between humans. Here the dream is instructive in at least three ways. First, in its insistence that the future is not marked out; second, in its demonstration of the negative effects of human disrelation; and third, by demonstrating the same for relations between humans and God. Together they depict God as absolutely relational.

While God is not directly invoked as the source of the dream, it is clearly implied. This is Lehi's third direct report of a dream, the fifth in all of his supernatural seeing. That Lehi received dreams from God when God wanted Lehi to know something is established in the text. Yet even as God is the source, Lehi directs the action. It was *after* Lehi decided to follow the man in a white robe that he beheld a dark and dreary waste. It was *after* Lehi prayed that he was delivered to the tree. It was *after* Lehi decided to eat that he had a redemptive experience. It was *after* Lehi called and beckoned that Sariah, Sam, and Nephi approached the tree. It was *after* Lehi disengaged with Laman and Lemuel that the scene exploded. In each instance, Lehi *could have* acted differently. If he'd done so, we'd be reading a different dream. The same is true of Lehi's first divine encounter. It was *after* Lehi "went forth [and] prayed unto the Lord" that he "saw and heard much" (1 Ne. 1:5–6). God seeks relationship, and of a certain kind, but in God's commitment to each, God forces neither the relationship nor its direction.

This kind of relational commitment is risky. While there is a future God intends, honouring human decisions means God is not the only one capable of shaping the future. Disrelation is a possibility. Having partaken of the fruit and experienced "exceedingly great joy" (v. 12), Lehi immediately turned to his family. However, this gesture aimed at right relation was actualised in disrelational ways. These include Lehi's almost immediate distraction from his search (vv. 13–14), and two very different interactions with his sons, which resulted in a number of disrelational consequences. While Lehi initially approached the tree unobstructed, for everyone else access became progressively more complicated. Rivers, paths, mists of darkness, and buildings full of people obscured the way. This progressive aggravation of the physical landscape mirrored the worsening of the dream's interpersonal relations. Lehi's disengaged interaction with Laman and Lemuel gave way to in-group pressing and finally to between-group scoffing. The physical landscape, that is, suffered the effects of humanity's increasing disrelation. This insight has much to contribute to a developing Latter-day Saint ecotheology, but for our purposes, a different observation: human disrelation not only complicates access to the tree, it also diminishes one's experience with the fruit. For Lehi the tree and the fruit represented redemption. More plainly said, then, disrelation amongst humans complicates right relations with God.

That human relations impact relation with God may initially seem surprising. It is, however, a necessary condition of God's being in relation. This is glimpsed intuitively every time a bad day at work is brought home or frustration with one child is carried into interactions with another. For beings in relation, each relation impacts other relations. When one is disrelated to others, one cannot relate rightly to God.[4] Given that humans are, in some way or other, perpetually in a state of disrelation, what hope is there of right relations with each other or with God? The dream hints towards an answer. Opening with a positive expression of salvation—"I have reason to suppose that they . . . will be saved" (v. 3)—it concludes with a negative one—"he feared lest they should be cast off from the presence of the Lord" (v. 36). This framing makes clear that in Lehi's mind, the dream's chief preoccupation is salvation, negatively expressed in the dream through those described as "lost."

Lost, it is clear, is a relational descriptor. One can only be lost in relation to something else. In the dream, that "something" is Lehi. Further, those that are lost are "lost from [Lehi's] view" (v. 32). When Lehi can no longer see them, they have travelled beyond the bounds of his relating and they are "lost." The problem is Lehi's sight, the limits of which demark the extent of his relational capacity. That this capacity is limited is made clear in at least four ways in the dream: (1) in Lehi's addressing only one part of his listening audience and then in his focus on the fruit of one tree, narrowing significantly the context of the dream's telling wherein "the seeds of fruit of every kind" (v. 1) were gathered; (2) in Lehi's immediate distraction when initially looking for his family; (3) in the distinction between "seeing" and "beholding" and the effect of disrelation on Lehi's ability to discern; and (4) in the things Lehi can't see, particularly those he once did but then "lost from his view." This linkage of sight and relation not only emphasises the personal nature of relation but also Lehi's finitude. "Lost" as a relational descriptor, this makes clear, applies to finite beings. What then of infinite beings? After all, Lehi is not God, and it is in God that salvation is found.

Included in 1 Nephi 10 is some of the preaching and prophesying mentioned at the dream's conclusion (v. 38). There Lehi's focus is on "a Messiah, or, in other words, a Savior of the world" (1 Ne. 10:4). Already, there is a distinction: while finite beings have relational limits, God saves the world. Further, this is no partial salvation. The Messiah is not "*part* Savior of the world" or "Savior *of part* of the world," but "Savior of the world." Complete. To this Lehi adds the claim that "all" are "lost" except "they should rely on this Redeemer" (1 Ne. 10:6). This places salvation firmly in the relational realm. It is found in relating rightly to the redeeming Messiah. However, considering the reading of the dream just offered, this presents a problem. Humans don't always relate rightly, and each instance of disrelation complicates relation with God.

Lehi and His Dream: A Relational Reading

If salvation is found in right relation, how can anyone be saved? Later, in very similar language to Lehi, Amulek contends that without Christ's atonement "all . . . are lost." This atonement he describes as "infinite" (Alma 34:12) and suggests it brings "means unto men that they may have faith unto repentance" (Alma 34:15). Atonement, that is, provides the mechanism for overcoming disrelation. Read this way atonement is not only the means by which relationships are restored, it is the infinite possibility of their restoration. Ultimately, God is capable of righting all relations. If the dream exposes the negative consequences of disrelation, atonement clears the ground. The tree *is* desirable, and eventually its fruit will make each one happy, even if it has not yet. The dream is about Lehi and yet in its focus on him, it transcends him. Lehi's humanity, revealed in the limits of his relating, exposes the majesty of God, the bounds of whose relating cannot be traversed. One, that is, can never be lost to God.

PLATE 3. Megan Knobloch Geilman, *Adaptations of Desire*, photographic print of mixed media collage, 16 x 20 inches, 2021. Photography by Samantha Zauscher.

Adaptations of Desire

MEGAN KNOBLOCH GEILMAN

WITH SO MUCH OF THE IMAGERY SURROUNDING LEHI'S DREAM being narrative in nature, I wanted to explore the psychological under-pinnings of this visionary scripture. The surrealists seemed like an appropriate vehicle for that thesis, and Salvador Dalí's *Accommodations of Desire* fit the bill. Although the painting was exploring Dalí's anxieties about a lover, I wanted to appropriate that into Lehi's desire for his children to partake of the fruit. The ceramic figs, a clear reference to the white fruit of the tree, are also a reference to the New Testament account of the Savior's parable of the fig tree. The fig has become, for me, a symbol of beckoning, an exhortation to pay attention to what is being presented. The bonsai helped with the scale of the display, while its undulating curves are reminiscent of a surrealist vision and anchor the com-position as the central figure of the tree in the vision. Other trees and other gar-dens come to mind, especially with the lion figure—a reference to Asherah and her exile as referenced in Kathryn Knight Sonntag's "The Tree of Life" poem, while also hearkening back to the original work where Dalí used a repeated image of a lion. The layout of the cloth, delineating a landscape, places the great and spacious building outside the frame, reminding the viewer that rather than falling into an "us vs. them" rhetoric, we should be sensitive to how often we might find ourselves in that large edifice. The moth—a symbol of decay placed on a mossy stone—is a foil to Joseph Smith's self-description of a "rough stone rolling," and is placed where we might expect to find the "river of filthy water" and/or the "mists of darkness" in a traditional image of Lehi's dream. Other symbols of eggs and seer stones, drawing attention to the allusions of divine parents and prophetic inklings, lend to this surrealistic and unconventional approach to Lehi's dream imagery.

Lehi's Parable of the Fruitful Tree

ROSALYNDE FRANDSEN WELCH

Early in June of 1829, Joseph Smith sat with his scribe Christian Whitmer in the upper room of the Whitmer log home in Fayette Township, New York.[1] The June morning dawned early and warm in advance of the summer solstice. The two men labored "from morning till night," the young prophet dictating and his friend inscribing the second chapter of the first book of Nephi, their friendship forming the first modern interpretive community to receive the dream of Lehi.[2] Beyond the windows the plowed wheatfields of the Whitmers' farm rolled out dark and moist.[3] Gardens and orchards girded the frontier farmstead, and woodlands extended beyond.

This was the physical environment in which Lehi's dream first found English expression and interpretation. What can we say of the *lexical* environment? What was the *language* world of the prophet and his scribe?

Smith was famously reticent about his translation method, saying only that it occurred "by the gift and power of God." Scholars have recently begun to investigate the process, mining clues from historical accounts and descriptions *within* the translated texts Smith produced. Some of these suggest that portions of the dictated text may have begun with pre-verbal impressions of the plates' ancient content, perhaps as images, panoramas, sensations, or notions, which Smith prophetically received and then expressed in early American English to his scribe.[4] This proposed model of translation foregrounds Smith's gift of seership: the power he received from God was the power of *seeing*, or spiritually perceiving, the Book of Mormon's meaning, and then, through inspired interpretation, rendering that vision in language mentally available to him and intelligible to the book's intended readership. Under this model, part of the task of investigating the text is to determine which meanings of a word or phrase were available as Smith brought forth the text's English form, and which of those meanings provides the best reading of a passage.

Like all social milieux, the family and community in which Smith produced his translation was structured by various overlapping lexical worlds. By "lexical world," I mean a set of verbal meanings loosely united by a shared setting or practice.[5] All proficient language users understand, as a practical matter, that a word may convey several meanings, depending on which lexical world is implied by its context. In a discussion of building construction, for example, centered on the lexical world of industrial equipment, the word "crane" indicates a heavy machine for lifting and moving loads; in a discussion centered on the lexical world of wetland ecology, the same word refers to a waterfowl. To infer the verbal worlds of which a speaker has knowledge, and further to identify the lexical realm in which a particular discussion unfolds, then, can help to interpret the meaning of a word or phrase. Applying this model to Book of Mormon translation, I take it that the lexical contexts available to the book's translator, Joseph Smith, necessarily influence the phrasing and verbal expression of the Book of Mormon as it was dictated. It thus falls to the book's interpreters to infer the language world in which any passage of the dictation operates and to wager interpretations based on the meanings that populate that world.

Working from this model of verbal dictation embedded in available language worlds, I propose that the agrarian world of the early American farm is a primary lexical context for the English translation of Lehi's dream. The dream has typically been interpreted in the lexical world of the King James Bible, an authoritative language environment in antebellum America that undeniably conditions much of the English in the Book of Mormon, including in 1 Nephi 8, as a source of words and phrases for religious ideas. It is my contention that the lexical world of farm ecology offers a compelling additional interpretive context for 1 Nephi 8. Both language worlds were prominent in Smith's family and local environment as he dictated the Book of Mormon in English. (To be sure, other early American language worlds were available to Joseph Smith and relevant to the Book of Mormon translation, but in this paper I limit my discussion to these.) The primary elements of the dream—wilderness, field, tree, river, rod, building—are intelligible in either context, but they yield subtly different meanings under each.

Consider, for example, the wilderness through which Lehi follows his guide as the dream begins. Pictured in the context of biblical narratives, the wilderness is a barren desert, dry and treeless, a place of testing and refuge in which the Lord's hand is miraculously bared. In an early American context, however, "wilderness" carries markedly negative associations. For the New England farmer, wilderness is a "waste" of forested (that is, non-arable) land that must be cleared of trees before being suitable for tillage. Webster's 1828 dictionary captures this distinction in its first definition of the word: "Wilderness: A desert; a tract of land or region uncultivated and uninhabited by human beings, whether a forest or a wide barren plain. *In the United States, it is applied only to a forest. In Scripture, it is applied frequently to the deserts of Arabia*" (emphasis mine).[6] In this note, Noah Webster captures both the adjacency and the division of the language worlds organized around pastoral ecology on the one hand and biblical narrative on the other.

Both meanings of "wilderness" were available to Smith and Whitmer, the book's earliest "intended audience"; the work of comparative analysis teases out the nuances of each meaning. These variant meanings, in turn, build toward larger differences in narrative, genre, and theology. If the language of Lehi's dream is best understood as a fabric of allusions and symbols linked to the biblical text, it sits comfortably in the genre of prophetic vision, which in turn suggests a set of typical theological concerns. But if, as I'll argue, the text of what is now 1 Nephi 8 is placed among the everyday scenes and objects of the agrarian environment in which its English form originated, it is better classified as a kind of parable, and its theological work is best understood within the characteristic concerns of that form.

Before diving into my argument, I offer two caveats. First, I want to make it clear that I write as a believer in the Book of Mormon, one who accepts its scriptural authority as a personal and spiritual commitment. Furthermore, I am convinced that the book's own explanation of its provenance and purpose, namely to bring the voices of ancient Christian prophets into the present in order to convince a modern world that Jesus is Christ, best accounts for the fascinating texture of its linguistic features. The Book of Mormon has never failed to respond to any question I've brought to it with astonishing theological richness and expressive depth.

Second, I acknowledge that I approach the scholarly task of interpreting the Book of Mormon with an intellectual modesty to match my confidence in the book's capacity to bear analysis. In that spirit of methodological modesty, I note that my interpretive skills are lexical, not historical. Furthermore, I acknowledge that lexical and historical contexts are not identical. My focus is limited to the immediate interpretation of the English text as dictated in 1829, and thus I limit potential interpretive frames to the lexical worlds available in that process. When I invoke a "biblical" lexical world, I mean the language, narratives, and cultural authority of the King James Bible in antebellum America. This differs importantly from an ancient Near Eastern *historical* context, which would broadly encompass the social, political, cultural, economic, and environmental features of the cultures from which the Hebrew Bible arose.[7] Granting as I do that the pre-verbal source of Joseph Smith's spoken words was the spiritual transmission of an ancient record, the dictation would have found its immediate interpretive context among the several available lexical worlds in which Joseph and his scribe were fluent.[8] Thus, I do not aim to *historicize* Lehi's dream as an early American artifact, a project that I am neither qualified as a scholar nor inclined as a believer to undertake. I aim instead to explore the agrarian milieu that may have informed its most immediate interpretation and reception, an analysis that, as I see it, is fully compatible with the book's ancient origin under any proposed model of inspired translation.[9] My claims are not historical but interpretive in intent and, as will be seen, theological in purpose. The earthy cultural immediacy of the language of Lehi's dream speaks, I'll argue, to its scriptural function as parable and its urgent concern to guide its readers to the gates of God's kingdom.

BIBLICAL WORLD: PROPHECY AND VISION

That Joseph Smith was weaned on the biblical rhythms and expressions of the Authorized Version is everywhere observed by scholars. Philip Barlow notes that Smith was "well exposed to the KJV, [and] that his language and thought patterns had been colored by it[.] . . . When Deity did come, Smith heard him speak in both biblical and Bible-like language."[10] That Lehi's dream accordingly brims with biblical phrases and echoes is likewise clear.[11] If we suppose that the Bible represents for 1 Nephi 8 not just a resource for religious language but indeed the primary lexical world for interpretation, the key images in the text come together in a particular dreamscape. I'll briefly sketch that picture here

Lehi's Parable of the Fruitful Tree

in order to better delineate, by contrast, the picture that emerges from an early American lexical world, which I'll explore at greater length below.

I noted above that early Americans understood the biblical *wilderness* as the Arabian desert, a "vast sandy plain."[12] A shroud of symbolic associations clings to the idea of wilderness. The parched desolation of the wilderness is divinely cursed, a realm of sin and death hostile to human life. The levitical scapegoat carries sin into the wilderness (Lev. 16:10). Under divine disfavor, the wicked lament that their "holy cities are a wilderness, Zion is a wilderness" (Isa. 64:10). Above all, the wilderness is waterless, a mortal danger for the children of Israel who wander through "that great and terrible wilderness, wherein were fiery serpents, and scorpions, and drought, where there was no water" (Deut. 8:15). Yet the Exodus narrative shows that, despite its arid perils, the wilderness is also a place of testing and refuge, purification and freedom, wherein a chosen people is prepared for the land of promise. The biblical wilderness is thus thematically ambiguous, both the scene of liminal wandering outside one's destined home and, perhaps consequently, the scene of transcendent encounter with God. In short, the desert wilderness of the Bible is a figure for the human condition in the world, where sin, death, and evil dwell, but an austere God may appear "in a flame of fire out of the midst of a bush" (Ex. 3:2).

Lehi's wilderness wanderings thus take him through a barren plain until he reaches a "large and spacious field" (v. 9). *Field*, in the Bible, most often refers to a tract of cultivated land. Lehi's crossing from wilderness to field is thus a scenic reversal of dramatic proportion. In contrast to wilderness, a field is a place that is watered, a domain of abundance and life sustained by the God "who giveth rain upon the earth, and sendeth waters upon the fields" (Job 5:10). As one scholar notes, if "drought and the resulting wilderness were thought of as the curse dispensed by the divine power in order to show his displeasure," then divine favor "meant an abundance of life-giving water."[13] Indeed, the "most pronounced figurative use of wilderness is in contrast to fertile ground, and God's power is frequently described as being able to turn the one into the other."[14] In the Bible, God's sovereign salvific power is illustrated by the transformation of dry wilderness into verdant landscape. Lehi's crossing from wilderness to field thus represents a scene of divine deliverance from the afflictions and toil of the world.

As Lehi is delivered, so is his dreamscape. If wilderness is a biblical figure for the world, a biblical field or garden is a figure of paradise, the symbolic opposite of wilderness. At the edge of the field, with a spring flowing past the fruitful tree at its center, then, Lehi stands like the prophet Joel surveying the day of the Lord, "the land . . . as the Garden of Eden before them, and behind them a desolate wilderness" (Joel 2:3). In the Bible, the messianic future is envisioned as the watering of the wilderness. Isaiah's song of the redeemed Zion, for instance, promises that "in the wilderness shall waters break out, and streams in the desert. And the parched ground shall become a pool, and the thirsty land springs of water" (Isa. 35:6–7). The wilderness is the world of human tribulation in its desert state; the field is a place of redemption, watered by the hand of God.

In broadest strokes, then, Lehi's journey, interpreted in the lexical world of the Bible, is a passage from earthly tribulation in the dry wilderness-world toward redemption in the field-paradise, where the fruitful tree and sweet fruit promise an eschatological feast. In this exegetical context, Lehi's dream fits well in the broad biblical genre of prophecy. Charles Swift has argued that Lehi's dream belongs to a subset of prophecy identified as "visionary literature."[15] Reading the dream in the biblical genre of prophecy in turn alerts us to the presence of theological concerns characteristic of the genre. The prophetic form's theological work is, in part, to comfort God's people in the wilderness (the dark and dreary waste), to proclaim the future paradise that awaits the righteous (the tree at the end of the path), and to celebrate the unfathomable transcendence of God and his marvelous intervention in salvation history (the exceeding whiteness of the fruit and the watered paradise of the field).

A picture of God begins to take shape from this approach to the dream, a text that notably lacks any direct representation of the divine. If God is the source of life-giving moisture, then the salvation represented in the well-watered dream field is a blessing granted by divine hand, a demonstration of God's transcendent sovereignty and power. Isaiah affirms a similar link between humankind's dependency on life-saving rain and a theology of divine sovereignty:

> For as the heavens are higher than the earth, so are my ways higher than your ways, and my thoughts than your thoughts. For as the rain cometh down, and the snow from heaven, and returneth not thither, but watereth the earth, and maketh it bring forth and bud, that it may give seed to the sower, and bread to the eater: So shall my word be that goeth forth out of my mouth: it shall not return unto me void, but it shall accomplish that which I please, and it shall prosper in the thing whereto I sent it. (Isa. 55:9–11)

Just as rain falls from the high heavens to the dry earth, God's sovereign words and ways are higher than humankind's. The contrast between the parched earth and the aqueous heavens—figured in Lehi's crossing from wilderness to field—parallels the absolute disparity between human finitude and divine power to "accomplish that which I please." God's relationship to his creatures is one of elevation, otherness, and dominion, as the rain, foreign to the thirsty earth, falls from unfathomable heights to moisten the dust. Lehi the desert prophet prays to a rain God from a barren sandflat and is delivered to the fields of paradise.

Under a reading of 1 Nephi 8 as biblical visionary prophecy, then, a particular existential picture emerges. Lehi's wandering in the wilderness is our life in the world, lost and lonely and afflicted. Yet we aim for a better place, God's well-watered field where salvation awaits in the tree's sweet fruit. Bruce Jorgensen movingly summarizes this reading:

> Ultimately, as in all Judeo-Christian figures of pilgrimage, [Lehi] goes through the wilderness of a fallen world toward a redeemed world abounding in the joy of God's loving presence. Call it quest or conversion, at bottom the pattern is a simple transformation: from dark and barren waste by means of the Word to a world fruitful and filled with light.[16]

I've briefly explored here a reading of 1 Nephi 8 that takes the lexical world of the King James Bible as the verbal context for the English translation. In this vein, I've suggested that the exposition produced by the selection of lexical world in turn points to a classification of the text among the various scriptural genres. Generic classification then highlights for the reader characteristic theological concerns, and finally a particular existential meaning may give itself from that series of interpretive moves. The latter stages of this sequence, the theological and existential, are the questions that most interest me, not the historical and linguistic. But I hope I've shown that the earliest interpretive choice—namely, identification of the lexical world in which the text is to be read—can be decisive for the *kind* of existential structure that scripture offers its readers.

The biblically-inflected reading I've just outlined—which, as noted, is not original to this essay and has been widely developed by scholars—yields a plausible interpretation of the text and a meaningful performance of its power as scripture.[17] Yet every scriptural text will exceed any single interpretive frame, and the lexical world of the Bible cannot easily account for some aspects of Lehi's dream. For example, 1 Nephi 8:20 plainly identifies the *field*, not the wilderness, as the "world" in which moral choice unfolds. But in the lexicon of the Bible, as I've shown, the *wilderness* represents the world, while fruitful fields most often represent paradise. Neither can the lexicon of the Bible readily explain the dream's emphasis on the darkness of the wilderness, noted in verses 4, 7, and 8 (absent any suggestion that the narrative occurs at night). The desert of the biblical prophets is a shelterless landscape. A sun-baked setting makes sense of Isaiah's promise that in the day of the Lord, "there shall be a tabernacle for a shadow in the daytime from the heat" (Isa. 4:6, see also 2 Ne. 14:6). The dark wilderness through which Lehi wanders is strikingly different. The historicizing approach to Lehi's dream, which compares the text to extra-biblical ancient sources, has suggested an explanation for the anomalous darkness of Lehi's wilderness: a desert storm.[18] But a lexical approach focused on the linguistic resources of the Bible makes little immediate sense of a "dark wilderness" without inventive interpretive work to explain the darkness.[19]

Other elements of the dream pose similar puzzles, lacking a ready verbal antecedent in the King James Bible. In particular, the rod of iron, as its use and form are described in the dream, has no clear referent in the Bible, though scholars have made several suggestions.[20] Even the impressive sweetness of the fruit, the sensory centerpiece of the dream, is somewhat puzzling in a biblical context, where sweetness overwhelmingly describes the odorous incense of sacrifice ascending to God. Less frequently, the sweet tastes of honey, cane, or wine are praised (see Judg. 14:18; Psalm 19:10; Isa. 43:24; Isa. 49:26). On a single occasion, in the Song of Songs, is sweetness attributed to fruit (Song. 2:3).

To be sure, a reader may find ways to fit these elements of Lehi's dream into the verbal world of the Bible by proposing various exegetical solutions. Still, one begins to wonder: might a different verbal context shed light on these exegetical puzzles in Lehi's dream? If so, does the resulting exposition of the text suggest that the dream partakes of a different biblical genre? And if that is the case, does that genre point toward a different set of theological concerns and a different existential effect on the reader? I'll argue that the answer to each question is yes.

FROM WILDERNESS TO FIELD

Beyond the cabin on the American frontier where Joseph Smith dictated the dream of a Jewish prophet stretched a landscape of wilderness, fields, fruit trees, and creeks draining to the Seneca River. The farmstead and its flora were intimately familiar to Smith; the rhythms of frontier farming ordered every year of the young prophet's life. The Smiths' hundred-acre farmstead in the Genesee River valley included cultivated plowland, meadowland, apple orchard, and woodlot.[21] Practical husbandry passed through generations of farmers yielded a deep store of tacit and local knowledge, transmitted orally and in farmers' almanacs. These practices and objects produced, beyond bushels of wheat and barrels of apples, an informal lexicon, a working vocabulary of terms and ideas related to the farmstead. In this language world, the oral dictation of Lehi's dream would have unfolded as a passage through frontier countryside of cleared fields and deciduous forests, burgeoning villages and developing waterways, each vista freighted with tacit meanings and practical relationships.

While my ultimate interest in this world of meanings is theological, my first aim is straightforwardly exegetical, namely to propose for six elements of the dream meanings embedded in the pastoral world I've marked here. In addition to wilderness, broached in the introduction, I'll consider the field and the building, and the tree, fruit, and rod of iron. For each element, I'll sketch its significance in and briefly consider its relationships to other elements of the agrarian language world. It's worth noting, with regard to the language of landscape and ecology, the singular character of Lehi's dream as a pericope or portion of the Book of Mormon. Shawna Norton has observed that "despite The Book of Mormon's deep interest in territory, we receive few actual descriptions of the landscape."[22] Instead of evoking visual pictures or sensory descriptions, Norton shows, Book of Mormon authors tend to write about land as either a "land of promise" or a "land of inheritance," linking the land to ethnic identity and covenant relationship to God. Strikingly, Lehi's dream speaks of land in a different register. There is no mention of "land of promise" or "land of inheritance"—indeed, there is no talk of "land" as a territory at all. Instead, there is a sensory ecological description of landscapes, evoking pleasure, color, and sensation, quite unlike anything else in the Book of Mormon (aside from in quotations of Old Testament poetry). To be sure, Nephi soon "translates" Lehi's dream into the more familiar Book of Mormon themes of promised and inherited lands (1 Ne. 12). But inasmuch as Lehi's dream stands as an identifiable narrative unit, it seems to draw from both a different language world and a different genre than the reportage and prophetic passages that precede and follow it. This means, for one thing, that the early American agrarian language world I propose here is likely a suitable interpretive context only for Lehi's dream, not a general interpretive strategy for the entire Book of Mormon. But it also points, as I hope to show, toward the unique *theological* resources offered by Lehi's remarkable dream of the sweet, white fruit.

Wilderness, Field, Building

The forests of North America were a defining ecological fact of early American experience. Forests represented the material substrate of frontier settlement and a crucial source of timber and fuel.[23] They were also an implacable foe. Wilderness stood in the way of the young society's hungry demand for grain and cider. The shady earth under the forest canopy could not be cultivated; farmers were faced with the daunting labor of felling trees and clearing stumps to bring sunlight to arable plowland. After clearing, resurgent wilderness threatened to reclaim hard-won plowland.[24] Darkness and gloom defined wilderness in the early American imagination.[25] An imagined moral taint clung to the forests, linked by colonial racism to the indigenous peoples who, with the forests, represented the continent's primitive "savagery."[26] The romantic view of American wilderness as a place of ennobling grandeur, so familiar to modern readers, arose among educated city-dwellers later in the nineteenth century.[27] To the early American farmer, the endless wilderness signified darkness, death, and depravity.

By the same token, a tilled field signified much beyond its black earth. A field represented wilderness vanquished, a transformation from "waste" to abundance wrought by human toil. The word "field" evoked an entire pastoral context. The first definition of *field* in Webster's 1828 Dictionary is "[a] piece of land inclosed for tillage or pasture; any part of a farm." Demographic growth and partible inheritance laws meant that the young republic's hunger for plowland was insatiable.[28] Families and fields were closely joined: as sons became men and required fields of their own, wilderness was cleared at an increasing rate. Peak deforestation in New England occurred from 1830 to 1860 when 60-80% of the land was cleared.[29] An Irish traveler noted that "To [the Americans] the sight of a wheat field . . . would convey pleasure far greater than that of the most romantic woodland views. They have an unconquerable aversion to trees; and whenever a settlement is made, they cut away all before them without mercy."[30] The Smith family lived out this collective story. Lucy Mack Smith reported her husband and sons Alvin and Hyrum cleared thirty acres during their first year in residence. They would eventually clear sixty.[31]

Early America was a society in flux: local agrarian worlds once bound by family and community turned to wider worlds of commerce and market.[32] As wilderness gave way to field, field yielded to city. Demographic growth and transit infrastructure, including the Erie Canal, transported families to new population centers, where field harvests became market commodities. City streetscapes sprang up to house the new commercial activity. For many, rising cities with their demographic brawn marked the final stage in a providential civilizing and populating of the continent. An Ohio newspaperman extolled "wilderness, once the chosen residence of solitude and savageness, converted into populous cities, smiling villages, beautiful farms and plantations!"[33] But this

Lehi's Parable of the Fruitful Tree

process left bitter social division in its wake, as a prosperous merchant class and subsistence farming families faced off across a growing socioeconomic chasm that pitted growing capitalist markets for American commodities against the kinship and communal practices of the poor backwoods. Prosperous agrarian merchants "excoriated backwoods farming practices and anti-market ideologies."[34] Merchants regarded pioneer farmers as backward and benighted; farmers regarded merchants with resentment and suspicion.[35]

The progress of Lehi's dream from wilderness to field to city seems to reflect this early American lexical world in many particulars. The prophet begins in the wilderness. The darkness of the wilderness is noted three times in quick succession, and the epithet "dark and dreary" is repeated twice (vv. 4, 7, 8). Lehi calls the wilderness a "waste," an undeveloped tract unsuitable for cultivation (v. 7). The wilderness is endless and empty; Lehi wanders alone, apparently abandoned by his guide, "for the space of many hours" (v. 8). The dark wilderness is a place of stasis, sin, and isolation; it imposes a blindness that separates him from God's love and from which he must be rescued by God's mercy (v. 8). The wilderness is a narrative parallel to the "mists of darkness" that will separate the multitudes from the love of God later in the dream (v. 23). Notably, the wilderness of Lehi's dream is dissimilar from the wilderness of Lehi's desert migration. The wilderness through which the Lehite band travels closely recalls the biblical wilderness of the Israelite exodus—a place of refuge and testing, of divine nourishment and guidance, of law-giving, covenant, and theophany. By contrast, the dark and dreary wilderness of the dream is God-forsaken, empty, and trackless.

From this dark wilderness, Lehi comes upon a bright field. The passage from American wilderness to tilled field again marks a dramatic transformation of the dreamscape, but with a different set of theological and existential connotations than that implied in the biblical context explored above. The stark contrast lies in the disjunction between the wasted wilderness and the fruitful field, and in the engine of human labor that accomplishes the transformation. Imagine the sweat and toil required to clear a field as "large and spacious" "as if it had been a world"! (v. 20) The field is a place of pleasure and light, with a clear view of earth and water, and rich soil underfoot waiting to receive seed. It is a domain bound first by family ties, as Sariah, Sam, and Nephi appear at the spring (v. 14); it is only later that "numberless concourses" appear to populate the great field. The field is Lehi's world, and it is a good world. But it is no biblical paradise; no wall girdles the field to repel sin and death. The dark mist, echoing the dark wilderness, threatens to rise and blind other travelers in its shadow, just as the forest threatens resurgence (v. 23). For all its goodness, the dream field remains open to contingency and risk.

Lehi's dream seems to track the course of early American experience as it moves from empty wilderness to family fields to populous buildings. The "large and spacious field" with its humble seekers stands across from its market-like "great and spacious building," replete with high society and fine commercial goods. The resentment of the frontier farmer before an ascendant elite is clear in the bitterly noted "mocking and pointing [of] fingers" (v. 27). Yet the prophet's dream departs clearly from the historical logic of American settler colonialism. The great building and its populace are not the providential aspiration and destiny of the godly society; this is no simple fantasy of subduing and filling an empty wilderness. Rather, the *field* is Lehi's destination; the family farm is the good world that the dream imagines. The field exists in a state of moral and ecological tension between a fearsome wilderness on one side and a polluted market center on the other. Salvation is found in a pastoral family world, not in a prosperous, populous city.

Tree, Fruit, Rod

No sooner had a frontier farmer cleared the deciduous hardwood trees from his acreage, than he began planting new trees—apple trees, whose fruit could be eaten, preserved, or pressed into cider. Fruit trees tolerated marginal soils where grains struggled; farmers accordingly reserved their prime tillage fields for wheat and sited their orchards on rocky slopes.[36] Productive fruit trees were prized as markers of a developed farmstead because they required ten years or more to mature. Once established, an apple orchard could provide a perennial harvest for decades, proving a valuable, reliable investment when grain crops failed. The Smith farm boasted an apple orchard of 200 trees, as did the Whitmer farm where Joseph Smith dictated the dream of the Jewish prophet.[37] Today, a bounteous apple tree stands outside the window of the Whitmer cabin reconstructed on its original foundation.

Apple trees are rooted deep in human history, having made their way from central Asia across the globe in prized cultivars. The species is unique in the diversity of its genome and the resulting variability of its fruit. To plant an apple seed is to roll genetic dice: the resulting fruit exhibits dramatically variable characteristics, most often small, bitter, and unpalatable. Occasionally, however, a tree yields fruit of exceptional quality— large, sweet, and fair.[38] In early America, these lucky apples, if they escaped the apple scab fungus, were prized for eating at table, rather than consigned to the cider barrel. Further, its branches were cut for grafting onto established rootstock, thereby cloning the plant and preserving its felicitous genes. In colonial and antebellum America, the grafting of apple trees came to be associated with agricultural reform and prosperous commodity farming, while seedling apples were linked with "the poor, the idle, the unambitious, the primitive frontier family eking out a subsistence, [and] those who sought isolation from the markets."[39] Whether to graft or seed new apple trees was thus implicated in early American culture wars over commercial expansion.

The division of the farmstead into orchard, plowfield, meadow, woodlot, and pasture was carefully fitted to the microecology of its land—its soils, elevations, and waterways. Plots were surveyed and measured with specialized surveyor's tools. Among these, the metal surveyor's rod, sometimes called a "pole" or a "perch," was an essential tool for marking property lines and determining acreages. This meaning is the sixth of Webster's twelve definitions for the word "rod": "An instrument for measuring; but more generally, a measure of length containing five yards, or sixteen feet and a half . . . In many parts of the United States, rod is universally used for pole or perch." An iron surveyor's rod, often broken into attached segments for portability and known thus as a "surveyor's chain," would be staked at a lot corner, extended in a straight line, and staked at the far end, to mark one unit of distance.[40]

Such tacit cultural knowledge of local husbandry, the tools and rhythms and practices of the New England farmstead, would likely have informed the conceptual horizon of the Book of Mormon's first interpreters. Lehi's fruitful tree, in particular, takes on a special character when received in this world of farmstead and field. The presence of a mature tree heavy with fruit implies a caretaker who has nurtured and pruned it for many years. That it stands in a field, not an orchard, suggests that it was carefully sited in the choicest soils. But this tree is not a financial investment; its fruit is not bound for market. The fruit is freely offered to all "without money and without price" (Isa. 55:1). The fruit is "desirable to make one happy," not rich (v. 10). Indeed, desire is central to the tree's effect. Lehi underscores the desirability of the fruit five times in his account (vv. 10, 12, 12, 15, 17). The tree's capacity to stimulate desire links it in complex ways to the commercial world figured in the great building. Markets function by stimulating desire to produce demand, but—at least as depicted in the dream—they catalyze the potency of desire into scorn, pride, and mockery. The tree stimulates desire, but its fruit catalyzes desire into happiness and the love of God.

That the tree stands in the field of the despised, not the prosperous proud, suggests that the tree has grown from a seedling, not a graft, and thus that the quality of its fruit may be in question as Lehi approaches the tree. But he finds it neither bitter nor scabbed, but sweet and white. This may explain Lehi's excessive delight: "I beheld that it was most sweet, above all that I ever before tasted. Yea, and I beheld that the fruit thereof was white, to exceed all the whiteness that I had ever seen" (v. 11). The text dwells not on the fruit's value, but on its quality—or better, its *qualia*, the subjective experience of taste and color and joy that it produces in those who eat. Its sensory intensity seems to produce a kind of synesthesia in Lehi, who appears to see its flavor: "I beheld that it was most sweet" (v. 11). (Alma's parable of the seed, which seems to build on Lehi's parable of the fruitful tree, reverses the synesthetic motif and speaks of "tast[ing] this light" (Alma 32:35)).

What of the rod? How might the book's earliest interpreters have pictured it? The rod of iron has remained an exegetical challenge for various interpretive approaches to the dream.[41] In modern artistic renderings, the rod of iron is most often depicted as a kind of handrail, but Webster's 1828 dictionary records no architectural rail-related definition for early American usage of "rod." Suggestions that the rod of iron is a kind of handheld staff or weapon—or, alternately, a wand or dowsing rod—do not correspond with its description and function in the dream. An iron surveyor's rod both fits an early American pastoral context and seems to match the dream rod's properties. The rod is said to "extend along the bank of the river" (v. 19), just as a surveyor's rod or chain is unfolded and extended to its full measure of distance. Moreover, the straight linear extension of the surveyor's rod was a primary feature of the tool's use. Royal Skousen argues that the correct textual variant of verse 20, which describes the path that runs beside the rod, is "straight and narrow," not "strait and narrow," as it has appeared since the 1981 edition.[42] The rod functions in the dream to guide and orient one toward the tree, which broadly fits the purpose of the surveyor's tool. The dream rod is grasped by those who "caught hold of the end of the rod of iron" and follow it to the tree (v. 24); notably, surveyor's chains are fabricated with a handle at each end.

When these six elements are considered together, the lexical world of the early American farm offers a compelling interpretive context for Lehi's dream. The dark and forbidding wilderness, the large cleared field, the fine building, and the numberless concourses of people fit together in the vocabulary of frontier expansion and demographic growth. The opposition between the "large and spacious field" and the "great and spacious building" is legible in light of the war of words between subsistence frontier farming and urban commercial development. The objects, places, and practices in the dream are interrelated by the argot of agrarian ecology. But in crucial ways the dream rejects the historical logic of antebellum America. It resists powerful currents in Jacksonian

Lehi's Parable of the Fruitful Tree

America—commercial striving, the expansion of white urban population centers, and the dissolution of local worlds of family and farm. The dream may be clothed in the language of early America, but it turns that language toward a radically different vision of the good.

THE PARABLE OF THE FRUITFUL TREE

Earlier in this essay I offered a brief reading of Lehi's dream within the lexical world of the King James Bible, a key language environment for the dictation of the Book of Mormon. I suggested, following Charles Swift, that this interpretive approach sorts the text into the biblical genre of prophetic *visionary writing*, alongside texts like the visions of Daniel and Ezekiel. Biblical genres display distinct features, conventions, and purposes, and a method alert to genre can reveal currents of meaning in a scriptural text. Swift, for instance, building on the work of scholar Leland Ryken, finds that Lehi's dream displays hallmarks of visionary writing in a kaleidoscopic structure, an ambience of surreal otherness, and a heavily symbolic dreamscape.[43] For a frontier farmer like Joseph Smith and the early American readers whom the Book of Mormon addresses, a dreamscape of vast barren plains and exotic gardens would indeed summon an imposing alien mood of exposure and divine transcendence.

The centerpiece of my argument, however, has been to show that the dream may also be fruitfully interpreted in the pastoral world of the early American farm. In the context of its most immediate modern interpretive community, the scenes of 1 Nephi 8—forest, fields, fruit trees, surveyor's rod, and rising urban cityscape—summon the humble stuff of everyday life and labor, not exotic scenes from the elevated and set-apart world of the Bible. And within an antebellum agrarian lexical world, the dream loses the austere strangeness characteristic of the genre of Old Testament visionary prophecy. Instead, it resembles something like a parable, a short story-form that sets out ordinary objects and scenarios to convey hidden dimensions of spiritual meaning. Parables in the Old and New Testaments are often set in agrarian scenes featuring fields, trees, and farmland; similarly, parables take up social relations between fathers and sons, rich and poor, merchants and farmhands.[44] In these ways, the narrative subject of Lehi's dream fits well within the genre of parable.

Though the parables recorded in the four gospels are the most familiar examples of the genre, the parables of Jesus are firmly rooted in the themes and metaphors of the Old Testament: they "belong with, rework, reappropriate and redirect Israel's prophetic and apocalyptic traditions."[45] We might go further to say that Jesus's parables, homespun as their fabric may be, audaciously proclaim and enact the messianic kingdom prophesied by the Hebrew prophets. Thus to classify Lehi's dream as an agrarian parable is not to discount its relevance to the prophetic and apocalyptic genres in which it most naturally fits when read within the lexical world of the Bible. It is rather to note that Lehi's dream amplifies these prophetic and apocalyptic themes in the homely-but-transformative mode of the parable when routed through the early American pastoral world in which it was dictated.

It might be objected that parables and other figurative story forms are uncommon in the Book of Mormon. Uncommon perhaps, but they are not unknown: Alma 32 has recently been analyzed as the "parable of the seed," for instance.[46] Moreover, it is true that biblical writers typically do not recount parables as dreams in the first-person narrative voice, as Lehi does. But first-person narrative dreams are very rare in the Bible—dreams related to the Genesis tale of Joseph in Egypt being the only instances—and thus Lehi's dream will sit a bit askew in any scriptural genre. I suggest that framing Lehi's dream as a *parable*—"the parable of the fruitful tree," formally distinct from, though related to, Nephi's allegorical vision that follows—is both textually justified and theologically productive.[47]

Just as biblical prophecy reflects a characteristic (if informal) theology, biblical parables explore a set of distinctive theological issues. As noted above, the parables of Jesus famously concern the inauguration and character of the kingdom of God, as Jesus brought historical Israel to the portal of the messianic Kingdom and invited his people to enter. Botanically-themed parables like Lehi's are, in particular, oriented toward eschatology and the kingdom of God.[48] Biblical parables depict men and women encountering the hidden kernel of the kingdom in the midst of their ordinary activities, as a woman bakes bread or a farmer sows seed (Matt. 13:33; Mark 4:26–29). They emphasize the modest face of the divine kingdom, a mustard seed or a single pearl, which conceals the immense value and breadth of the Kingdom's new reality. The parables often juxtapose wealth and poverty and celebrate a reversal of conventional values, offering a new paradigm for human relationships that dramatically upsets social and economic hierarchies in scenes of feasting banqueters and joyful merchants (Luke 14: 15–24; Matt. 13:44–46). They urge the protagonist (and the reader) toward a crisis or reckoning, wherein he or she must decide whether and how to enter the Kingdom of God, represented as the coming of a bridegroom or a master, and then must account for that decision (Matt. 25:1–30).

Read alongside the pattern of biblical parables, Lehi's dream lights up with theological meaning. The imagistic narrative of 1 Nephi 8, interpreted in the vocabulary and visual scenes of a working American farm, shows men and women approaching or retreating from God as they go about the daily labor of clearing forest, surveying fields, and harvesting fruit. If Lehi's narrative is a parable, then the implicit object of his seeking is likely to be the kingdom of God, with the white fruit as the promised eschatological feast, a sacramental meal shared by believers in the presence of the Lord. Interpreted as American farmers, Lehi and his family encounter this love and this kingdom in the heart of their world, a cleared field, not in a transcendent otherplace. Embedded in the scenes and objects at hand, anchored by routine practices of labor and care, the love of God is an immanent dimension of present experience. The kingdom gives itself modestly, as a humble apple tree grown from seed in the poor man's way. Yet the tree's fruiting maturity and its placement at the center of a tilled field, the most valuable and labor-intensive of the colonial farm's several acreages, suggests its great value. The finely-dressed denizens within the great building act as a foil for the humble seekers of the kingdom. The rich mockers would seek the tree's fruit not as an eschatological feast in God's kingdom but as commodity for the marketplace; they are brought low in the parable's spiritual upending of social and economic hierarchies of value. Finally, the narrative structure of 1 Nephi 8 builds to a moment of existential inflection, in which first Nephi with Sariah and Sam, then Laman and Lemuel, and finally "numberless concourses of people" must decide whether to grasp the rod of iron to gain the tree or to wander in forbidden paths. In this way, the reader, too, is urged to recognize God and his kingdom in ordinary experiences and the modest entities at hand, to cast aside conventional status markers, and to ready himself for the kingdom by deciding to grasp the rod with measured steps toward the tree.

One theological element of Lehi's parable stands out: namely, the presence of risk and contingency in the field-world. On a frontier farm laboriously carved from the forest, the dark wilderness always threatens to regrow and the field to relapse into wilderness, if encroaching saplings are not cleared. This implies a world in which risk and danger persist—even in the midst of the bright field charged with the presence of God. With wilderness crowding its edges, Lehi's field of dreams is not fully subject to divine will and desire, much less to human efforts to control it. Indeed, the very portal to the immanent kingdom, the tree whose shining fruit is a heavenly meal to all who grasp it, contains some element of chance. Recall that apple saplings planted from seed, rather than grafted from known stock, are subject to the contingencies of plant reproduction and may produce bitter or sweet fruit. The very emergence of the promised kingdom from its immanent potentiality in the world is, it seems, contingent in some way—conditioned at least upon the presence of hands to grasp the fruit of the tree and mouths to eat.[49] Is the fruit of the tree sweet in the absence of a tongue to enjoy it? This is a sharp departure from the sovereign and self-sufficient God of the desert prophets in the Bible, a confident God whose "word . . . goeth forth out of my mouth: it shall not return unto me void, but it shall accomplish that which I please" (Isa. 55:11). The God of Lehi's dream must, with his children, contend with resistant forces beyond his control and labor continuously to clear space for moral choice in a universe that may oppose him.

When read as a parable against the backdrop of an early American word world, 1 Nephi 8 produces a portrait of God that in some ways anticipates the vulnerable God of Joseph Smith's later revelations, a deity who exists within a universe ontologically prior to himself and within currents of time, space, and agency that exceed his control. This portrait differs significantly from the transcendent, sovereign God of biblical prophecy. Within this array of comparators, however, the portrait of God in 1 Nephi 8 departs sharply from all in one notable way: God is absent from direct representation in Lehi's dream. God is famously developed as an embodied being in Joseph Smith's later revelations (D&C 130:22). The Book of Mormon contains two climactic encounters with the immortal person of Christ (see 3 Ne. 11 and Ether 3). And God is represented directly in the throne theophanies of biblical prophets—indeed, Lehi himself sees the enthroned God directly in vision at 1 Nephi 1:8.[50] But the theophany of Lehi in 1 Nephi 8 contains no such direct representation of God. Instead, God is known through superlative sensations of sweetness, light, and joy that stimulate his desire:

> I did go forth and partake of the fruit thereof; and I beheld that it was most sweet, above all that I ever before tasted. Yea, and I beheld that the fruit thereof was white, to exceed all the whiteness that I had ever seen. And as I partook of the fruit thereof it filled my soul with exceedingly great joy; wherefore, I began to be desirous that my family should partake of it also; for I knew that it was desirable above all other fruit.

Note that the fruit, a representation of the love of God, is described in terms of the *qualia* it produces for those who consume it. Qualia are the subjective sensory perceptions—of color, taste, texture, pleasure—that, taken together, weave the personal character of one's experience. Qualia are the first-order building blocks of experience. As noted above, the extraordinary whiteness and sweetness of the fruit are emphasized in part to distinguish between the humble seekers who grasp the fruit to enjoy the fullness of its experience, and those in the great building who see the fruit as commodity. But more salient still, the qualia themselves constitute the experience of God's saving love and are the only way in which God is known in the dream. In the ordinary objects and scenes of pastoral life, the parable discovers a kind of experiential theophany—a union with God in the form of a heightened qualitative experience.

Lehi's parable thus offers something quite extraordinary in the Book of Mormon: a direct experience of God not in the form of a transcendent deity but in the form of a superlative sensation or experience—an immanent phenomenon. This could be seen as a kind of narrative concealment of the "real," directly-personed God behind the literary symbol of the fruit, as if direct representation of the divine would be unseemly or overwhelming; indeed, if we read Lehi's dream as an allegory, as Nephi does in the chapters that follow, this is precisely the interpretation one must reach. But reading 1 Nephi 8 as a parable draws out a different interpretation of the text's "concealment" of God. Hiddenness is a frequent topic in the parables, and it is also a central narrative mode. Jesus often concluded his parables with the aphorism, "He that hath ears to hear, let him hear," which he explained to his disciples in this way: "Unto you it is given to know the mystery of the kingdom of God: but unto them that are without, all these things are done in parables: that seeing they may see, and not perceive; and hearing they may hear, and not understand; lest at any time they should be converted, and their sins should be forgiven them" (Mark 4:11–12). This seems to suggest that the narrative concealment of the parables is analogous to—or, better, an enactment of—the existential concealment of God: the esoteric meaning of the story, like the portal to the kingdom, is abundantly present for those to whom it is given but remains hidden from those who will not understand and enter. The genre form of the parable activates at least two different ways of using language: on one level, plain referential language describes an everyday scenario comprehensible to all hearers; on another level, language assumes a creative power to reveal the mysteries of God. In a similar way, the kingdom of God as described by Jesus is mysteriously available to one person but absent from his fellow:

Two men [shall be] in one bed; the one shall be taken, and the other shall be left. Two women shall be grinding together; the one shall be taken, and the other left. Two men shall be in the field; the one shall be taken, and the other left. (Luke 17:34–36)

Just as a parable activates different modes of language to unveil the spiritual mystery in an ordinary story, the kingdom activates different modes of experience to unveil God in ordinary life. Lehi's parable, we might say, doesn't merely describe or explain God's real love in literary symbols; it existentially *performs* the reality of God as a qualitative experience of love and desire. Though constructed of words, it works to create a first order experience outside of language and description.

This account of parables owes much to the theologian N. T. Wright, who describes the work of the parable in this way:

> The parables are not simply information about the kingdom, but are part of the means of bringing it to birth. They are not a second order activity, talking about what is happening at one remove. They are part of the primary activity itself. They do not merely give people something to think about. They invite people into the new world that is being created, and warn of dire consequences if the invitation is refused. Jesus' telling of these stories is one of the key ways in which the kingdom breaks in upon Israel, redefining itself as it does so. . . . The parables are not merely theme, they are also performance. They do not merely talk about the divine offer of mercy; they both make the offer, and defend Jesus' right to make it.[51]

I've argued previously that Lehi's dream works in precisely the performative mode described here, a mode that acts directly on the heart and desire of the reader to *bring to pass* the substantive change we know as conversion; Nephi's dream, by contrast, works in a semantic and historical mode that aims to explain and describe events that occur "in real life."[52] Lehi's dream, a parable, works directly to bring into reality the very conditions of salvation that Nephi's vision describes as transpiring in future historical events. What to Nephi is a promised future, to Lehi is an experienced reality.

Readers have long recognized the Book of Mormon's unique and forceful attestation of the divine incarnate person of Christ.[53] It has been my aim in this essay to show that Lehi's parable of the fruitful tree opens for the reader another way to God. I've offered contrasting interpretations of 1 Nephi 8 within each of the two language worlds most salient at the moment of its rendition in English, namely the trove of language, images, and narratives derived from the King James Bible, and the world of objects, practices, and landscapes associated with early American farming. The dream of Lehi takes on a powerful devotional dimension when interpreted as its earliest readers would have, among the images of frontier forests, cleared fields, apple orchards, family economies, urban development, and agrarian technologies of colonial and antebellum America. In light of this language world, we recognize in the English text of Lehi's dream an unmistakable contextual immediacy with the scenes and experiences of its original readers' everyday lives. This literary effect plausibly places 1 Nephi 8 within the genre of parable and consequently highlights its theological interest in the character or mode of the kingdom of God as an immanent dimension of a present reality. Several provocative implications about God's nature emerge from this interpretive move, including echoes of Joseph Smith's later revelations on God's passibility and immanence. But perhaps the most striking theological offering of Lehi's parable of the fruitful tree is its revelation of God infused in the qualia of life: God gives himself as direct experience in a world of taste, color, pleasure, joy, and desire. To paraphrase Wright, the parable is not simply information about God but is a means of realizing God on earth. It is not a second order activity, describing God at one remove. It aims to illuminate God directly, in the light of the reader's own experience. The first course of that sacramental meal in the kingdom of God may be an improbably sweet and shiny apple plucked today from a tree in the field down the road.

PLATE 4. Sarah Winegar, *Rod of Hands and Feet*, relief print, 26 × 26 inches, 2020.

Artwork:

Rod of Hands and Feet

SARAH WINEGAR

WHEN NEPHI ASKED THE ANGEL TO KNOW THE INTERPRETATION OF the tree from Lehi's dream, the angel showed him Mary, the mother of Jesus. When Nephi saw a child in her arms, the angel asked "knowest thou the meaning of the tree which thy father saw?" (1 Ne. 11:21) and Nephi said "yea, it is the love of God, which sheddeth itself abroad in the hearts of the children of men, wherefore it is the most desirable above all things." (1 Ne. 11:22) Nephi learned the meaning of the dream when he saw a mother and her child. Likewise, it is through loving relationships that a child comes to know the meaning of the love of God. The rod that leads us home is one made of flesh, not iron.

Lehi's Dream:
Desire for God and Endless Progress

ANDREW R. TEAL

THERE IS SOMETHING WONDERFULLY PRIMORDIAL ABOUT DREAMS. They are vivid encounters of a reality which projects us beyond the merely physical or temporal into an awareness of the profound totality of the human person, and our life as mystery. If that's true in the realm of psychology and self-understanding, how much more is that the case in scripture? Our creativity and receptivity to God when we are awake and active is echoed with profound symbolism in our sleep and dreams.

Consider how the Lord puts Adam into a "deep sleep," and then works creatively to bring Eve out of his flesh (Gen. 2:21). Note the many rich and powerful prophetic dreams throughout the Hebrew Bible and New Testament whereby God communicates his purposes and instruction.[1]

Dreams, indeed, carried such weight that the practice of falsifying dreams or their interpretation draws particular censure (see Zech. 10:2). They are a vivid and valid means of connection to eternity and engagement with the true

God. Angels communicate and guide those whom God blesses through dreams, not least around the incarnation of Jesus Christ.[2]

LEHI'S DREAM THAT LOVE MAY NOT FAIL IN THE DARK AND DREARY WILDERNESS: AN ENGAGEMENT WITH THE TEXT IN ITS CONTEXT

This volume draws from many backgrounds to consider Lehi's dream in 1 Nephi 8. The reflections articulated in words are put alongside careful engagements in art—highly appropriate for the subject matter. Responses to Lehi's vision of multi-valent images work together to explore this passage: understanding and imagination together illuminate Lehi's response and parental impulse, whilst he remains faithful to this commanding vision.

After an imaginative engagement with the text from the Book of Mormon, this reflection will attempt to connect the narrative with other approaches from holy scripture and broader spiritual Christian traditions, particularly in early Christianity. My motivation for this endeavor in collaboration with The Church of Jesus Christ of Latter-day Saints is rooted in a series of encounters with its leaders and members, which fuels a commitment to reconciliation and understanding through an engagement with scripture.[3]

The section we are exploring in the volume comes at the outset of a series of profound challenges and tasks for Lehi, his wife Sariah, his four sons and their families. Lehi has already seen a vision with a pillar of fire—an image of divine presence in the theophany to the prophet Moses (Ex. 3: 1–4:17), for example, and of God's shepherding of his people in the wilderness after escaping from Egypt (Ex. 13:21). In the Exodus narrative, as in the promptings of the patriarchs in Genesis, God's disturbing presence accompanies, rebukes, sustains, and illuminates his chosen people through all the twisting and dangerous paths of their pilgrimage journey to God's promised land, preparing and honing the people of Israel until they are ready to take the next step in understanding and commitment, even when they have fallen from obedience. The vision is, therefore, challenging and commanding. The coming of the Messiah is predicted, as is the destruction and fall of Jerusalem. Note that human agency even here is both blamed for the moral collapse of Israel and the subsequent fall of the holy city, but this in no way cancels or frustrates the purposes of the Lord. Though Lehi's faithful witness calling his people to repentance leads to his own persecution, he will not abandon them to their fate without inviting them to turn and live (1 Ne. 1:18–19), even if the impact of the vision was terrible and disturbing (1 Ne. 1:6–7). Not least disturbing is the cultural dislocation that obedience to God causes. Nephi insists that, throughout the narrative of this new Exodus,

> Behold, I, Nephi, will show unto you that the tender mercies of the Lord are over all those whom he hath chosen, because of their faith, to make them mighty even unto the power of deliverance. (1 Ne. 1:20)

So, to reiterate, the dream of Lehi that we are primarily considering is not a "one-off," but part of a network of revelation where dreams are not merely to be valued as depth-psychology but divine revelation. It is because of Lehi's initial vision that he takes the step to flee into the wilderness in obedience to God (1 Ne. 2:2–4). This, then, leads to the experience of the family fleeing empty-handed to camp near the Red Sea (1 Ne 2:4–5); God still provides for their needs as he is worshipped at an altar of stones which they construct (1 Ne. 2:7), and Lehi blesses even his stiff-necked sons (1 Ne. 2:8–11), Laman and Lemuel, as they murmur and resist (1 Ne. 2:11–13). There is a resentment at their father's obedience to his vision of God, and although his strong rebuke in the power of the Spirit makes them shake (1 Ne. 2:14), they resent the loss of their property, stability, and identity. It is this last recognition that is addressed in another of Lehi's dreams:

> Behold I have dreamed a dream, in the which the Lord hath com-manded me that thou and thy brethren shall return to Jerusalem (1 Ne. 3:2).

The family's identity was their most valuable possession and the "record of the Jews" and their genealogy would be an indispensable guide on the unknown pil-grimage ahead (1 Ne. 3:3). The brothers, therefore, are commanded to return by their father Lehi in obedience to the Lord, and they attempt to reason with Laban yet to no avail (1 Ne. 3:13). The brothers represent a "type" similar to the Hebrew spies sent to Jericho (Josh. 2:9–13),[4] leading to the slaying of Laban, the disguising of Nephi in his clothes (1 Ne. 4:19–27), the recovery of the engraved plates, and the redemption, not of Rahab and her family, but of Zoram, the servant of Laban (1 Ne. 4:35).

Lehi and the anxious Sariah rejoice at their sons' safe return, and the recov-ery of valuable records in obedience to God's instruction to carry with them into the wilderness, ultimately across the seas to the new Zion God would prepare. In all the anguish and darkness that lay ahead on that journey, Lehi insists on the loving purposes of God in redeeming his family as a remnant:

if I had not seen the things of God in a vision I should not have known the goodness of God, but had tarried at Jerusalem, and had perished with my brethren. (1 Ne. 5:4)

The holiness and commandment of God, robed in majestic truth, has provoked the flight from Jerusalem and the gathering of the plates, but the foundational motif that is most striking is that this is all a revelation of the Lord's goodness, kindness, and love, his *hesed*, that love that fulfils his covenant in every situation and change, and that engages human imagination and invites a change of heart and mind, bringing

> to the fore the mutual nature of the covenant-bond. There is indeed from God's side faithful love and compassion, but for a true relationship these must be answered with loyalty and trust, from which is born a purity of heart and an abhorrence of evil-doing. disciples must be responsive in trust and purity on the daily path.[5]

The core is that perpetual patience that works at enlivening human agency, whatever the messes and disrupted relations in which people find themselves.

Indeed, the depiction of the pain of Lehi floods the senses when reading this prelude to the fraternal conflicts that replay in different contexts throughout the Book of Mormon. Lehi and Nephi and Sam strive to remain loyal to God, the Lord's promises, and each other; whereas Laman and Lemuel persist in rebellion and resistance. Although they behave as sons of perdition, Lehi remains both tender and true to them, persevering and modelling pastoral and missionary care. Yet the interior cost of this determination to save by love and truth is the fear that is the context for Lehi's dream:

> Behold, Laman and Lemuel, I fear exceedingly because of you; for behold, methought I saw in my dream, a dark and dreary wilderness. (v. 4)

The reader can see that Laman and Lemuel obviously inhabit this fearful gloom, but the broken-hearted father Lehi, who has obediently responded to God's command, and follows the one who invites him in a bright robe, he, too, finds himself in a dark dreary wasteland that is not readily shaken-off but has to be endured painfully (vv. 7–8a). Lehi is broken-hearted and torn as a loving father who wants only the best for his rebellious sons Laman and Lemuel; he has to bear the dark and bitter pain of that love. He pleads with the Lord to have mercy upon him (v. 8b). Here is no angry, resentful, or authoritarian father demanding obedience. Lehi, rather, models the nature of his Heavenly Father who, above all, longs to pour out blessings upon each soul that lives, has lived, or ever will live in the temporal condition. Lehi knows the overwhelming mercy of God because that is what he himself lives and holds for all his family, his good sons and his perverse, rebellious children. Thus Lehi "did exhort them with all the feeling of a tender parent" (v. 37).

A further important point is that this wonderful dream is not a "silver-lining theology." It, rather, grows out of Lehi's wrestling honestly with the situation and clinging to remain faithful to God. Like the fourteen-year-old Joseph Smith centuries later, in his bewilderment and perplexity, Lehi *asked* God.[6] God, in both cases, kept faithful to his love, fulfilling his covenant-promises, and did not despise either request. In neither example, though, does God make all things instantly better, and wipe away pain and anguish without struggle and the possibility for Lehi (and Joseph Smith, Jr.) to grow further in love, even as the pain carved-out thus creates the space for them to love more profoundly and with an eternal dimension.

The dark and dreary waste, however, gives way to a large and spacious field (v. 9). Lehi is also granted to see the tree whose shining white sweet fruit endued happiness. There is great joy in the vision God has granted Lehi. But the connections in the dream, the motivations of the longing, loving father for his family's happiness and unity are further revealed:

... it filled my soul with exceedingly great joy; wherefore I began to be desirous that my family should partake of it also. (v. 12)

However, by the head of the river that appears to water the tree, Lehi saw Sariah, Sam, and Nephi. Lehi manages to beckon and guide them with his loud voice. These are they that have heeded the clear instructions given to Lehi by the Lord, with obedience and diligence; they thus are united with Lehi and eat the fruit (vv. 15–16). By contrast, but according to their character types, Laman and Lemuel, like much of their seed after them, resist: "they would not come unto me and partake of the fruit" (v. 18).

Nonetheless, God provides a safe, if narrow, path, and a rod of iron, a secure hold for all amid serious danger. This made it possible for people to approach the fruitful tree even when there arose "an exceedingly great mist of darkness" (v. 23). However, the dangers are not passed—it is as if the human pilgrimage has inevitably to move from one challenging episode to another—as dangerous as the sheer pathways in Zion National Park in Utah, even with the handrail.

The issue is not really topography, though. It is the disobedient desire of some to make their way to the tree on their own terms, thereby wandering off in the darkness and mist and getting lost (v. 23). In contrast, those who cling to the secure handrail—the iron rod—make it to the tree and eat the fruit (v. 24). At this point, were it a fairy tale aimed at a happy-ever-after ending, the gloom would disperse and all would be well.

However, after eating the fruit of the tree, those eating rather surprisingly seem to be granted the gift of shame: "after they had partaken of the fruit of the tree, they did cast their eyes about as if they were ashamed" (v. 25). The tree of life thus also represents in some way the tree of the knowledge of good and evil, whereby Adam and Eve knew their nakedness and shame by eating of its fruit in *disobedience* of the Lord's command, bringing a cursed temporal existence (Gen. 2:16; 3:1; 3:14–19). This self-consciousness in the vision introduces the next threat.

In contrast to the rural and agricultural imagery thus far in the vision, there now comes an enormous urbane contrast—the lofty and elegant spacious and high building. Unlike the narrow path, this is a broad place of wealth, sophistication, and finery, and, with that, not gracious charity but cruel mockery. Were this but a dream rather than a vision, one might analyse it as a fear of exposure—a fruit of imposter syndrome or resentment at seeing worldly wealth. But it's clearly not that. There is a strong degree of pathos, as those who had made it through the mists and danger, having tasted the wondrous luminous white fruit, are now shamed by the mockery. They are living examples of Jesus's parable of the sower, the seed which takes root quickly, but because there is no depth, withers quickly away (Mark 4:1–20). Nephi breaks off the dream in a way that alludes to the deep sadness of Lehi but gives way to still reflection (v. 29). Nephi does reiterate the tragedy—those who use all their effort to reach out to the guiding rod persist and partake of the fruit, while others are lured by the spacious grandeur of the building, only to find destruction and loss (v. 32). This seems to cause disdainful ridicule and further mockery of the journey of faith from the haughty. There is a downward spiral in these bitter images aimed at distracting, shaming, and preventing the invitation to life. The combination of evil oppressing, demeaning, bullying, and destroying the image of God in others is profoundly offensive and disturbing—and "as many as heeded them, had fallen away" (v. 34).

The chapter concludes with Lehi not desisting his earnest work as a kind and loving father of Laman and Lemuel, for whom he "exceedingly feared . . . lest they should be cast off from the presence of the Lord" (v. 36). The story of the vision or dream of Lehi ends with a reiteration of the motivation of his determination to save his sons were it at all possible. In that way, the vision reflects the open heart of the Heavenly Father in his persistent patience and kindness, and Lehi reflects an image of God like that of the father of the prodigal son, constantly looking for his beloved to appear on the horizon and waiting to embrace him on his return (Luke 15:11–32). There is a profound empathy evoked in the reader that longs—for the tender Lehi's sake—for that to be the case, that Laman and Lemuel turn around and come home. The reader will return to the power, pain, and poignancy of this vision through all the turns in the lives of the brothers as they sojourn in the desert and make the journey to settle in the New Zion.

There are interesting asides in the story. One example is the reference to multitudes who are drawn to the tree. Are they drawn by Lehi's prophetic witness? Is it a foretaste of the enormous mission that will happen in the name of his people—or generations of his own yet to come? No answer is given because that is not the point. Wherever the multitudes come from, each one of them will need strength of character, the power of fellowship, and a focus on the mission of the Lord to all in the world, that each and all may be led safely home by the Good Shepherd. There is a burden shared with Lehi, and through his witness to Nephi, to each of us, to be faithful ambassadors of the Lord in binding up the wounded, leading the lost, and bringing all our brothers and sisters home. Whoever the multitude is, the crowd is truly *our* people: the wonder of a multitude clamouring through a field, along a narrow path, and to taste of the fruit of the tree—we belong together.

Yet the vision is far from triumphalist. Rather, again and again, come temptations and the need to meet these by exercising faithfulness to the commands of God, loyalty to family, and the autonomous exercise of agency in reaching out both to the iron guiding rod and to neighbours in trouble. Communal and personal loyalty will be necessary to resist the caustic acidity of bitter disdain and humiliation. This vision is an *overture* of the life of faith—but not all is sweetness and light, delectation and ease: in fact, very little is. In Churchillian language, the lively faith depicted in this vision offers us the constant mission of "blood, toil, tears and sweat."[7] Lehi's vision holds together urgency and patience. There is a real danger that people drift off to destruction, even if safeguards are provided. The multitudes "feeling the way" are all "journeying by stages, as the Lord commanded" (Ex. 17:1). Our urgent temporal care must not lose eternal perspective, and a good shepherd in the Lord's stead constantly represents the patient love with a profound awareness of the stages each member of the multitude is on. A genius of the Book of Mormon is that it holds together this generous understanding without losing the urgency to be *winsome*.

Another observation is that *everyone*, including Lehi, knows the fear and desolation that comes with finding themselves in the dark and dreary waste (vv. 7–8; 14; 17–18; 23; 24). Faithful pilgrims are not more beloved of the Lord than anyone else, however fallen others currently may be. All are loved and longed-for, Nephi and his loving faithfulness fulfilling the covenant with the Lord, no more and no less than embittered Laman and Lemuel, or the cruel tormentors in the spacious house of luxurious disdain. Hatred of another is not on the agenda, but mission, to those even violently opposed to the Lord, is. As repugnant as it is to see, for example, how fickle and cruel and destructive human beings so often can be, it is a denial of the Lord who has granted Lehi this vision to hate those who hurt others. Rather, Lehi's vision prompts us to see the truth even in its most challenging dimensions, without ever losing hope in God's power and mercy.[8] Moreover, belonging to the Lord does not mean inoculation from difficulties and failure, nor not having constantly to begin again—it means sharing the mist and wasteland that others inhabit with a deliberate intention to be committed to our enemies and urgently making peace before the sun sets. Daily doing whatever we can—in the pattern of Lehi—means to commit ourselves to mending relationships, not by denying difference or emotions, or by repression, but by committing ourselves to the narrow path even in the darkness, holding on to the iron rod, promising not to hide from our brother and sister, and at times encouraging others not to hide. This robs the house of mockery of the power of its contentious ridicule.

But what might we understand to be the house of mockery in today's contexts? I offer but two of many possible thoughts, both of which emerge from my context as an academic and a churchman from a different denomination.

Firstly, there is the suspicion of (post-)Modernity of any notion of specific revelation. Whilst vague or poetic inspiration is appreciated and relished, particularly in small soundbites of text or story, overarching narratives which enable lengthy engagements with whole texts and their teaching in worship are eschewed. Reading and learning the Psalms, for example, is valued less than garnering selections of religious and spiritual nuggets.[9] Though these are often tender and poignant, and accessible from religious and non-religious perspectives, immersing oneself in the broad scope of scripture's narrative seems increasingly ridiculed as naïve or unintelligent, undermined by psychological suspicion.[10] Within the academy, the experience of ridicule and shame is far from unusual. After the Reformation, theology faculties in mainland Europe divided into Catholic and Protestant. Theology was pursued according to the theological emphases of each tradition. Protestant faculties soon found it hard to justify studying Patristic and medieval theology at all, although strategies were devised

Lehi's Dream: Desire for God and Endless Progress

to include some writings composed around the time of the New Testament (by inventing the category of "Apostolic Fathers," for example).[11] The study of the Old Testament was soon bullied in Protestant faculties to prove itself a scientific enterprise worthy of the academy and not merely Sunday school with a scattering of Hebrew words. Elaborate literary and source theories sought to make the reading of the Bible scientific, and therefore an intellectually credible subject. One of the first casualties was the sense of poetry, imagination, literary integrity or reader-response in texts studied. So Wellhausen developed his source criticism of the Torah, gone were Genesis, Exodus, Leviticus, Numbers, and Deuteronomy as literary works with integrity, to be replaced by postulating redactions and sources—the Yahwist (J), the "E" source which uses Elohim (or God(s)) rather than "the Lord"; the Deuteronomist historian (D), and the liturgical, temple-based Priestly source (P).[12] Obsession concerning compliance with academic convention meant expelling all supernatural or substantially theological discussion. This also extended into New Testament study, with similar consequences—"acceptable" questions included textual and form criticism and historical enterprises, but not an answer to the question "Who do you say that I am?"[13] Looking from a perspective of western academic traditions as taught in secular and Protestant faculties, it is not difficult to understand the historical background within The Church of Jesus Christ of Latter-day Saints of a traditional reluctance and suspicion of theology as authoritative, though this is far from the current engagements with theology, as the Enlightenment project lost its grasp on the academic curriculum, prohibiting certain areas of investigation. Interestingly, the infiltration of literary theory from the study of texts since the late twentieth century has moved from an obsession with notions such as "authorial intent" to more fruitful possibilities of "reader response."[14] Nonetheless, whilst the young Joseph Smith was taking James 1:5 at its word and asking for the gift of wisdom, theological academies in Europe were ruling out the very possibility of asking God, and ridicule was poured out at the suggestion that God might indeed answer. The academy has a tainted history as one of the cultured despisers of religion.[15] It is positive to see trends in contemporary scholarship that are now much more respectful of the integrity of narratives, and there is an increased awareness of the validity and significance of streams of wisdom beyond the Western academic tradition. But it remains the case that there are constantly new approaches that present afresh a hermeneutic of suspicion and ridicule, attacking and dismissing concerns for the substance of *theological* engagement.[16] The University of Oxford's motto, *Dominus Illuminatio Mea* ("The Lord is my Light") is generally now viewed as a rather quaint historical throwback to its medieval roots, and Theology faculties in Britain are now ubiquitously named Theology and Religious Studies.

It is to a model of Patristic engagement and creativity that we now turn. There follows a sustained focus on two distinct elements of Lehi's dream through early Christian texts and traditions. Firstly, the tree motif, and subsequently the priority of the path as the model of necessary perseverance.

TREE OF LIFE, TREE OF KNOWLEDGE, CROSS: UNDERSTANDING THE CHRISTOLOGICAL TREE

The tree of life is an archetype in world religions far beyond the Judeo-Christian canon of texts.[17] In Kaballah mysticism, the tree of life is nothing other than the receptacle of all lives—blossoming to produce new souls which the archangel Gabriel protects, and which the angel of conception guards in embryonic form until each is born.[18] Christian creativity, likewise, seems particularly fruitful contemplating the tree of life. The approach of the early church to texts (before some ossification into categories and restrictive rules of interpretation) is marked by extraordinary, imaginative associations:

> texts from right across Scripture that either contained the word *xylon* [tree, wood, staff, etc.] . . . [were interwoven] so as to demonstrate their fulfilment in the cross of Christ. Justin's *Dialogue with Trypho* 86 provides instructive examples: Isaac carried his own "wood," as did Christ; Moses' "staff" parted the Red Sea and turned sweet the bitter waters of Marah; Aaron's "rod" blossomed; God appeared to Abraham from a "tree" at Mamre, and comforted David with his "rod and staff"—so Christ redeemed the people by being crucified on a tree. . . . Justin opens his list by suggesting that "this man, of whom the Scriptures declare he will come in glory after his crucifixion, was symbolised by the tree of life."[19]

Xylon is also the Greek term not only for the tree of life (Gen. 2:9) but is used interchangeably to refer also to the tree of knowledge of good and evil (Gen. 3:22–24). Irenaeus, for example, seems to identify them as the "tree of death *becoming* the tree of life through Christ's obedience."[20]

So, for all the wonder of bright fruit, and Lehi's longing for his family to come to the life-giving tree of Christ, the reception of its sweet bright sacramental fruit is a typological foretaste, a prophecy rather than a final accomplishment or possession. Perhaps for those who longed for final security after eating the fruit, therein lies the opening of shame and disillusionment—not merely from the external scoffing, but from the thwarting of impatient, temporal desires to come to perfection. Subsequently, many leave the true way and are lost on forbidden paths (1 Ne. 8:28). There are journeys new now to be made, refreshed by the sacramental food. St. Ephrem the Syrian expounds:

> Two trees did God place
>   in Paradise
> the Tree of Life
>   and that of Wisdom,
> a pair of blessed fountains,
>   source of every good;
> by means of this
>   glorious pair
> the human person can become
>   the likeness of God,
> endowed with immortal life
>   and wisdom that does not err.[21]
> **For God would not grant him the crown**
>   **without some effort . . .** [22]

The tree, even if it is the figure of the life-giving cross whereon did hang the Savior of the world, appears less significant in this vision than the path. Of course, the path leads to the tree, but the tree is not the end of the journey. Scoffing leads some to be so ashamed of the tree that "they fell away into forbidden paths and were lost" (1 Ne. 8:28). We have observed that *xylon* in addition to "tree" also means staff, club (with which people come to arrest Jesus)[23] and even rod—the instrument by God to Moses to bring plagues, divide the Red Sea, and bring water out of the rock. The rod is a sign of authority and a means of restraint and punishment.[24] This rod in the Book of Revelation and the Prophecy of Jeremiah is a rod of iron. The motif of restraint and security is clearly found in 1 Nephi 8 but with a transforming dimension. Agency is imaginatively called upon as if it is the solid root of the tree of life, guiding, restraining, and supporting those journeying to it as a rod of iron. Once the fruit of the tree is eaten then the rod is interiorised—those receiving the life-giving sweet sustenance now are required to exercise their discipleship in resilience, commitment, and perseverance. The external rod of iron is now transformed into the multiple overwhelming and constantly renewing presence of the Holy Spirit—God's own self equips human agency to be worthy of the crown of life.

But with this great entrustment, there is an immense obligation—a motif echoed again and again in Hebrew Scripture, the New Testament, and the Book of Mormon: the necessity of persevering, making personal autonomy count by continuing to choose the right, grasping the spiritual rod by exercising appropriate agency. Above all is the need to keep travelling the true path. Christ the Tree of Life, Christ pinned to the tree of the Cross—the Cross has a central place, but it is not a talisman—Christ our constant companion, instilling the necessity for us to continue to travel with him by the power of the true guiding rod—the Holy Ghost.

EQUIPPING AGENCY: PERSEVERANCE ON THE STEEP AND NARROW PATH

> Better is the *Torah* to one who observes it and walks in the paths of the way of life, than the fruit of the tree of life; for the word of the Lord prepared it for humanity to keep, that they would be established in the world to come.[25]

New Testament scholarship has conventionally constructed early Christian history particularly from the writings of St. Paul (and St. Luke). But the New Testament reflects the diversity, conflict even, between Jewish and Gentile Christian communities in coming to correlate Jewish identity as norms with emerging Gentile practice.[26] To the diverse witness of the New Testament might be added two important early texts concerned with discipleship and which both emphasise the notion of keeping walking the path, personally and in communion with the Christian community: the anonymous *Didachē*[27] and St. Irenaeus' *Epideixis* or *Demonstration of the Apostolic Preaching*.[28] Both describe rules of faith to form a community culture of faithfulness in different contexts.

The Didachē

> There are two paths: one of life, and one of death.
> What a vast distinction (*diaphora*) there is between the two ways.[29]

After a list of specific grave sins and the rehearsal of a list of specific commandments,[30] the anonymous author offers careful examples of actions and attitudes that are characteristic of these two ways: life is characterised by love, death by hate:

Do not hate any person:
Though reprove some,
Pray for others;
Some you will love above your own soul.[31]

Likewise, anger is the path leading to murder and other violent crimes:

Do not be angry
For anger is the path to murder.[32]

The *Didachē*'s instructions to early Christian communities, then, offer both practical ethical boundaries, rods of iron to grasp which secure continuance on the path of Christ, whilst also urging understanding and an interiorising of spiritual guidance, grasping the spiritual principle whereby attitudes become vices. By the Christian's flexing of moral and spiritual muscles, obedience on the path of life is established as a rule of life.[33] Paradoxically, travelling faithfully establishes a stability that is maintained in and through movement.

The Epideixis

There is a wonderful tenderness in the writings of Irenaeus of Lyons (ca. 130– ca. 202 CE), a maturity, wit, and perceptiveness that marks him as a pastoral theologian and attentive missionary. His *Epideixis* appears to be his honouring of apostolic teaching, even as his *Against the Heresies* is an attempt to unpick heresies which would diminish not only matter but God the creator, the real humanity assumed by Jesus Christ, and the openness of Christian revelation. In the Rule of Faith that he passes on to believers, he outlines continuities between the Testaments and the centrality of Jesus Christ in making sense of faith and life.[34]

Most poignant is Irenaeus' observation that humanity is immature, needing to be led, taught, and guided throughout life. This was especially the case in Paradise.

> . . . Adam and Eve . . . "were naked and were not ashamed," since there was in them an innocent and childlike mind and they thought or understood nothing whatsoever of those things which are wickedly born in the soul through lust and shameful desires . . . without comprehension or understanding of what is evil: and thus "they were not ashamed," kissing [and] embracing each other in holiness as children.[35]

As wonderful as this state was, it is not to be regained by going in reverse. Regaining ignorance would not be bliss, it would not be paradise regained. Irenaeus instead argues that Jesus Christ has recapitulated all things and redeems us not to take us back, but to lead us forward. He does that by teaching us, equipping us with the Holy Spirit to walk the true path. With echoes of both Titus 2:8 and Lehi's dream, Irenaeus urges us to make our way by faith:

> For the way of all those who see is single and upward, illumined by the heavenly light, but the ways of those who do not see are many, dark and divergent; the one leads to the kingdom of heaven, uniting man to God, while the others lead down to death, separating man from God. Thus it is necessary for you and for all who are concerned about their salvation to make [your] way by faith, without deviation, surely and resolutely, lest in slacking, you remain in gross desires, or, erring, wander far from the right [path].[36]

Travelling the path with Christ brings us to ripening maturity, and that maturity is nurtured by the teaching of the Church, until we understand fully, when that which is truly real and secure will be within us, rather than depending upon the boundaries of external commandments (such as the Law) as an iron railing to keep us secure. But it is always "necessary to take great care of it"[37] to attend to the disciplines whereby the Holy Spirit will dwell in us as his temple, and nurture us into maturity in Christ by keeping to the path of life.

The Pilgrim's Progress

A concern to equip Christians—or, in his text, Christian—in the perilous journey of faithful discipleship forms the motivating centre of John Bunyan's The Pilgrim's Progress.[38] This early modern story has many parallels which in itself could form a chapter in this collection. Space restricts a full analytical discourse here, but note the character and plot comparisons, and theological similarities and differences with Lehi's vision, not least the Hill Flashing Fire;[39] Evangelist in the fields;[40] the necessity of boldly confronting Giant Despair;[41] the obligation to conquer Hill Difficulty;[42] the difficulty of ascent;[43] the need to confront proud lions at the Palace;[44] the imperative of passing through Perilous Valley;[45] and the necessity of there being Great Heart helper.[46] Clearly, there is no suggestion of textual dependence here, simply a flagging of the spiritual parallels in the communication of a vision "Delivered under the Similitude of a Dream, Wherein is discovered, The manner of [s]etting out, His Dangerous Journey; and [s]afe Arrival at the De[s]ired Countrey."[47]

The imperative in Bunyan is keeping the movement of faith through all discouragements to be a pilgrim, a theme powerfully parallel to the message of 1 Nephi 8.

God's Action & Human Delight—Gregory of Nyssa

The upsurge in interest in the work of Gregory of Nyssa (ca. 330–ca. 395) is evident not only in patristic studies but particularly in modern Systematic study of theology and religion, not least in Latter-day Saint circles, as "the youngest of the so-called 'Cappadocian Fathers', and in many ways the most subtle and intriguing."[48] The Nyssen emphasises struggle, self-transcendence, and infinite ascent as one might expect in a neo-Platonic context, but matter is purposeful in that it leads to God's heavenly presence. The key connection and mitigation of neo-Platonic norms is the sacramental in his thought.[49] Gregory demonstrates the goodness of matter and materiality, as created by God and shared by the incarnation of God, and ultimately destined to participate in the dynamic life of God himself. The notion of redemption and exaltation is presented in terms of *perichoresis*, an interweaving circular dance, where matter is enlivened in the dancing movement between the persons of Father and Son in the Holy Spirit.[50] In a similar way to Origen, Gregory insists on the present goodness, the perfectibility, and the ultimate glory of matter.[51]

That ultimate destiny of matter to be flooded with divine glory must not be conceived of as being brought to an end:

> Never will the soul reach its final perfection, for it will never encounter a limit . . . it will always be transformed into a better thing.[52]

The very model of salvation then, as sharing the life of the Father and the Son in the power of the Holy Spirit, is fluid. This echoes the infinite perfections of the divine personages, as well as human experience: life in mortal bodies continues because the force of being doesn't cease to move. Human life, authentic discipleship, is movement and balance, neither tearing the fabric of our materiality nor loosening it to dissolution.[53] Stability is given to earth and matter to enable the journey, the movement to the heavens. Creation is thus a wonderful kinship, with matter sharing a divine *destiny* because of this *destination*.[54] This is an extension and contemplation of an eschatological orientation, focused on the end and glorification of temporal life (*apokatastasis*), a spirituality which unsurprisingly finds welcome among, and correspondence with, Latter-day Saint thought and practice, as these examples illustrate:

Terra stat in aeternum! [The earth stands eternally] But what is more tedious than . . . fixity without movement? The sea is stirred up with boundless   movement—yet what is more meaningless?[55]

To wish ever to possess more fully the beautiful is perhaps the perfection [*teleiotēs, end*] of human nature.[56]

The materiality, changeability of human being make Man [and Woman] the microcosm of the Universe.[57]

For Gregory of Nyssa, the destiny of human being is to journey infinitely:

All limited computations henceforth disappear. Once the soul has arrived at a new summit, it is as if she had not yet taken her first step. It learns that it is as far from having reached its end as those who have not yet undertaken their first faltering steps.[58]

Matter, energy, is—far from being diminished in the environs of neo-Platonism—exposed is "eternal delight."[59]

The story of Lehi's dream, then, as revelation, connects with a host of Christian reflections, though we have encountered but a few of these here kaleidoscopically—from the earliest reflections on the steep path of Christian perfection in the *Didache* and Irenaeus' *Demonstration of the Apostolic Preaching*, through Gregory of Nyssa and John Bunyan—all pondering the paradox that stability requires movement. Thoughts on the fruitful tree and its connection with the biblical trees of Life and Knowledge set in Eden have likewise utilised patristic imagination and association, which engaged texts from across scripture and spiritual writings in an interweaving that pointed to the mystery of the tree of the cross, bearing its eternal fruit, a tree of shame becoming the means of glory. Reflections on the rod of iron, given by God to guide all to life, give way to the observation that, having eaten the fruit of the tree and continuing in fellowship, heeding neither shame nor mockery, the guiding rod to be grasped becomes an internal spiritual orientation, a tiller in our own hand, the helm we learn to steer through the continued exercise of agency in discipleship together:

Its errors forgiven, may our Vision come home.[60]

These considerations, if undertaken ecumenically among Christian traditions and between faiths, could illuminate theological priorities and difficulties in evaluating, for example, faith and works which have marred Christian discourse since New Testament times, but most specifically since the Reformation, and which draws caricature from some antagonistic groups anxious to caricature The Church of Jesus Christ of Latter-day Saints as a movement of works-righteousness. Further words are needed to bring these issues explicitly into consideration.

But not all words can be spoken (v. 29): the Lord Jesus Christ is *more* than all this.

There remains the silent promise of infinite atonement and redemption. Morning breaks day after day, and the vision of the glorious sunrise red of eternity invites us ever to embody Lehi's mystical vision to be more than we can even imagine, with him who transcends all things even as he inhabits all things.

> He is the Way.
> Follow Him through the Land of Unlikeness;
> You will see rare beasts, and have unique adventures.
> He is the Truth.
> Seek Him in the Kingdom of Anxiety;
> You will come to a great city that has expected your return for years.
> He is the Life.
> Love Him in the World of the Flesh;
> And at your marriage all its occasions shall dance for joy.[61]

PLATE 5. Hildebrando de Melo, *Tree of Life "LDS"*
(Lehi's Dream Series I, II, III), acrylic on canvas,
35.45 × 35.45 inches (90 × 90 cm), 2020.

Artwork:

Tree of Life "LDS"

HILDEBRANDO DE MELO

WHEN I STARTED TO THINK ABOUT THIS PROJECT AND BEGAN READING about Lehi's dream, I realized that there was a relationship with what God had previously announced. The tree in Lehi's dream may be the same tree of life that God has repeatedly mentioned throughout the aeons, or eternity. Being a sacred symbol, the tree connects with the whole. This idea hovered in my mind for some time as I thought about producing a work with a new approach to Lehi's dream.

On a recent trip to Portugal, I lay on the bed, exhausted after my arrival, and while looking at the ceiling I had an epiphany. I thought of the acronym "LDS" that stands for "Latter-day Saints" and realized it could also stand for "Lehi's Dream Series." It was like a revelation. When thinking about the tree that appears in the middle of paradise as the same symbol that appears in Lehi's dream, I thought inwardly, "This tree is very much described by God, Christ, and the Bible."

Then the painting process followed, the production of the work. I wanted an immediate process, for the idea not to escape me. As I typically work with acrylic on canvas and spatulas that give a corporeality to painting, this engagement for me was excellent. I wanted this work to be a series—a multiplicity of painting and probability, "Sequence-Cause-Effect." Why is it not representative of my most abstract form? I had to navigate between representative figuration and abstraction, because it made more sense in this plastic discourse and with this subject matter to be more figurative. The perception of color results in a similar chain of events, so I didn't use green just like traditional trees. Instead, I used the mind suggestion trick (the green color isn't there, but the viewer immediately thinks of it). The ebullient formal vitality in this context works to show there are no mutable truths in this tree of life, so that in the end the subject and God would speak for themselves, not the artist.

The Tree of Knowledge and the Pedagogy of Lehi's Dream

KIMBERLY MATHESON

LEHI'S DREAM HINGES ON AN ICONIC IMAGE: A TREE WITH WHITE, luminescent fruit that draws Lehi magnetically toward its branches, spurs Nephi's visionary impulse (1 Ne. 11:3, 8), and has since inspired decades of Latter-day Saint artists to pursue creative visions of their own. Described in vivid sensory terms, the tree commands a striking vista on an otherwise empty landscape, suggests to Lehi the possibility of being made "happy" (v. 10), and serves to define the trajectory of every other character for the remainder of the dream. Given the prominence and charisma of the tree, it is little wonder, then, that it becomes a recurring feature of the Book of Mormon and Latter-day Saint imaginary.

What's more, it seems that this captivating tree is also readily identifiable; its fruit is described as joy-inducing and superlatively sweet, and the tree itself is described in later passages as "a tree springing up unto everlasting life" (Alma 32:41; see also 1 Ne. 11:25). Quite naturally, therefore, readers of the Book of Mormon have tended to associate this tree with the biblical tree of life. Within

Lehi's dream proper, however, identifying the tree is not quite as simple as the dream's reception has sometimes made it appear. As Grant Hardy points out, "Latter-day Saints usually refer to this vision as 'Lehi's dream of the tree of life,' but it is striking (and significant) that Lehi never uses that term from the Garden of Eden. . . . Lehi's tree is not in a garden, there is no angel guarding it, and it does not confer eternal life."[1] These are only the first of several clues that the tree is more ambiguous than many readers have assumed. As the dream goes on, we find Lehi's tree associated with thematics of desire and knowledge, an obviously fallen landscape, and the specter of familial rift.

I wish, therefore, to pose an alternative possibility: what if we imagined the tree of Lehi's vision as the biblical tree of *knowledge* rather than the tree of life? What new angles on Lehi's dream might reveal themselves to readers if the tree at its center were imagined in parallel with the tree that inaugurates the fall rather than the tree that overcomes it? This interpretive possibility is made especially poignant by the dream's central concerns: corporate sin, pedagogical struggles, and intergenerational conflict—themes that also reverberate through the story of Adam and Eve's fateful decision in Genesis 2–3. For Lehi, these themes take the shape of anxiety about Laman and Lemuel's rebellion in the wilderness, their unreceptivity to the knowledge he offers them, and the specter of a centuries-long schism between his sons. At its heart, Lehi's dream is about extending spiritual knowledge to a generation that seems unreceptive; it expresses Lehi's religious anxiety for his two oldest sons and concludes with a new kind of pedagogy in Lehi's exhortations "with all the feeling of a tender parent" (v. 37).

My essay, then, is an exploration of how we might read Lehi's vision after reimagining its central image and also a reflection on dreams and allegory, on the passage of knowledge between fathers and sons, and what it might mean for another iconic scriptural family to begin its story at the foot of a knowledge-granting tree. I will proceed in four sections: first, a look at what Lehi's time in the "dark and dreary waste" may imply about the anxieties that spark this unconscious therapeutic; second, a look at the tree itself together with all the details that suggest its kinship to the biblical tree of knowledge; a third section then explores the theological implications of that reimagining, especially as it focuses attention on Lehi's sharing of the fruit with others and his pedagogy vis-à-vis Laman and Lemuel; finally, a fourth and concluding section asks after God's own pedagogy, imagining what it might mean for God to offer the tree and its fruit to Lehi in a dream just as Lehi offers it to his own sons in the dream's retelling.[2]

The dream opens with Lehi wandering through a "dark and dreary waste" (v. 7). Although the text lingers here for little more than a few verses, Lehi himself notes that he spent "many hours" of dream time wading through this gloomy wilderness (v. 8). Suspended in something closer to a nightmare than the foyer of a joyous Edenic return, Lehi reaches for a devotional lifeline and begins "to pray unto the Lord" (v. 8). It is what he prays *for*, however, that is especially noteworthy; he requests, the texts reports, "that [the Lord] would have mercy . . . according to the multitude of his tender mercies" (v. 8).

At first glance, it is easy to assume that Lehi asks for mercy because he finds himself lost in a frightening landscape, but there are hints that his thirst for divine compassion is prompted by more than unsettling terrain. 1 Nephi 8:8 is a quotation from the opening line of Psalm 51 where "tender mercies" are associated with forgiveness rather than general aid. The psalmist begs: "Have mercy upon me, O God, according to thy lovingkindness; according unto the multitude of thy tender mercies *blot out my transgressions*" (Ps. 51:1, emphasis added).[3] Readers, it seems, are meant to imagine Lehi relying on the language of the biblical psalter rather than praying extemporaneously; as such, Lehi is imagined not merely to crave relief from a nightmarish landscape that surrounds him but rather to crave relief from burdens he carries within him. To respond to the waste with a prayer for mercy may suggest that Lehi has begun to wonder whether this frightening wilderness might reflect things he himself needs to address. Indeed, to take seriously the Book of Mormon's presentation of Lehi as a sixth-century Judean man steeped in the psalmody of biblical Israel, readers must entertain the possibility that Lehi spends the opening hours of his dream meditating on Psalm 51 and experiencing the waste as a kind of divine punishment rather than accidental happenstance.

What heaviness, then, might weigh on Lehi's mind so heavily that he takes to his bed only to find himself wandering for hours in darkness? For a concern substantial enough to give Lehi nightmares, readers need look no further than the previous chapter, which contains Laman and Lemuel's first overt rebellion and near-fratricide in the wilderness (1 Ne. 7:6–7, 16)—a rebellion resolved only by corporate expiation in the form of burnt offerings (1 Ne. 7:22).[4] 1 Nephi 8 thus opens in the aftermath of Laman and Lemuel committing the kind of sin that divides entire families and cannot but make parents wonder what more they can or could do. We can imagine Lehi newly cognizant of his eldest sons' growing resentments and feeling moral responsibility for the violence breaking out among the next generation. For anyone with strong investments in the moral and religious formation of their children, these worries are familiar. Given the events of the previous chapter, it is little wonder that Lehi's nighttime journey thus begins in darkness and anxiety.

What's more, worries over sin and forgiveness are not the only themes of Lehi's dream metonymically compressed into this brief citation of Psalm 51. The psalm opens with the speaker's wish to be "wash[ed] . . . thoroughly from . . . iniquity" (Ps. 51:2) and traces this sinfulness all the way back to his birth ("in sin did my mother conceive me" [Ps. 51:5]). This latter phrase, however, takes on a new cast in the context of Lehi's dream. As we will see, the tree at the center of the dream has much more in common with the biblical tree of knowledge than it does with the tree of life, such that the psalmist's image of a woman conceiving children in sin begins to foreshadow Eve as much as it also foreshadows Lehi's worries about sin being transmitted across generations. When the psalmist anticipates divine expiation such that he "shall be whiter than snow" (Ps. 51:7), readers of 1 Nephi 8 might be reminded of the whiteness of the fruit in verse 11. The line "O Lord, open thou my lips" (Ps. 51:15) likewise anticipates Lehi's eating of the fruit just as the psalmic plea to "restore unto me the joy of . . . salvation" (Ps. 51:12) anticipates the "exceedingly great joy" Lehi experiences as a result of the fruit (1 Ne. 8:12). With its invocation of "burnt offering and whole offering" (Ps. 51:19), Psalm 51 echoes the expiatory rites that form part of the context of Lehi's dream (see 1 Ne. 7:22) and with its future-looking promise to "teach transgressors [God's] ways" (Ps. 51:13), the psalm even foreshadows the pedagogical concerns that will be Lehi's own takeaway from his nighttime journey. Readers are perhaps meant to understand this echo of Psalm 51, then, as not only a piece of Lehi's psychological landscape at the beginning of the dream but also as an implicit anticipation of everything that unfolds in following scenes. Lehi's anxieties in the dark, the affective reversal that comes from eating the fruit, and even his pedagogical reinvigoration at the end of the dream all find expression in the piece of Israelite scripture that Lehi carries with him as he sets foot in the waste.

Lehi's dreamscape, then, is not dark and dreary as a matter of fictional weather or climate; it is dark and dreary because this is a *moral* landscape—an allegorical expression of Lehi's spiritual worries and anxieties. The invocation of Psalm 51 in 1 Nephi 8:8 gives readers a window into the patriarchal and educational worries that we are meant to imagine as motivations for this dream. Lehi is a man coming face to face with the challenges of teaching wayward sons, one with especially high stakes as he tries to lead his family through a literal wilderness in search of God. What began as heel-dragging from Laman and Lemuel has ballooned into something more sinister, leading Lehi to pray

The Tree of Knowledge and the Pedagogy of Lehi's Dream

desperately by night for expiation from the corporate sin their murderous rage has brought on the family. Wrestling, then, with next steps, potential correctives, and how he might better reach his oldest sons, Lehi finds himself in a dream concerned with precisely these themes. Contemplating how to better teach his transgressing sons, Lehi suddenly finds himself at the foot of a tree.

TREE

Lehi reports: "after I had prayed unto the Lord I beheld a large and spacious field" and in that field "I beheld a tree" (vv. 9–10). The tree is described as fruit-bearing and "desirable to make one happy" (v. 10). Reoriented by the sudden appearance of this new landmark, Lehi exchanges his directionless wandering for a taste of the fruit. The response is immediate: "it filled my soul with exceedingly great joy" (v. 12). Importantly, though, Lehi next doubles down not on his joyous affect but on the continuance of his desire: "I began to be *desirous* that my family should partake of it also" (v. 12, emphasis added). And when Lehi goes on to explain this expanded desire, we find the culminating result of the fruit to be not only a third iteration of desire but also a question of knowledge: "I *knew* that it was desirable above all other fruit" (v. 12, emphasis added). Before the vision is populated with other characters or busy allegorical details, there is first simply a tree with desirable fruit and the knowledge that accrues to Lehi after he eats. What might readers gather from the tree's immediate imbrication with these themes?

First, at least, this: Lehi's dreamscape remains moral. The dark and dreary waste, with its echoes of spiritual confusion, is not the only dream element thus far to be charged with ethical weight. The tree, too, is described in ethical terms as joy-inducing, desirable, and knowledge-granting. Happiness, desire, and knowledge are the parameters that define every moral instruction because, if moral instruction is the business of shaping human subjects for how they *ought* to behave, these three themes are the tools one uses to do that shaping. Happiness names the consequence on the far side of right action; desire for that happiness is the motive force that urges one through the difficult work of changing habits and attitudes; and knowledge considers the content of that work, the "what" and the "how" of moral growth. Whatever else Lehi's dream is or will become, its concentration on happiness, desire, and knowledge should alert readers that it is morally charged from the beginning.

Second, these themes should give readers pause when they consider biblical precedents for Lehi's tree. A fruit that is triply desirable, whose immediate effect is to grant knowledge, and which spurs the taster to share with family members—one does not have to read far in the Hebrew Bible to find a parallel. The tree of knowledge in Genesis 3 is also described as knowledge-granting and "a tree to be desired" (Gen. 3:6) and, immediately after taking its fruit, Eve attends to passing that fruit on to her husband. Similarly, the first person Lehi sees after taking the fruit is his wife, Sariah, followed shortly by their children (vv. 14, 17–18). Like the Bible, the Book of Mormon opens with an eating of fruit that involves a spouse and brings children onto the scene. And while readers might be tempted to view these as so many motifs of life and fecundity, the text presses on us the theme of knowledge instead. Sariah, Sam, and Nephi are first characterized in the dream as lacking knowledge: "they stood as if they *knew not* whither they should go" (v. 14, emphasis added). Their collective lack, as well as Lehi's initial motivation for offering the fruit, remains a question of knowledge.

Two additional features of the dream suggest that this tree is more like the tree of knowledge than the tree of life that readers, following Nephi's later guidance, naturally assume it to be. First, it is no exaggeration to say that Lehi's eyes are opened after he eats the fruit (compare Gen. 3:5–7); only after partaking does he begin to see the details with which so many Latter-day Saint readers are familiar—"numberless concourses of people" (1 Ne. 8:21), a path, a rod, and a great and spacious building. In a very real sense, Lehi's vision only gets underway after he tastes the fruit. A second feature of the fruit is equally suggestive, though it occurs much later in the chapter when readers watch the fruit's effect on whole "concourses" of anonymous "others" who also reach the tree (vv. 21, 24). The effect of that same fruit on later (less eager) partakers is, strikingly, a question of "shame" (vv. 25, 28; see Gen. 3:7) that, just as for Adam and Eve in Genesis 3, is a matter of clothing. Across the river from the tree, the eaters are being mocked by people whose "manner of dress was exceedingly fine" (v. 27). The tree is therefore not only desirable and knowledge-granting but also invokes a bodily indignity marked by the question of apparel.

But the kinship between the tree of knowledge and the tree of Lehi's dream is especially clinched by their shared stakes. At its core, Lehi's vision concerns a rift both domestic and existential, as did Eve's decision in Eden. Shortly after Sariah and her younger sons take the fruit, Laman and Lemuel appear on the stage. Interestingly, they show up already separated from their mother and brothers, a distinct familial group to which Lehi again reaches out in desire: he "was desirous that Laman and Lemuel should come and partake of the fruit also" (v. 17) but, alas, "they would not" (v. 18). Laman and Lemuel's appearance as a second, separate group of sons foreshadows the fraternal division that will only worsen over the course of 1 Nephi and whose first intimations here trouble Lehi's sleep. Here again Lehi echoes the matriarch of biblical Eden, whose own bite of fruit was soon followed by violent fraternal division—fratricide of the sort just narrowly avoided in 1 Nephi 7. Like Eve, Lehi sees his family fractured when he takes the fruit. Indeed, as the dream concludes, Lehi worries out loud that Laman and Lemuel will be "cast off from the presence of the Lord" (v. 36), language used throughout the Book of Mormon to refer precisely to Adam and Eve's fall from Edenic grace (see 2 Ne. 9:6; Alma 42:7, 9, 11).[5] Wandering in a fallen landscape, anxious about his patriarchal responsibilities, and troubled by the sin the family has had to address because of the actions of his sons, Lehi encounters a tree that seems to have much more to do with knowledge, sin, and domestic division than with eternal life.

The tree at the heart of Lehi's dream thus carries not only Edenic parallels but also Edenic hazards. In this regard, it is easy to identify the source of the tree's undeniable moral weight. The tree is symbolically overdetermined, to say the least, laden with biblical resonance and ethical stakes and parental affect. It is no wonder that this tree occupies the gravitational core of the dream that follows. This is a moral landscape and Lehi stands poised at its center, wondering how to parcel out the prophetic and spiritual knowledge he holds. And nowhere are those stakes more fraught than in the case of Laman and Lemuel who, when Lehi desires their arrival with the rest of the family, "would not come . . . and partake of the fruit" (v. 18). This is, readers are meant to assume, a devastating moment for Lehi. It is what charges the dream's introduction with "exceeding" "fear" (v. 4) and motivates its conclusion in precisely the same terms (v. 36). Laman and Lemuel do not come to the tree, and, behind these words, readers are given to imagine Lehi tossing fitfully in his sleep.

What are we to understand by Laman and Lemuel's failure to join their family in eating the fruit? Why would his sons' not-partaking of something like a tree of knowledge constitute a nightmare for Lehi? Especially given that the events of Genesis 3 inaugurated the Fall, wouldn't Laman and Lemuel's abstinence from a tree of knowledge be viewed positively from a biblical perspective? Here, however, we would do well to remember that Genesis presents Eden's trees with more nuance than simply "the good tree" and "the bad tree." Recall that the tree of knowledge was not *bad*, per se, so much as its fruit was simply untimely taken and paired with specific consequences. One of those consequences was in fact desirable enough to motivate Eve's tasting in the first place: knowledge, and more precisely, knowledge *of good and evil*. At stake in Eden's fateful tree was less a negatively valued disobedience and instead a specific capacity of discernment. Indeed, this is precisely how the tree functions for Lehi, as well. After taking its fruit, he begins to discern various features of his dreamscape and can discriminate more clearly the position of his sons. It may be, then, that the resonance between the tree of Lehi's dream and the biblical tree of knowledge is not meant to invoke the full weight of humanity's fall from grace, but perhaps invokes a narrower slice of existential drama. Laman and Lemuel's failure to eat fruit from something like a tree of knowledge is meant simply to highlight their lack of spiritual comprehension relative to the rest of their family. Indeed, in Laman and Lemuel's failure to come to the tree, we see encapsulated their posture through all of 1 Nephi: they lack the spiritual knowledge and discernment that their parents and siblings have managed to acquire.

Lehi's family dynamic is a question of knowledge as early as 1 Nephi 2 where Laman and Lemuel "knew not the dealings of . . . God" (1 Ne. 2:12) whereas Nephi had "desires to know" of God's mysteries (1 Ne. 2:16), not only explaining his compliance but suggestively tying knowledge to desire, as in Lehi's dream. Nephi's famous speech about commandments in the following chapter is also a question of knowledge ("I *know* that the Lord giveth no commandments," he says [1 Ne. 3:7]). When an angel appears to Laman and Lemuel, their chastisement reads "know ye not that the Lord hath chosen [Nephi] to be a ruler over you"? [1 Ne. 3:29]) and Nephi's moral struggle before the body of Laban also entails a recital of what he "knew" (1 Ne. 4:11, 16–17). Nor are these instances of knowledge limited solely to Lehi's sons. Lehi "knows" himself to be a visionary man (1 Ne. 5:4–5) and Sariah has a related testimony confirmed by her sons' safe return from Jerusalem (1 Ne. 5:8). In fact, by the time Lehi's dream rolls around, each of the family members figured in the dream is characterized by knowledge at one time or another. Nephi knows, Lehi knows, Sariah comes to know, and Nephi "makes known" to Sam, but Laman and Lemuel's knowledge is always in question; they either "know not" or are on the receiving end of incredulous questions such as "wherefore can ye doubt?" (1 Ne. 4:3). The opening chapters of 1 Nephi read as a serial genealogy of how Laman and Lemuel continue to lack knowledge while everyone else in the family comes to possess it.

Amplifying the tree's emphasis on discernment changes the stakes of Laman and Lemuel's failure to arrive at its branches. Their immobility need not read as a sinful refusal of redemption but can be read, instead, as a less defiant lack of discernment, an absence of the knowledge necessary to navigate this moral and familial landscape. Laman and Lemuel may be undiscerning and undecided, in other words, more than actively rebellious—at least at first, as they in fact seem to have been. Notice, for instance, that for all their centrality and importance to the dream (serving as its frame [vv. 4, 35] and narrative center [vv. 17–18]), they are surprisingly static—in fact, arguably the most static elements of the whole vision. Everything else in Lehi's dream is profoundly in motion, including especially people. Whole crowds of people progress in turns toward the tree on a shifting landscape in which plants crop up where there had been wasteland only moments before and iron rods appear in midair alongside entire rivers that come into focus without warning. In this way, Lehi's dream is admirably dreamlike, but it heightens Laman and Lemuel's immobility by contrast. They stand statically, framed on each side by *other* people journeying to the tree with various degrees of difficulty.

But motionless sons are not the same thing as actively rebellious ones—certainly at first. Although Laman and Lemuel may fail to come to the tree, their future remains initially unclear; they are certainly not, for instance, depicted walking off to the great and spacious building or mocking other characters. They simply stand there, no trajectory yet decided and no vector yet embarked upon. When Lehi's gaze finally rests on his eldest sons, he sees them at a proverbial fork in the road. In a way, part of what is so terrifying to Lehi—what causes him to "fear exceedingly" (v. 4) for his eldest sons—may be less that they're actively rebellious and more that they remain so opaque to him; he cannot see where they're headed, and yet they clearly are not headed toward the tree and family in any decisive fashion. Where a tree-of-life model would have us read Laman and Lemuel as rebellious sons rejecting salvation, a tree-of-knowledge model complicates that portrayal somewhat. They may be, at the point the dream depicts them, undecided and indiscernibly oriented. They are figures of open-ended potential, poised statically on a morally fraught landscape, having not yet made their decision. Lehi may in fact be recounting his dream to these sons in the hopes of *spurring* the decision he sees they need to make.

What Lehi has gained by partaking from the tree in his vision is not life but knowledge—specifically, knowledge about his own sons. Taking the fruit allows Lehi to see where Laman and Lemuel stand, the obstacles by which they are surrounded, their proximity to which paths and which temptations. They may not have chosen one path over another just yet, but their very indecision leads Lehi to worry. Though he holds in his hands a fruit that he values above anything else, his oldest sons do not seem to immediately recognize its value. Worried about their sin, the consequences for his family, coming to see more clearly the specter of fraternal division, possessing knowledge and anxious to instill it in a new generation who shows signs of disinterest in what he offers— *this* is the situation the dream speaks to through the symbol of a tree.

What, then, happens in that pivotal moment between Lehi's seeing and Laman and Lemuel's failure to come to the tree? If this is a tree of knowledge, in some sense, all the weight of biblical precedent would have us focus on the moments when Lehi, like Eve, offers its fruit to others—the moment, in other words, when the fruit changes hands.

FRUIT

Like all dreams, this one too has a symptomatic center, tucked away in the space between Lehi's desire and Laman and Lemuel's immobility. For all his anxiety that his sons join him at the tree, it appears that Lehi *never offers the fruit to Laman and Lemuel.* Though he shouts and beckons to Sariah, Nephi, and Sam, the chapter never reports a parallel beckoning to Laman and Lemuel. Lehi's fruit-distribution is narrated in two distinct scenes, but any explicit invitation to his elder sons is noticeably absent from the latter. This may be ultimately immaterial, but it is interpretively suggestive. Verse 12 reports that Lehi was initially "desirous that my family should partake . . . also" and then cashed out this wish in an explicit invitation: "I beckoned unto [Sariah, Nephi, and Sam]; and I also did say unto them with a loud voice that they should come unto me, and partake of the fruit" (v. 15). But when Laman and Lemuel appear and Lehi feels a second surge of desire, no such invitation follows. The verse reads: "I was desirous that Laman and Lemuel should come and partake of the fruit also" (v. 17) but the immediate aftermath is only this: "I saw them, but they would not come unto me and partake of the fruit" (v. 18). Here there is no beckoning or saying with a loud voice. We find only Lehi's desire and its unfulfillment, without any of the intermediate steps he employed with his wife and younger sons.

While it is possible that such an invitation *was* present in Lehi's dream, elided only for reasons of space or forgotten by Nephi in his retelling, even such a possible elision would be suggestive. Even if the narrative intends readers to assume an invitation, in other words, choosing to leave it merely implicit in the text may suggest that Lehi's pedagogy toward his eldest sons has been more implicit than explicit as well. Perhaps Lehi has too-quickly presumed that instruction calibrated for Sariah, Nephi, and Sam might work sufficiently for the eldest sons—a kind of one-size-fits-all pedagogy. Or, again, perhaps readers are meant to understand that Lehi *really did* fail to invite Laman and Lemuel to the tree; perhaps their immobility in verse 18 stems from a lack of summons rather than any individual stubbornness on their part. Whether readers are meant to understand the invitation to be actually lacking in the dream or merely implicit, the fact remains that nothing Lehi does in the dream initiates any real movement on their part.

The dream thus reveals a symptomatic moment in the relationship between Lehi and his eldest sons and, in this instance at least, tells readers something more about the dreamer than about the people and objects that populate his vision. The force of Lehi's dream seems intended not just to reveal Laman and Lemuel's immobility, in other words, but also to show Lehi's anxieties about whether he might have done something more or something different to overcome their indecision. By the close of the dream, then, Lehi has learned that Laman and Lemuel stand apart, at an alienated remove from their mother and younger brothers; he comes to see that their pedagogical situation is unique and distinct, that they are not standing on the same terrain as the rest of the family, that they won't simply "come around eventually." Alarmed by their failure to come to the tree, Lehi—like any concerned parent—may wonder whether some of that failure may be due to a less-than-explicit or a less-than-perfectly-calibrated invitation keyed to the specific needs of his sons.

What Lehi sees when he looks at his eldest sons, then, may not be rebellious children who openly disregard him. With the loving but concerned eyes of a parent, Lehi may instead see a reflection of *his own frustrated attempts to teach them.* He sees opaque, immobile characters; he feels desire for their movement toward the tree but witnesses the ineffectuality of that desire. The point of the dream may thus be to focus readers less on Laman and Lemuel as soteriologically defiant and more on how *Lehi* grows increasingly self-aware about what it really means to reach out to wayward sons.

This, too, may lie behind the tree's resonance with themes of knowledge and desire. Like Eden's arboreal dilemma, pedagogy is always a question of these two subjects. Any experienced teacher can tell you that education is less about the transmission of information and more about packaging that information in a way that makes the student crave it; it is not just about delivering facts and answers but about creating minds that thirst with questions. This, too, is Lehi's dilemma: he holds something in his hands that is both knowledge-giving and desirable, something he hopes to make his sons crave. The difficulty, of course, is that Laman and Lemuel do not come. They possess neither the knowledge it offers nor, more alarmingly, any desire to reach after it, and so Lehi's question becomes the dilemma of every instructor standing in front of her pupils: how to make them receptive to this fruit? How to overcome their current indifference? How to instill in them the desire necessary for moral instruction?[6]

Fired by that question, shaken by a nighttime glimpse of where waywardness can lead, and receptive to the pedagogical cues of his dream, Lehi ends its retelling with a new exhortation. "After my father had spoken all the words of his dream or vision," Nephi explains, "he did exhort [Laman and Lemuel] then with all the feeling of a tender parent . . . yea, my father did preach unto them" (vv. 36–38). And not only preach, as we come to see—he also "prophesied unto them of many things" (v. 38), a taste of which comes in 1 Nephi 10. Readers are given no indication of Laman and Lemuel's reception of these teachings, however, until 1 Nephi 15 where we encounter the two brothers "disputing one with another" about Lehi's words (1 Ne. 15:2). Nephi interprets this animated conversation as faithless, diagnosing their conceptual difficulty as a refusal to ask God for the dream's interpretation as Nephi himself had done, but their questions do not suggest lukewarm indifference. On the contrary, Laman and Lemuel begin to pepper Nephi with deeply invested queries about Lehi's dream. Remaining on their mind for the intervening seven chapters, it seems, are the allegorical details that Lehi offered to them as part of his reinvigorated moral instruction. "What meaneth this thing which our father saw in a dream?" they ask (1 Ne. 15:21). "What meaneth the tree which he saw?" "What meaneth the rod of iron"? "What meaneth the river of water"? (1 Ne. 15:21, 23, 26). Though Nephi is discouraged by what we might call their lack of knowledge, Laman and Lemuel display another necessary ingredient of effective pedagogy—indeed, arguably the more important ingredient, and the very one they were shown to lack in the dream: desire. They want to know what the dream means, and they're willing to grant their younger brother an opportunity to talk about it in order to get to the bottom of things. Something about Lehi's dream has stuck with them.[7]

What's more, Lehi's renewed pedagogy following the dream shows signs of having been effective. Though Laman and Lemuel protest that Nephi's words have been "hard things, more than we are able to bear" (1 Ne. 16:1), it is not clear whether they are genuinely confused or simply smarting from Nephi's chastisements. Although they push back against *Nephi's* words, there are signs that *Lehi's* words, at least, have taken effect. For instance, after the exchange between brothers, Nephi reports that Laman and Lemuel "did humble themselves before the Lord" (1 Ne. 16:4). This humbling may be due above all to the lingering after-effects of Lehi's pedagogy, however added to by Nephi's additional explanations. Each of Laman and Lemuel's questions had to do with Lehi's words and especially Lehi's dream. Their growing resistance to Nephi's role as teacher sparks resistance (see, again, 1 Ne. 16:1). In fact, when they do humble themselves in the end, readers might mistake Nephi's degree of influence. It would be appropriate if it was Lehi's (their father's) instruction, not Nephi's (their brother's), that made the most difference.[8]

And when the scene concludes with a final note about Laman and Lemuel's moral reform, the summary again bears echoes of Lehi's intervention rather than Nephi's. Despite his harsh criticism of his brothers, Nephi reports: "I had joy and great hopes of them, that they would walk in the paths of righteousness" (1 Ne. 16:5). Some major improvement is evident in Laman and Lemuel; something has altered their course more substantially than previous interventions, or even angelic appearances. Suggestively, Nephi describes that change in terms that put the brothers right back on the terrain of Lehi's dreamscape: Nephi names the "joy" he feels when contemplating the pedagogical improvement in his brothers, and pictures them "walk[ing]" on new "paths." Though Lehi's dream never imagined Laman and Lemuel as mobile, Nephi can picture them striding along a road toward a joyful destination.

Lehi's dream reimagines for itself something like a fallen Eden with a desirable and knowledge-granting tree at its center and with a domestic rift hanging in the balance. At the heart of that dream is a scene where, as in Eden, fruit and knowledge should exchange hands but this time fail to do so, with the failed exchange correlating to some sort of culpability on Lehi's part. The dream, then, becomes an expression of Lehi's parental anxieties and a revelation of the pedagogical undercurrents in Lehi's relationship with two different pairs of sons. Spurred by this moment of failed exchange, Lehi becomes a new kind of teacher as a result. A moral landscape and a pedagogical revelation—these, too, are part of the dream's invocation of a tree of knowledge.

GOD

Where, though, is God in all of this? This is one of the most well-known and best-loved scenes in the Book of Mormon, and yet God is nowhere to be found. He doesn't speak directly to Lehi, he doesn't appear visually in the dream, and he isn't even found on the lips of the characters (who, as a general rule, are mostly silent in the chapter). And if God doesn't speak, appear, or figure in the dream at all, then what kind of God is imagined by 1 Nephi 8?

This is not the only passage of scripture in which God takes a low profile. We might compare 1 Nephi 8 to the book of Ruth, for instance, which is biblically unique for a similar reason: it contains no angels, no divine voices, no miracles; God doesn't speak from heaven in the book of Ruth, he doesn't directly inspire narrative action, he doesn't send prophets who intervene in the lives of characters—nothing transcendent or supernatural happens at all. This is not, however, to Ruth's theological detriment. On the contrary, the book of Ruth thus becomes a powerfully relatable story about everyday people living loyal to a God they cannot see, trusting that there is a divine order at work behind the scenes. In a similar way, 1 Nephi 8 represents a family struggling across an ambiguous landscape, trying to act in light of a God who is not immediately present and whose will is not immediately clear.

But there is a touch more divinity implicit in 1 Nephi 8 than in the book of Ruth because, according to Nephi, his father had not simply "dreamed a dream" but, more precisely, had "seen a *vision*" (v. 2, emphasis added). More than simple subconscious happenstance, on Nephi's telling, Lehi's dream is properly visionary, implying that God is part of this dream as its *giver*. If this is right—that is, if readers are meant to locate God primarily in the fact of the dream's happening—what are we to make of this God who gives dreams? Indeed, given that we've reflected especially on Lehi's pedagogy as revealed by the dream, what can we now learn about *God's* pedagogy in offering this dream to Lehi in the first place?

The dream grants Lehi a chance to see Laman and Lemuel without any of the obscuring trappings of day-to-day life. Here the daily rigors of a household economy are suspended; there are no meals to prepare, no animals to care for, no provisions to procure, no children to tend, no tents to take down and set up. All daily pragmatics are filtered out until Lehi can see, with stark clarity, the religious and spiritual position of each of his family members. In effect, the dream offers Lehi a kind of allegorical clarity about his sons, a simplifying mirror of his family situation that is (at least in certain respects) clearer than daily life. And precisely because the day-to-day world is reduced out from the dream, the dream can then serve as a place of ethical and spiritual imagination. It is a space in which Lehi can explore alternatives to everyday life, see things in a new light, and imagine people in a different setting. In order to change daily realities, Lehi needs a space where he can both see the situation clearly and imagine alternatives to the way things actually are. God provides him just such an imaginative and clarifying space with a dream.

Lehi's dream is not, however, merely simplifying; it is also profoundly complicating and ambiguous. The vision reminds Lehi of all the things he can*not* see—the fuzzy edges of the dream where people and paths "were lost from his view" (v. 32) and Laman and Lemuel stand before him in frightening opacity. There may be an allegorical quality to Lehi's dream, but this does not, therefore, render it transparent and easily digestible. On the contrary, this dream provokes new emotions in Lehi; it raises new questions; it requires time and pondering and careful interpretive work. When God sends Lehi a dream, then, we might notice what he has *not* sent: no list of doctrinal propositions or bullet-pointed action items, no black-and-white commandments or easy answers. The dream may be simplifying in the way it reduces out the day-to-day pragmatics of the world, but it is deeply complicating in all the ambiguity it reveals just below that world's surface.

The God of Lehi's dream, then, is a teacher of a very specific sort. He loves ambiguity and the learning that comes from wrestling with situations that are not immediately clear. He is not the kind of teacher who lists facts and figures for memorization, or the kind of professor who relies on the transparency of textbooks. This is a hands-on instructor, taking Lehi out onto a practice field so "large and spacious" that it might have "been a world" (v. 20). It is a God whose pedagogy, we might say, consists in giving his children life rather than downloading all the right propositions into their heads. The God who gives dreams in 1 Nephi 8 is a God who cares less about brains thinking rightly and cares more about hearts and bodies and emotions, the much messier and more ambiguous work of moral instruction. Lehi is not a mind to be filled with propositions, on this model, because God is not invested in Lehi learning *about* his sons but rather in Lehi's loving them and feeling the terrain under their feet and passing on, with sticky fingers, a succulent fruit to the people he loves best. By the same token, then, God is not invested in teaching his children *about* the plan of salvation so much as he's invested in us actually *living* it with these messy bodies and these overwhelming hardships and these lived desires that have to be tamed.

And in the same way that the God behind 1 Nephi 8 offers Lehi a landscape on which he can see more clearly and imagine alternatives to daily life, so too God offers us a religious life full of occasions to suspend the worldly order of things. Scripture, Sabbath worship, temples, prayer—all the trappings and rituals of discipleship function like dreamscapes of our own, spaces where we can suspend the pragmatics of everyday living in order to examine spiritual undercurrents, see one another more clearly, and train ourselves in moral alternatives. The God of 1 Nephi 8 is a teacher who instructs us in the same way he instructs Lehi—with gifts of dream space where we can imagine things differently.[9]

There is knowledge on offer in that imagining, to be sure—the tree of knowledge stands at the heart of Lehi's dream for a reason—but this is not knowledge of the sort invoked by textbooks and exams and letter grades. This is knowledge of the sort invoked by discernment and experience and the wisdom of a life well and fully lived. The God of this dream, then, is the God who stands behind the tree of knowledge asking us not to copy down, memorize, or dictate, not to imbibe correct propositions, but to wrestle with ambiguous landscapes, to wager interpretations on dense and opaque symbols, and to reach after one another in clear-eyed love and honesty. There is knowledge on offer in Lehi's dream, but it is not knowledge for rote memorization or catechistic recital. This is the kind of knowledge that God hangs on trees in lush gardens lovingly crafted for humanity—knowledge to be touched, and tasted, and dreamed.

Lehi's Dream

PLATE 6. Caitlin Connolly, *Lehi's Dream*, pencil sketch, 7 × 9 inches, 2020.

Artwork:

Lehi's Dream

CAITLIN CONNOLLY

I DREW THIS SKETCH OF LEHI AND SARIAH, MEDIATING THE SEPARATION of their sons, and haloed by their ongoing posterity. I enjoyed drawing Lehi and considering the tenderness he was feeling as a parent and how that emotion may have dictated the details of his dream. I found myself feeling drawn to and curious about Sariah and unsure of how to depict her. I am eager to understand the tenderness she was feeling as a parent and what vision she had for her posterity. In this drawing I also see my own belief: that despite a separation of differing paths, there is joy in the journey, a distant reunion, and redemption available to all.

Symbolic Seeds and Separated Sons:
Understanding Lehi's Dream as a Setting for Unity and Division

KYLIE NIELSON TURLEY

SIDNEY SPERRY ARGUES THAT LEHI'S DREAM SHOULD "NOT BE PRESSED too far" because "the moral and religious implications of it are fairly obvious and certain."[1] Sperry sums up the vision easily: it is a warning to Lehi that Laman and Lemuel "would eventually depart from the faith" and an example of "spiritual symbolism" that is profitable to "all."[2] Despite the suggestion of simplicity, Sperry's two main conclusions alert readers to a vision that is at the very least a split message for a split audience. And that is just the beginning of the splitting, dividing, and doubling in 1 Nephi 8.

The focus on division in Lehi's vision begins with 1 Nephi 8:1, a strange sentence about gathering seeds. At this point in time, Ishmael and his family have arrived at Lehi's tent, "give[n] thanks," and "offer[ed] sacrifice and burnt offerings" unto the Lord (1 Ne. 7:22). The story then comments that the Lehites "had gathered all manner of seeds of every kind," repeating "of every kind" three times before clarifying that *every* kind is only two kinds: fruit seeds and grain seeds (v. 1). In a modern Book of Mormon, this seed sentence derives unearned prominence as the first verse in the chapter about Lehi's vision, but in the original Chapter II this sentence seems to be merely a clumsy transition between Ishmael's arrival and Lehi's vision, between leaving one place (Jerusalem) and going toward another (promised land), and between plot episodes about sacrifice and Lehi's mystical dream. Yet these disjointed words are actually the building blocks of Lehi's vision; the gathering of seeds is not a bungled divider of stories but a symbol-laden, two-seed introduction to a vision brimming with two-word pairs and a critical two-step process.

This paper analyzes the seed sentence and its pairing of fruit and grain seeds. The seeds introduce readers to thematic doubling and divisions, but not in a neat or tidy manner. The seeds allude to creation, create a symbolic relationship with depth and nuance, and invite readers to see doubled words, people, places, and plants that resist categorization. Unlike easy synonyms or predictable antonyms, the seeds—and Lehi's sons—are intertwined with and defined by each other, even when they are slighted, rejected, or refined by each other. Forming a complex relationship of commonalities and oppositions, the seeds invite readers to see and understand Lehi's vision in terms of word pairs. Yet readers may be so familiar with the paired descriptions of buildings and fields and paths that they have ceased seeing anything but the veneer of single-sighted visual description. The oversight bulldozes variation and neglects nuance, same-sizing what should be unique, especially the distinct movements of *coming forth* and *partaking* of the fruit.

Splitting word pairs apart defamiliarizes the vision and demonstrates the complexity of seed symbolism, which is written onto Lehi's sons and their posterity. Filtering the seeds, the vision, and the sons through the lens of basic literary devices such as diction, characterization, narrative structure, and setting suggests that labelling all pairings as visually-oriented adjectives generalizes to the point of inaccuracy. The pairings are different, and the parts are unique; generalizing in these pairs overlooks doctrinal gradation, personal responsibility, and real and symbolic change. Ultimately, Lehi's vision may not convey the message readers assume (a warning) about the people they think (Laman and Lemuel) for the reason they think is obvious (the brothers' unrighteousness) to the person they think received it (Lehi). Lehi had a vision, and Nephi's rendering of that vision reveals a multiplicity of small and important insights, while slowly outlining a paradox that Lehi seemingly understood by the end of his life and that Nephi seemingly portrayed with subtle literary finesse. At the heart of seed symbolism is a question for today: what can hold together a family or world that is being shattered by difference even while it is being simultaneously disfigured by over-simplification and uniformity?

SEED SYMBOLISM: STRUCTURE

When informed that the Lehites "had gathered together all manner of seeds of every kind" (v. 1), the most obvious assumption is that these are literal seeds. Though not the only necessity, seeds are an essential provision for Lehi's journey. And yet the past perfect verb tense jars readers out of narrative time with its indication of past sequenced action. Apparently, the Lehites "had gathered" these seeds previously, and they had done so either before or after doing something else. The change in narrative time unhinges the geographical setting. Readers cannot be certain if the next verse will be about more seeds from the past, about Ishmael and his family's adjustment to wilderness life, or about Lehi's continued sojourn in the valley of Lemuel. A solid transition should smooth connections between stories, but the seed sentence is jolting. When the next verse returns readers to Lehi's present, the seed sentence is orphaned. Rather than transitional and connective, the seed sentence is disruptive and dislocating. Why do readers need to know about these previously-gathered seeds? Why do they need to know this now? This seed sentence appears without prior context, disappears without explanation, and states non-essential, non-plot-forwarding information—and then exacerbates those infelicities by being highly repetitious: the gathered seeds were "of every kind," "both of grain of every kind, and also of the seeds of fruit of every kind" (1 Ne. 8:1, my emphasis).

The seed sentence appears to be an inept transition, yet appearances can be deceiving. The phrase of every kind alludes to creation, and it marks a moment of naming and differentiating, similar to the Genesis creation. Like the re-creation story of Noah and his ark,[3] Lehi's story is about gathering necessary pairs for a journey on water to a better place. The seeds reappear in 1 Nephi 16:11 when the Lehites "gather together . . . the remainder of [their] provisions," but, again, only the "seed of every kind" is singled out (and is, notably, singular). Noel Reynolds observes that 1 Nephi 8:1, 1 Nephi 16:11, and 1 Nephi 18:24 are "the only three references to these seeds"[4] and argues that the seeds in chapters 8 and 18 should be paired as one link in a holistic chiasm encompassing 1 and 2 Nephi. Yet the creation phrasing is repeated only in 1 Nephi 16:11, suggesting that 1 Nephi 8:1 and 1 Nephi 16:11 form an inclusio around a subtle structured story of creation. Encompassed within the verses is a story of two visions about fruit and seeds,[5] two explanations of visions,[6] two interruptions,[7] and a mass marriage of Lehi's sons and Ishmael's daughters (see 1 Ne. 16:7). The seed sentence and its echo function as weakened chapter breaks as they effectively insert a beginning and cut a conclusion. They bookend a story about the creation of Nephite society, which is essentially a story about seed (posterity). However overlooked by modern readers, the subtlety was not missed by Nephi: less than a chapter later Nephi explains that "our women did bear children in the wilderness" (1 Ne. 17:1).

SEED SYMBOLISM: DICTION

Charles Swift notes that readers often approach Lehi's symbolic vision by "mak[ing] a list of each symbol in the dream and what each one represents, as though they were making a list of mathematical formulas," but, Swift argues, "symbolism rarely works that way."[8] Symbols—such as the seeds in Lehi's vision—evoke a complex web of meaning. On a literal level, Richard Rust suggests that gathering seeds in an agrarian society meant the Lehites had eaten fruit recently. When Lehi speaks of fruit that is "most sweet, above all that I ever before tasted," he is speaking to people who have a fresh and personal connection with fruit (v. 11).[9] Rust's comments ground Lehi's symbolic dream in an earthy reality, which makes sense given the seeds' concrete tangibility. The gathered seeds are real seeds; they are collected and carried by Lehi's family to the promised land, and then planted "into the earth" (1 Ne. 18:24). The seeds will produce fruit that will sustain life. Yet Lehi later equates *fruit* with *seed*,[10] using the words synonymously to mean posterity, thus doubling the possible meanings. In both English and Hebrew *seed* can refer to seeds "that are planted in the ground . . . as well as human seed or offspring."[11] Within a few short verses, the text uses both: seeds are literal seeds (plants), but Lehi then expresses his worry for Laman and Lemuel, and his joy in Sam and Nephi and their "seed," meaning posterity (v. 3).

The variety of meanings is complex: the word *seed* refers to plants and progeny; both seed (plants) and seed (posterity) are related to fruit (plants) and fruit (posterity); and both seed (plant) and seed (posterity) are present in the introductory verses. Seed refers to "that from which any thing springs" or something that is the "original" or the "first,"[12] while fruit means broadly the "effect or consequence" or "that which is produced."[13] Seed and fruit (plants) are at opposite ends of a growing cycle, invariably linked but separated by time and effort. Yet growth is not linear in an agrarian society; it is circular. On one hand, seeds are retrospective, connoting the past and symbolizing the beginning of a growth process. Fruit is prospective. It is what one looks forward to as the hoped-for outcome of the planted seeds. And yet, as Rust noted, the seed is embedded within the fruit. The fruit is the effect of planting and nourishing a seed, but the seed is also the effect of having grown and eaten the fruit.

Seed (plant) and fruit (plant) emerge in a cyclical fashion, the one producing the other. Seed (posterity) and fruit (posterity) are synonymous, which only adds to the confusion. Both words have doubled meanings, and both meanings define both words. The text plays with the dozens of references to both seeds (plants) and seeds (posterity) and fruit (plants) in these sermons as well as to fruit (posterity) in other sermons. The word *seed* is used more than 40 times in Lehi's and Nephi's visions, bringing a depth of symbolic meaning to any particular use. Seed (posterity) and fruit (posterity) are completely unified; seed (plant) and fruit (plant) are separated by oppositional but related definitions. In one usage, the words are interchangeable. In the other, they refer to oppositional points of a cyclical process. Gathering all these seeds may be necessary, but the complicated wordplay hints at convoluted relationships and a troubled past even while it foreshadows the difficulty of gathering these volatile seeds and sons for their journey to the promised land; they are bound by definitions, but those definitions are interwoven in thorny ways on both literal and symbolic levels.

SYMBOLISM: CHARACTERS AND CHARACTERIZATION

Before Lehi begins narrating his dream, fruit and grain seeds are named and divided (1 Ne. 8:1) and then sons are named and divided. When he categorizes four sons into two groupings and then specifically refers to his sons and their "seed" (v. 3), Lehi links sons and seeds. Sam and Nephi are the sons who eat the fruit, changing spiritually by choice and physically by eating. But what about the sons who do not partake? Laman and Lemuel refuse to consume fruit (plants), but, as symbolic seeds, they are left with only one option: to be symbolic grain seeds. Obviously, they are still Lehi's seed (posterity), but the decision not to partake changes them in Lehi's eyes. In Lehi's world, sons and seeds are divided and then categorized. But whereas fruit and grain seeds are then united as seeds "of every kind"—repetitively (v. 1)—Lehi's sons are separated further by judgment: Lehi speaks of sons in whom he has "reason to rejoice" (v. 3) and sons about whom he has reason to "fear" (v. 4). How is Lehi supposed to gather all of these seeds together for the journey to the promised land? There are seeds of plants and seeds of posterity; seeds of fruit and seeds of grain; seeds of rejoicing and seeds of fear; seeds of obedience and seeds of disobedience.

Unlike Nephi, Lehi has not asked what his vision means, at least not in recorded scripture. Nevertheless, Lehi has gleaned meaning from his vision. He is definite: "because of these things which he saw in a vision, he exceedingly fear[s] for Laman and Lemuel" (v. 36). This vision-induced anxiety weighs on him, altering how he speaks, what he says, and what he does not say. Based on parental fear or favor, Lehi's evaluations begin changing relationships. When Lehi tells Laman and Lemuel that he fears for them, he does not refer to their seed. Lehi restates his fear for Laman and Lemuel—and no seed—at the conclusion of his dream. When the family packs to move further into the wilderness, a singular "seed of every kind" is gathered, unlike the "seeds of every kind" the family gathered earlier. Even in his final words to Laman and Lemuel, Lehi speaks about their personal righteousness, which has "been the anxiety of [his] soul from the beginning" (2 Ne. 1:16).

The oversight is stark since Lehi's final words to everyone else focus fixedly on seed: the promised land is Joseph's—and his seed's—"inheritance" (2 Ne. 3:2).[14] Sam's blessing is short, but entirely seed-centric (see 2 Ne. 4:11). Lehi even blesses Zoram that his "seed shall be blessed . . . forever" because he is a "true friend" to Nephi (2 Ne. 1:31). The silence about Laman and Lemuel's seed is consistent and distressing, especially because Laman and Lemuel do have children. Perhaps foreshadowing loving and inclusive Lamanite family relationships,[15] Lehi speaks to both Laman's and Lemuel's sons and daughters. He re-establishes the Lehite covenant with them and promises that they—and their "seed"—shall "not utterly be destroyed" (2 Ne. 4:9) because any "cursing" will be "answered on the heads of [their] parents" (2 Ne. 4:6). Readers may wonder about this uneven interaction.

It is within the context of the Abrahamic covenant that Lehi's silence becomes meaningful. Nephi explains to his brothers that "our father hath not spoken of our seed alone, but also of all the house of Israel, pointing to the covenant . . . made to our father Abraham" (1 Ne. 15:18). To Abraham, the Lord promised, "In thy seed shall all the kindreds of the earth be blessed" (1 Ne. 15:18). When Lehi never speaks about Laman's and Lemuel's seed *to them*, he leaves Laman and Lemuel as stranded as the seed sentence. He leaves a clear message that he believes they are cut off from the Abrahamic covenant, no longer receiving the blessing or opportunity to have their seed bless the kindreds of the earth.

Lehi and Nephi and Laman and Lemuel seem trapped in a circular cycle of destruction rather than growth. The vision plants seeds of fear in Lehi. The fruits of these seeds are words and silences that are likely to produce Laman's and Lemuel's anger and hostility. The brothers plant their jealousy of Nephi, dwell on slights, cultivate resentment and antagonism, and grow the fruit of enmity. Perhaps Laman and Lemuel are motivated by threats of "be[ing] cast off from the presence of the Lord" (v. 36). Perhaps they will change after being compared to the brothers who cause Lehi to "rejoice in the Lord" (v. 3). Perhaps they will understand that their anger is just sinful anger while Nephi's anger is "the sharpness of the power of the word of God" (2 Ne. 1:26). Watching Laman and Lemuel causes Lehi to feel "anxiety" (2 Ne 1:16) and to be "weighed down with sorrow" (2 Ne. 1:17) and to "[fear]" Laman and Lemuel will be "cut off" (2 Ne. 1:17). What should Lehi do? Readers may relate to Lehi's concerns and fears as well as the difficult parenting choices he must make. Gathering "all seeds of every kind" is a literal gathering. Both seeds and sons must be gathered together for the journey to the promised land. And yet this compound is a volatile mixture. The complicated wordplay and the symbolism of the seed sentence hint of a troubled past and foreshadow familial relationships in a troubled future.

WORD PAIRS

The naming and dividing of difference and the gathering of diversity is the Book of Mormon's creation story. As in Genesis, Lehi's vision has a multitude of word pairs or what James T. Duke labels as "standard, formulaic combinations of two words."[16] Biblical scholar Leland Ryken cautions readers that the "interpretive importance" of word pairs "has been generally exaggerated,"[17] but it would be difficult to exaggerate their importance in Lehi's vision. If readers finish the vision thinking of an iron rod, a tree with sweet fruit, and a big building, then they do so because these paired, "standard, formulaic combinations of two words,"[18] are, despite their unpoetic name, the basis of parallelism in biblical poetry, and they play a significant role in the Book of Mormon, as well. Cynthia Hallen, Professor of Linguistics, had her students study various chapters, including 1 Nephi 8, looking for "conjoined words," or words that are connected by a conjunction and have lexical, syntactical, and semantical relationships.[19] Hallen's students found six conjoined word pairs in 1 Nephi 8: dark and dreary, large and spacious, strait and narrow, great and spacious, old and young, and dream or vision.[20] Hallen's students labelled most word pairs as synonymous adjectives with similar meanings, such as the *dark and dreary* waste in which Lehi is lost (1 Ne. 8:7), the *large* field that is so *spacious* that it seems to be a world (1 Ne. 8:20), and the *strait* path that is also *narrow* (v. 20).

Readers may try to visualize the dark waste, the field's spaciousness, and the constricted path, but if they do, they will realize that Lehi's vision is not easily imagined—or at least, not imagined similarly by different readers. That occurs in part because function, not visual impact, is the basis of these descriptors. For example, the field is "large and spacious" (v. 20), but neither word is a specific size. Instead, the words focus on the field's capacity to hold "numberless concourses of people" (v. 21). The capacity of the field is similarly matched by the capacity of the "great and spacious building," which is "filled with people, both old and young, both male and female" (v. 27). A *dark* waste could be mysterious, empty, windswept, or frightening, but Lehi's dark waste is *dreary*, evoking emotional hopelessness in the darkness. *Old and young* function as a merism, a literary device in which a few words represent an entire group. Saying that there were *old and young* people in the building does not mean there were no middle-aged people or little children, but, rather, that anyone within the boundaries of old and young could be found inside. In Lehi's vision, word pairs abound, and they are never simply doubled, visually-focused descriptors.

Word Pairs: Diction

Unlike the adjectival word pairs, the verb pairings in Lehi's vision often go unnoticed. Nevertheless, paired actions are plenteous.[21]

Some people "come forth and commence in the path" before they are confused by the mists of darkness and "[wander] off and [are] lost" (v. 23). Others "come forth and [catch] hold of the end of the rod of iron," clinging to it until they "come forth and partake" (v. 24). After partaking, they "cast their eyes about" (v. 22) and feel "ashamed" (v. 28) because the people in the great and spacious building are "mocking and pointing" at them (v. 27). These people "[fall] away into forbidden paths and [are] lost" (v. 28), a significant movement that is adopted into Nephite culture and phrasing. Religious leaders such as Abinadi (Mosiah 16:5) and Alma (Alma 9:32) re-purpose the action into description, labelling people as "lost and fallen."[22]

The paired verbs are action-oriented, character-defining movements. The man dressed in a white robe doubles his actions from the beginning: "he came and stood" before Lehi, then "spake and bade" Lehi to follow him. But Lehi initially moves in simple motions: he follows the man, travels, prays, beholds the capacious field, and then beholds the tree. Things begin to change, though, when Lehi makes the fateful decision to double his actions and "go forth and partake of the fruit" (v. 11). Emphasizing the two-part movement, Lehi invites Sariah, Sam, and Nephi to "come unto [him] and partake" (v. 15). Rather than simply summarizing their compliance, Lehi reiterates that they "did come unto me and partake" (v. 16). Similarly, Lehi desires that Laman and Lemuel "should come and partake of the fruit" (v. 17), and then announces that they "would not come unto me and partake of the fruit" (v. 18). In his vision, Lehi either invites or describes people *coming forth and partaking* eight different times.

Many of these doubled actions are examples of literary hendiadys, or "nouns or verbs of the same case or tense" that work together to "signal a deeper unity of meaning."[23] While much can be learned from the joining, these word pairs—particularly *come forth* and *partake*—should not be joined so seamlessly that the parts cease to be seen as separate, definable movements. "Coming" typically denotes a movement of drawing closer, moving towards, or advancing near.[24] The word *forth*, used regularly with *come* in Lehi's vision, refers to moving across a boundary or a "progression or advance from a state of confinement."[25] People "come forth and commence" in the path, and others "come forth and [catch] hold at the end of the rod," and even Lehi "did go forth and partake." *Coming forth* is the initial step, but it can be conjoined to a variety of second steps. Lehi most often followed *coming forth* with *partaking*, which can mean simply to eat, but also can mean "to take a part, portion or share in common with others"[26]—an apt description of Lehi's actions at the tree. Notably, the last group participates in a three-step process when they "came forth and fell down and partook of the fruit of the tree" (v. 30), splitting *coming forth* from *partaking* with proskynesis.

Word Pairs: Setting and Characterization

Lehi's decision to go forth and partake is based on a critical realization. Lehi explains, "I beheld myself that I was in a dark and dreary waste" (v. 7). Readers may skim over the phrase, "I beheld myself" (subject-verb-direct object) and assume it reads "I, myself, beheld . . ." (subject-reflexive pronoun-verb). But Lehi is not merely emphasizing that he, personally, had a dream. Instead, he sees himself. Is Lehi watching a vision of himself or is this beholding of self a metaphor indicating he saw his dreary spiritual state? Hallen notes that dark and dreary come from "two Old English roots that mean 'without light' and 'bloody,'" and labels them as a synonymous and complementary word pair.[27] There is no dark and dreary waste in the previous chapters, though Abinadi and Christ both refer to the "waste place of Jerusalem,"[28] an Isaian quotation. The allusion seems important, given that Lehi "dwelt at Jerusalem in all his days" (1 Nephi 1:4). In an intriguing antithetical description, the first plot action that happens in the Book of Mormon is in 1 Nephi 1:5 when Lehi "went forth" and "prayed," apparently leaving Jerusalem in a two-step process that reverses Lehi's actions of praying and then going forth in 1 Nephi 8. In 1 Nephi 1, Lehi leaves Jerusalem, a place so wicked that "many prophets" are "prophesying unto the people that they must repent, or . . . be destroyed" (1 Nephi 1:4).[29] In 1 Nephi 8, Lehi prays and then goes forth from a god-forsaken lightless waste rendered desolate by blood and violence.

In his reality, Lehi "prays with all his heart, in behalf of his people," praying generously and wholly for others (1 Nephi 1:5). The answer Lehi receives to his first vision is personal and intense: he sees a pillar of fire, which causes him to "quake and tremble exceedingly" (1 Nephi 1:6). This is not how Lehi reacts to all spiritual experiences. Just a few verses later, Lehi has a second vision (1 Ne 1:8–15), and his reaction there is to praise the Lord and rejoice. Readers should note that when Lehi and his family are chastised by the Lord for murmuring about Nephi's broken bow, he again "fear[s] and tremble[s] exceedingly" (1 Nephi 16:27). In his last words to them, Lehi tells Laman and Lemuel that he "exceedingly fear[s] and tremble[s] because of you" (2 Nephi 1:25). It seems that Lehi is moved to the point of physical shaking in his worry and concern for others. He wants all of his sons—and indeed all of his people—to leave the spiritual waste of Jerusalem. Lehi, himself, *went forth* from Jerusalem, and he wants others to follow, but that will require change.

The idea that Lehi *went forth* from spiritually-darkened Jerusalem explains many odd statements about time and change. Nephi notes in 1 Nephi 5:20 that "thus far [he] and his father had kept the commandments," a statement that hints at a distinct moment when Nephi's and Lehi's commandment-keeping began. Lehi later pleads for his wayward sons to "rebel no more against your brother, . . . who hath kept the commandments from the time that we left Jerusalem" (2 Ne. 1:23, 24), a specificity that dates a moment of leaving a sinful spiritual state with leaving a sinful physical state. Similar timing is suggested by Nephi's statement that he "should have perished also" in Jerusalem if he had not had a vision (1 Ne. 19:20). *Coming forth* is an important step. It is the step of emphatically leaving a place of sin and sorrow. Lehi knows that to stay in Jerusalem is to perish. Years later, Lehi tells Laman's children that he "know[s] that if ye are brought up in the way ye should go, ye will not depart from it." Readers can easily figure out that Laman's struggles to keep commandments are why his children will struggle similarly. What explains Laman's struggles? Instead of being "brought up in the way [he] should go," Laman was brought up in Jerusalem, and he is "desirous to return" both before Lehi's vision (1 Ne. 7:7) and after (1 Ne. 16:36). The parallels between Lehi's experiences in Jerusalem and his vision, the trembling reactions to only some visionary experiences, and the numerous odd statements are all explained by the idea that Lehi needed to symbolically *come forth*. This is not a slurred half-step inside a generalized word pair, but a distinct and difficult step of its own. That Lehi made that step seems likely, which makes Lehi's invitation to Laman and Lemuel to "come forth and partake" sad and poignant; these words come from a father who has lived all his days in Jerusalem, a dark and dreary waste place. He has valid reasons to fear

Symbolic Seeds and Separated Sons

for his sons or anyone who chooses to remain in Jerusalem. That fear begins his vision, ends his vision, and is the most likely motivation for him speaking about his vision at all: he is clearly speaking directly *to* Laman and Lemuel and *about* Sam and Nephi until 1 Nephi 8:16.

Years later, in his last words to them, Lehi does not even ask them to partake but merely counsels his wayward sons to "awake" and "shake off the chains with which you are bound, and *come forth* out of obscurity" (2 Ne. 1:23, my emphasis). This counsel alludes to Nephi's prophecy that the Lord will bring his covenant people "out of obscurity and out of darkness" and "gather" them in the "lands of their inheritance" (1 Ne. 22:12). Ironically, Nephi's prophecy alludes to his vision of Lehi's vision.[30] Lehi seems to know exactly what his words imply since he follows up his plea to Laman and Lemuel by calling on them to "rebel no more against your brother, whose views have been glorious" (2 Ne. 1:24). Given Laman's and Lemuel's hostility toward Nephi, readers may wonder whether hearing their father quote their brother who was quoting their father will inspire the elder brothers to *come forth* in anything but anger. Similarly, readers may wonder how likely Nephi's prophetic answer is to calm the situation, especially considering he concludes his answer by speaking of "my father" (1 Ne. 22:31). The fact that Nephi sometimes speaks of "our father" and sometimes of "my father" when addressing his brothers suggests that the possessive pronouns do rhetorical work. In this instance, Nephi's "my father" locates both Nephi and Lehi in a line of authoritative teachers: "ye need not suppose that I and my father are the only ones who that have testified, and also taught them." This question of authoritative teaching is the source of much of Laman and Lemuel's hostility toward Nephi. It is this question, ultimately, that splits the family in two.[31]

Word Pairs: Narrative Structure

If Lehi's first vision (1 Ne. 1:5–6) parallels the *going/coming forth* action, then readers might expect his second vision (vv. 8–14) to correlate with partaking. Both begin with a statement of what Lehi *thinks* he sees, followed by an entire vision that declares unflinchingly what he did see (see 1 Ne. 1:8; 8:4). Only two other people *think* they see something in the Book of Mormon—and one is clearly quoting Lehi (see Alma 36:22 and 3 Ne. 11:8). Unsurety abounds in this book,[32] but only rarely about what one sees. Lehi thinks he sees something twice, both times at the beginning of visions. The visions also provoke similar joy. In the vision of the tree of life, Lehi explains that "as [he] partook of the fruit thereof it filled [his] soul with exceedingly great joy" (v. 12). After his second vision in 1 Nephi 1, Lehi's "soul did rejoice and his whole heart was filled because of the things which he had seen" (1 Ne. 1:15). Problematically, the last recorded detail from Lehi's second vision is that Jerusalem "should be destroyed" and the inhabitants "carried away captive into Babylon" (1 Ne. 1:13). The next verse describes Lehi's joy, a literary non sequitur that can give readers the impression that Lehi is happy that his neighbors and friends are going to be captives or destroyed (1 Ne. 1:5). This occurs because of the decision to emphasize Lehi's joy. It seems possible that Nephi wanted readers to see parallels between Lehi's vision of the tree of life and his two visions in 1 Nephi 1. To help readers notice the overlap, he emphasized Lehi's joy in 1 Nephi 1:14 as a match to Lehi's joy in 1 Nephi 8:12. The parallels are striking, but focusing on joy creates a "surprising"[33] reaction to learning of Jerusalem's destruction.

The content of Lehi's second vision in 1 Nephi 1:8–15—what Michaël Ulrich calls Lehi's "throne theophany"—does not seem highly related to Lehi's tree of life vision. Yet the many parallels between the throne theophany and Nephi's vision of the tree of life lead Ulrich to argue that "we can see in 1 Nephi 11–12 five different visions that fit into the pattern of Lehi's previous throne theophany."[34] Though drawing parallels between Lehi's tree of life vision and Nephi's vision, as well as between Nephi's vision and Lehi's throne theophany, Ulrich does not take the final step and clearly connect Lehi's theophany and Lehi's tree of life vision.[35] Since neither Lehi's second vision (throne theophany) nor his vision of the tree of life are complete (see 1 Ne. 1:16; 8:29),[36] readers cannot be certain that these visions are the same. What readers know is that Lehi recounted his vision "while [he] tarried in the wilderness" (v. 2). What they do not know is when that vision occurred, although the two-step process, the unsure beginnings and joyous endings, and the incomplete state of these visions open the possibility of the visions being the same. At the very least, Lehi's visions in 1 Nephi 1:5–6 and 1 Nephi 1:8–15 are a foreshadowing of the *come forth* and *partake* process found in Lehi's vision of the tree of life.

Interactions and Complications

The two-step process is powerful; it changes people. Afterwards, Lehi "*began* to prophesy" (1 Nephi 1:18, my emphasis), wording that again pinpoints a moment of change. Whatever he was before, Lehi is now a prophet who calls people to repentance despite death threats, and who obeys unhesitatingly, simply "depart[ing] into the wilderness" with provisions and a tent when commanded to do so (1 Ne. 2:3). From this point until the outside frame of the seed story, readers are reassured more than a dozen times that Lehi has not returned physically to Jerusalem but is still dwelling in his tent.[37] Lehi's physical location is connected to his spiritual welfare, and both correspond to his

vision. Lehi has lived "all his days" in Jerusalem, a real-physical location populated with wicked people who need to repent, and thus a real-spiritual location
of darkness. Comparatively, Lehi spends "many hours"—the only measurement
of worldly time in his vision (v. 8)—in a dark and dreary dream-physical location. Lehi's decision to go forth from real-physical Jerusalem initiates a process of change that ends with his journey to a tent, an unworldly real-physical
location. Lehi's decision to go forth from darkness is a two-stepped journey
to a tree, a naturalistic setting with dream-physical fruit that brings great joy.
Planted firmly, Lehi stays at the tree, calling out to loved ones to come forth and
partake but not venturing forth to lead them. He stays just as firmly planted in
his tent, sending his sons back to Jerusalem twice but not personally returning.
Real-physical geography symbolizes real-spiritual location, a metaphor doubled with dream-physical and dream-spiritual locations.

Lehi's movement is coherent in reality and coherent in his dream, though
visionary literature is typified by episodic setting. Calling the structure "kaleidoscopic," Charles Swift explains, "[S]uch visions typically do not begin at the
beginning and then seamlessly flow through the middle to the end."[38] Swift
notes how Lehi "does not see the river until he is looking for his family" and
how the rod of iron "does not even exist when Lehi and his family are making their way to the tree."[39] The geography is fragmented and volatile, but the
vision reads smoothly because the temporality is coherent. The timing glides
effortlessly: Lehi is led to darkness by a man in white (vv. 5–7) and wanders
for "many hours" (v. 8) before he begins to pray for God's mercy (v. 8); "after"
[he] prayed, he saw a field and a tree (vv. 9–10). Somehow inherently aware
of its goodness, Lehi "did go forth and partake" of the fruit (v. 11). "[F]illed . . .
with exceedingly great joy," he "beg[ins] to be desirous" to share with his family (v. 12). The story continues in this manner, using time-marking words and
phrases consistently. Though not measurable in terms of seconds and minutes,
Lehi's vision is grounded in sequencing. Even after Lehi finishes his narration,
the timing remains steady: "after" narrating his dream (v. 36), Lehi "did exhort
[Laman and Lemuel]" (v. 37). And "after he had preached . . . and also prophesied," he asked them to follow the commandments, and then "did cease speaking"
(v. 38).

The setting is split: the physical landscape is sporadic and intervallic, mud-
dled enough that no one would be surprised if time suddenly twisted or flashed
forward or backward, but it never does. Instead, time proceeds in a realistic
manner, so functional that it fades inconspicuously to the background. And yet
time connects disjointed geography and allows Lehi's decisions and movement
to have meaning. Because readers can see a progression between past, present,

and future, they see that Lehi left a dark and dreary wilderness and came to a tree. They can see that his movement through a fragmented dreamscape is a journey and that the sequences compare with his past physical—and spiritual—movements. Time stabilizes the vision so completely that the calm progression into the visionary state and back out is barely noticed. Time also connects, allowing readers to see that this warning about Laman and Lemuel and their future choices can simultaneously be a confirmation to Lehi of change in the past. If Lehi ever questioned himself about prophesying or leaving Jerusalem, his vision provides reassurance.

Joseph Spencer also believes timing is critical in understanding Lehi's vision. He notes that a "sudden shift in the dreamscape" occurs the moment Laman and Lemuel will not come forth.[40] Abruptly the landscape fills with "numberless concourses of people" who commence in the path (v. 23). Some "lose their way" in the mist of darkness (v. 23), "multitudes" search for the great and spacious building (v. 31), and "great [is] the multitude" that find it and enter (v. 33). The numbers are staggering. Who are these people? In Spencer's analysis, Laman's and Lemuel's refusal provokes the populating, and thus these people are Laman's and Lemuel's posterity, a fascinating one-seed, one-set-of-sons interpretation.

There is another interpretation, however, and it explains Lehi's silence about Laman and Lemuel's seed as well as Nephi's pained reaction. Nephi feels "overcome" (1 Ne 15:5) after "behold[ing] the things that [his] father saw" (1 Nephi 11:3). He writes that his afflictions are "great above all because of the destruction of [his] people, for [he] had beheld their fall" (1 Ne. 15:5). What might Nephi mean here?? Looking out onto events hundreds of years in the future, Nephi expresses sorrow over the *fall* of his people, but in the course of his vision itself, what he sees is the "seed of [his] brethren . . . *overpower* the people of [his] seed" (1 Ne. 12:19). Might Nephi's use of the word "fall" here have other important meanings.

Why Nephi is sad rather than angry is explained, but readers must make connections: Nephi beheld "that the great and spacious building was the pride of the world; and it *fell*, and the *fall* thereof was exceedingly great" (1 Ne. 11:36, my emphasis). The angel agrees that the "large and spacious building . . . is the vain imaginations and the pride of the children of men" (1 Ne. 12:18) and also explains that the mists of darkness are "the temptations of the devil" (1 Ne. 12:17). Thus when Nephi unflinchingly reports in the next verse that the destruction of the Nephites occurs "because of the *pride* of my seed," he is invoking the symbolism of the great and spacious building (1 Ne. 12:19). When he further blames the destruction on "the *temptations* of the devil," he means the symbolic mists of darkness (1 Ne. 12:19, my emphasis). Regardless of the proximate cause of destruction, Nephi knows why his people are destroyed: they give in to the temptations of the devil, especially the temptation of pride. Pride is represented by the great and spacious building, and Nephi sees it fall. The "fall" of Nephi's seed is the fall of the great and spacious building.

This is a surprise. The most hostile element in Lehi's vision is the great and spacious building, and it is the people in that building—the old, the young, and everyone in between—whom Nephi identifies as his seed (posterity), meaning his own posterity as well as the posterity of Sam, Jacob, Joseph, Zoram, and Nephi's sisters (2 Ne. 5:6). From the great and spacious building and the mists of darkness to the path and the tree, the geographic edges of Lehi's dream represent the worst and the best choices that can be made—but only by those who begin to move. Nephi's people *come forth* as actors, and thus they populate the landscape of this dream. Laman and Lemuel—the seeds of grain—never step forward onto the large and spacious playing field. They disappear like visionary objects when they do not choose to "come unto [Lehi] and partake of the fruit" (v. 18). They only reappear in the last verse of Lehi's vision, which simply reiterates their non-movement: "Laman and Lemuel partook not of the fruit" (1 Ne. 9:33). Lehi's fear is sons who refuse to come forth and eat fruit. He fears they will be "cast off from the presence of the Lord" (v. 36), and they are if the tree represents the Lord's loving presence. Nephi's pain is realizing that the vision is not about his posterity at the tree while his brothers and their descendants reside in the great and spacious building. The numberless concourses are Nephi's people, and uncountable numbers of them are lost, wandering, drowned, or ashamed. Multitudes of Nephi's people are "feeling their way towards" the building and "great [is] the multitude" who enter in (vv. 31, 33). When the building falls, these people fall, as well.

This tragedy is implied in 1 Nephi 8:33. Nephi quits quoting Lehi in verse 29, but verse 33 suddenly slips into first person narration. Most likely Nephi is again quoting Lehi, who sees the multitudes in the building and then states bleakly that the people were mocking him. Nevertheless, if Nephi ever had a reason to interject, to impose his own perspective by fracturing his summary of his father's dream with his own voice, it would be this moment. Despite years and hindsight, verse 33 resounds with a bitter edge of pain when the first-person narrator announces that multitudes of people in the building "did point the finger of scorn *at me*." If this is Nephi, he is saying that he saw his children's children, generations of descendants—his own seed—mock and laugh, pointing their fingers and scorning him because he partook of the fruit (v. 33, my emphasis).

This reading is rather drastic, and it depends upon the seed introduction, likely written by Nephi. Moreover, practically speaking, Nephi's "seed" is interacting with, mingling, and becoming a "mixture" of all the seeds that "are among" Lehi's posterity (1 Ne. 13:30), especially during the 200 years after Christ comes in which there were "neither . . . Lamanites, nor any manner of -ites" (4 Ne. 1:17). And regardless of his silence, Lehi does not actually forget the seed of his older sons, but, rather, speaks directly to Laman's children, promising that the Lord God "will be merciful unto you and your seed forever" (2 Ne. 4:7), and blessing Lemuel's children similarly (2 Ne. 4:9). Nevertheless, Lehi fears for Laman and Lemuel, the sons who never come forth, and he never speaks of their seed to them. Nephi is devastated by this vision and blames his posterity, whom he refers to as "my people" (1 Ne. 15:5). Although Nephi has frequently referred to Lehi as "my father," he uses inclusive possessive pronouns ("*our* father," "*our* seed") while explaining Lehi's vision to his brothers in 1 Nephi 15. After seeing that his seed will be destroyed, he uses pronouns that connect him linguistically with Laman and Lemuel. Though exhausted at seeing his posterity be overcome by his brothers' descendants, Nephi is not angry, he is sad. Nephi suddenly begins speaking in a spirit of real unity, more so than in any other section of his writings. That this comes after seeing the vision of his people and their future seems significant. At this tender moment, he wants to stand together with his brothers of every kind as one family, each a son of Lehi and Sariah, each part of "our" family.

CONCLUSIONS

The story of Lehi's vision is the story of Lehi in his vision, and thus the story of any individual who chooses to interact personally with a merciful Savior. *Coming forth* is the first half of the journey to joy. It begins when Lehi evaluates his standing before God. Recognizing he is in darkness, Lehi *goes forth* from a spiritual wilderness, not in a simple half-step toward partaking, but in a critical movement that includes beholding oneself; those of us who leave the waste place of spiritual Jerusalem and move to the desert may need to plant ourselves solidly in a tent and not go back—not even when we think the lost and fallen people are our people. They are our people if we choose to become part of Lehi's vision because that vision expands into covenantal history and becomes the story of any seeds (posterity) who move into the space. This vision begins with a creation that names and divides seeds and people in "numberless concourses" based on their movement. The Book of Mormon is over when multitudes choose to join the scornful sons and daughters in the great and spacious building, rejecting the fruit and the tree, and shaming their ancestors who remain by the tree.

The Nephite fall is the end of the Book of Mormon, and that is a problem. Where are Nephi's brothers, the seeds of grain?

Nephi writes Lehi's story and some of his own, but he writes a one-sided, one-seeded story. The evidence is dramatic: the seed sentence is the only reference to grain in Nephi's writings, although there are over 50 references to fruit. Sporadic references attest that the grain seeds arrived in the promised land, but these references[41] are few in comparison to fruit and none are written by Nephi. Lehi's vision as written by Nephi begins with the dividing process of creation. This creation divides fruit from grain and brothers from brothers, but the division goes too far. That may explain why Nephi chooses to use the word *seed* in his vision, never *fruit*. Conversely, Lehi refers solely to *fruit* in his vision, never *seed*. Despite their often-overlapping diction, Nephi and Lehi behold a destructive growth cycle from opposite perspectives. As Nephi looks back toward the seeds with sorrow, and Lehi looks forward toward the fruit in fear, they both behold the enmity planted between brothers. Perhaps neither Nephi nor Lehi had the ability to prevent that seed from being planted, and eventually the Lord commands Nephi to "flee into the wilderness," severing completely the divided relationship (2 Ne. 5:5). But Nephi knows why the seed of enmity grew horrifying fruit: his posterity cultivated epic tragedy with their own pride. Moving from a painful vision is just moving to a painful reality.

And yet, if readers want to understand Lehi's vision, they must remember that Nephi is writing retrospectively, fully aware of the end of the vision and much more when he begins. He writes as if he were journaling each day, but a genuinely unaware Nephi would not create a seed sentence or a vision crammed with word pairs. A selfish Nephi would not write 1 Nephi 6 and 1 Nephi 9, interrupting his story with swaths of text that frame his father's vision with bizarre explanations of what he will *not* be writing about. The chapters are more jolting than the seed sentence, rupturing the narrative and reminding readers that while Nephi is an actor in the story, he is also the author of the story.

Nephi initially may seem to be the hero of the story. But careful readers will realize that this story is too structured and too symbolic to be a journal. Author-Nephi writes a story that begins in 1 Nephi 8:1 and concludes in 1 Nephi 16:11, leaving literary hints about the slow separation of his family. Author-Nephi crafts a story that uses pronouns to draw attention to 1 Nephi 15, the chapter in which he uses inclusive pronouns multiple times. This is the chapter in which Laman and Lemuel choose to "humble themselves before the

Lord" (1 Ne. 15:20), and it is the chapter in which Nephi chooses to portray dialogue with Laman and Lemuel, rather than simply summarizing it.

When Laman and Lemuel conclude that Nephi has "declared hard things" (1 Ne. 16:1), they sound as if they might be murmuring again. Nephi tells them, "The guilty taketh the truth to be hard, for it cutteth them to the very center" (1 Ne. 16:2). Readers may expect that this sibling encounter will end up as other encounters have: Laman and Lemuel will murmur (again), Nephi will call them to repentance (again), and the older brothers will threaten and become increasingly comfortable with the idea of fratricide (again). But the expected outcome is not what happens this time. Author-Nephi describes the scene with subtle finesse and expects careful readers to understand. Laman and Lemuel do murmur, and Nephi seems judgmental when he says, "if ye were righteous . . . ye would not murmur because of the truth" (1 Ne. 16:4). The dialogue is sharp, and the conversation is difficult. But no one walks away. In 1 Nephi 15, Nephi portrays brothers opting to remain in the discomfort of this strained relationship.

In Lehi's real world, the grain seeds disappear—at least they do in this book—and his visionary world is one in which sons disappear. While Lehi's dream may warn him of his most-feared future and comfort him about his repentant past, it also warns Lehi to behold his present with care, whether he beholds himself, the kaleidoscopic geography, or his sons of either kind. What Lehi beholds is rendered visible to him, but dividing splits what Lehi beholds. Rather than seeing difference, attention is often re-doubled on the one, making it difficult to see duality and distinctions. Lehi comments that he has "reason to suppose that [Nephi and Sam], and also *many of their seed*, will be saved," implying a knowledge that some Nephite descendants will fall (v. 3, my emphasis), but his fear for Laman and Lemuel is so overwhelming that he focuses almost wholly on them. Lehi knows that "it must needs be that [his family] should be led with one accord into the land of promise" if they are to "[fulfill] the word of the Lord" (1 Ne. 10:13), but his sons are fighting, his journey is floundering, he is living in a tent, and he has had a vision that is far from being a dream.

Is there hope for this family? Lehi does not know when he has his vision that a final pair of sons, Jacob and Joseph, will not be named as seeds, nor divided as rivals, nor explicitly in his vision at all. And yet Joseph stands with Jacob, willing to "answer the sins of the people upon [his] own head" if he does not teach the people (Jacob 1:19). Lehi blesses him with the blessings of his forefather, Joseph. That Joseph obtained a promise from the "Lord of the Fruit of my loins."[42] This promise is about how the writings of his seed and the writings of Judah will "grow together, unto the . . . laying down of contentions, and establishing peace among the fruit" (2 Ne. 2:12). Jacob warns the Nephites about their pride, speaks more compassionately than anyone but Ammon about his Lamanite brothers and sisters, and writes a lengthy allegory about the Lord of the Vineyard.

In his blessing to Jacob, Lehi teaches that "all things must needs be a compound in one" (2 Ne. 2:11). Seeming to contradict himself, Lehi then claims, "if it should be one body it must needs remain as dead" (2 Ne. 2:11). Lehi argues that forcing things to be "one body" creates lifelessness. Sin, happiness, the earth, and even God will "[vanish] away" if forced into absolute unified oneness (2 Ne. 2:13). Making fruit and grain the same will be a loss or vanishing of two into one; all will be fruit or all will be grain. And yet romanticizing difference is unwise: unfettered differences can shatter families, societies, and worlds, which is why Lehi begs his sons to "be men, and be determined in one mind and in one heart, united in all things" (2 Ne. 1:21). Lehi's answer to the paradox of unity and difference is tucked into the word *compound*. A compound is a non-homogenous, multi-faceted mixture—in this situation, it is a mixture of sons and seeds. Like a hendiadys, it holds unique parts together. Fruit and grain can be different and yet remain categorized together as *seeds of every kind*, just as Laman and Lemuel and Nephi and Sam are Lehi's *sons of every kind*.

That is good because the promised land is not the perfect destination for perfect people who partake of fruit and nothing else. It is a place for gathering a surprisingly diverse number of things *of every kind*: seeds, beasts in the forests, animals, sin, cattle, tools, riches, grain, ruins of buildings, weapons of war, fruit, cloth, fatlings, diseases, wild animals, trials and troubles, afflictions, flocks and herds, shields, many books and many records, precious ore, and precious things.[43] An abundance of oppositions fills the geography of the promised land, a virtual panoply of objects and structures and people of every kind. Does Lehi understand that his vision may be more great and spacious than he beholds? Does Nephi realize that the fall of his seed is not the end of the vision?

This father and son see visions, and their understandings of their visions cause real consequences. Yet what is critical is that at some point in his visionary experiences, Lehi beholds "a Savior of the world" (1 Nephi 10:4) who will "*go forth*" and partake of "suffering, pains and afflictions and temptations *of every kind*" so he can gather the sons and daughters *of every kind* (Alma 7:11, my emphasis). Nephi also sees the Savior "come down and [show] himself" to Lehi's descendants (1 Ne. 12:6). When he came to the promised land, Jesus called himself an inclusive and unique name: "Lord of the whole earth" (3 Ne. 20:19), encompassing every kaleidoscopic scene Lehi envisioned and more, and encompassing the vision's steady time, even as it continues well beyond the bounds of the book in which it is written. This is important because Ammon, alone, understands Nephi's metaphor. The seeds of grain were planted in the promised land and grew there because Ammon testifies in the middle of the Book of Mormon that the "sheaves" of grain are safe "in the hands of the Lord of the harvest, and they are his; and he will raise them up at the last day" (Alma 26:7).[44] That last day is not the day Lehi has his vision, nor the day Nephi has a vision. Lehi is overwhelmed by his fear for his sons, and Nephi cut off both visions "to be short in writing" and perhaps to move away from the pain of witnessing his seed's unrighteousness and scorn (v. 29).

Lehi is part of an irreconcilable family whose members are living in tents, and Nephi tells that story, leaving a variety of interpretive options available for readers. But Nephi also composes a sentence that is phrased in the past perfect verb tense. The awkward sentence contains symbolic depths about a past that was not perfect nor past. The decisions made about sons stubbornly impact this family and generations of their seed. But the sentence also plants hope. The words divide seeds but restrain judgment; they separate and categorize without losing uniqueness or connection. These words are important. When they name seeds and sons, they also name God—and then they wait for readers to make the connections. The Lord of the Harvest is also the Lord of the Fruit and ultimately he names himself as the Lord of the Whole Earth. In him, all things hold together, and he has covenanted to "gather" his people "together in [his] own due time" (3 Ne. 20:29, my emphasis).

Lehi saw a vision, and Nephi wrote that vision, and then both moved seamlessly from vision to reality because that is simply another step—difficult as that step may be—in and through a vision of eternity.

"Conjoined Words" found and labelled by Hallen's students	Book of Mormon References			References (Excluding Book of Mormon)		
	1 and 2 Nephi	(rest of) Book of Mormon	(total) Book of Mormon	Old Testament, New Testament, Doctrine & Covenants, Pearl of Great Price	(OT / NT / D&C / P of GP) usage	(total) non-Book of Mormon Usage
Dream /vision (synonymous) (nouns)	1 Ne 1:16; 8:2; 8:36 2 Nephi 27:3	Alma 30:28	5	Num 12:6 Job 7:14; 20:8; 33:15 Isa 29:7 Dan 1:17; :28; 4:5; 4:9; 7:1 Joel 2:28 Acts 2:17	11/1/0/0	12
Great spacious (synonymous) (adjectives)	1 Ne 8:26; 8:31; 111:36; 12:18	------	4			
Dark dreary (synonymous) (adjectives)	1 Ne 8:4,7		2			
Large spacious (synonymous) (adjectives)	1 Ne 8:9; 8:20; 11:35; 12:13		4			
Strait narrow (synonymous) (adjectives)	1 Ne 8:20 2 Ne 31:9, 18, 19; 33:9	Jacob 6:11 Hel 3:29 3 Ne 14:14; 27:33	9	Matt 7:14 D&C 132:22	0/1/1/0	2

Word Pairs in 1 Nephi 8 (Hallen list) [45]

"Conjoined Words" found and labelled by Hallen's students	Book of Mormon References			References (Excluding Book of Mormon)		
	1 and 2 Nephi	(rest of) Book of Mormon	(total) Book of Mormon	Old Testament, New Testament, Doctrine & Covenants, Pearl of Great Price	(OT / NT / D&C / P of GP) usage	(total) non-Book of Mormon Usage
Old young (antonymous) (adjectives)* *	1 Nephi 8:27	Jacob 5:63 Mosiah 2:40; 10:9 Alma 1:30; 5:49; 11:44 Moroni 9:19 *usage in poetic form (not use in narrative)	8	Gen 19:4 Ex 10:9 Deut 28:50 Josh 6:2 1 Kings 12:8 2 Chron 10:8; 36:17 Esther 3:13 Job 32:6 Psalms 37:25; 148:12 Prov 20:29 Isa 20:4; 30:6 Jer 31:13; 51:22 Lam 2:21 Ezk 9:6 Joel 2:2 Nahum 2:11 John 21:18 Acts 2:17 D&C 43:20	20/2/1/0	23

(More) Word Pairs in 1 Nephi 8 [46]

	Book of Mormon References			References (Excluding Book of Mormon)		
	1 and 2 Nephi	(rest of) Book of Mormon	(total) Book of Mormon	(OT / NT / D&C / P of GP) Scripture	(OT / NT / D&C / P of GP) Usage	(total) non-Book of Mormon Usage
Rejoice/fear	1 Ne 8:3–4	Alma 1:4	2	Psalms 2:1 Hosea 10:5 Joel 2:21 D&C 98:1	3/0/1/0	4

	Book of Mormon References			References (Excluding Book of Mormon)		
	1 and 2 Nephi	(rest of) Book of Mormon	(total) Book of Mormon	(OT / NT / D&C / P of GP) Scripture	(OT / NT / D&C / P of GP) Usage	(total) non-Book of Mormon Usage
Spake bade	1 Ne 8:6, 38	Mosiah 27:23 3 Ne 17:19	4	Num 15:38 2 Sam 14:19 2 Kings 5:13	3/0/0/0	3
Sweet white	1 Ne 8:11	Alma 32:42	2	-----		
Come partake	1 Ne 8:11*; 8:15, 16, 17, 18, 24, 27, 30 2 Ne 26:33 *go partake	Jacob 1:7 Omni 1:4 Alma 5: 34; 5: 62; 40:26; 42:27 Hel 6:26, 38 Ether 13:11	18	Rev 18:4 D&C 10:66; 29:40; 58:11 Moses 6:48	0/1/3/1	5
Come commence (as double action)	1 Ne 8:22; 14:17 2 Ne 30:8	3 Ne 21:27 War— Alma 35:13; 43:24 Hel 4:5	7	-----		
Wander lost	1 Ne 8:23, 32; 16:35	Alma 26:36	4	-----		
Partake/ ashamed or Taste/ashamed	1 Ne 8:25		1	2 Tim 1:8	0/1/0/0	1

	Book of Mormon References			References (Excluding Book of Mormon)		
	1 and 2 Nephi	(rest of) Book of Mormon	(total) Book of Mormon	(OT / NT / D&C / P of GP) Scripture	(OT / NT / D&C / P of GP) Usage	(total) non-Book of Mormon Usage
Male female *too difficult to differentiate between poetic use and narrative use. All included	1 Ne 8:27 2 Ne 10:16; 26:33	Alma 1:30; 111:44 Ether 1:41; 2:1	7	Gen 1:27; 5:2; 6:19; 7:2*; 7:3; 7:9; 7:16 Lev 3:1; 3:6; 12:7; 27:5; 27:6; 27:7 Num 5:3 Deut 4:16; 7:14 Matt 19:4 Mark 10:6 Galatians 3:28 D&C 20:18 Moses 2:27; 6:9 Abraham 4:27 * used twice	17/3/1/3	24
Mocking pointing	1 Ne 8:27		1	-----		
Fell lost	1 Ne 8:28; 10:6 2 Ne 25:17	*Lost Fallen:* Mosiah 16:4 Alma 9:30, 32; 12:22; 34:9; 42:6	14	-----		
		War Imagery Alma 43:38; 59:11 Morm 6:18 Ether 15:29 Moro 9:2		-----		
		Double Meaning Morm 6:18				

	Book of Mormon References			References (Excluding Book of Mormon)		
	1 and 2 Nephi	(rest of) Book of Mormon	(total) Book of Mormon	(OT / NT / D&C / P of GP) Scripture	(OT / NT / D&C / P of GP) Usage	(total) non-Book of Mormon Usage
Preach prophesy	1 Ne 8:38 2 Ne 25:26	Enos 1:23, 26 Omni 1:13 Alma 8:32; 30:6 Hel 3:14; 4:14; 6:2, 14; 7:2; 161:4, 7 3 Ne 2:10	15	D&C 35:23 NOTE: Many more verses in Alma and one in Jacob use both words but they do not appear to be parallel— Jacob 1:4 Alma 8:24; 9:21; 23:6; 434:2	0/0/1/0	1

PLATE 7. José de Faria, *Lehi's Dream*, oil on canvas, 35 × 27 inches, 2020.

Artwork:

Lehi's Dream

JOSÉ DE FARIA

A T THE WINDOW, YOU CAN SEE LUCIFER AND HIS FOLLOWERS WHO are invited to enter the strange, large and spacious building. The flames and smoke coming out of the chimney of the big house symbolize the fire of hell. The dense and misty atmosphere of the painting is intended to reflect the obscured and dramatic tone of the scene. Sam, Sariah, Lehi, and Nephi eat the fruit and do not let themselves be intimidated by the unbelievers who make fun of them, also trying to lead them on the way of the great and infernal house. Crowds also eat the fruit of the tree and, feeling ridiculed, they let themselves be carried on to hellish paths, walking in a long line towards the building that seems to hover high above the ground. The figure in red with his finger pointed at the house is an angel of Lucifer's hosts who also routes the crowds to dangerous paths. The figures who cling to the iron rod seem to walk with difficulty, but eventually mingle with the people who descend from the tree of life towards the crowd that lines up from the source of the river, all in a great mess. Laman and Lemuel stand still (on the left side) and don't seem to take the initiative to walk towards the family. The tree of life is a fundamental element in the scene. Very few approach it and eat its precious fruit, not fearing any kind of temptation. The other trees, the city in the background, the fish, etc. are figures of my imagination that have a very specific symbolism.

Returning to the Garden:

Augustine, Lehi, and the Arboreal Imagery of Eden

TIMOTHY FARRANT

A LOSS OF INNOCENCE

IN BOOK 2 OF HIS *CONFESSIONS*, AUGUSTINE RECOUNTS AN EPISODE from his adolescence in which he and his like-minded companions decide to steal pears from a tree near to their vineyard.[1] A first reading of the pear-theft episode is quite humorous, even enjoyable. Indeed, the very idea of a grown cleric of late antiquity retelling a boyish story of this sort with such soberness, before going on to berate himself endlessly, is almost laughable. Add to this the rhetorical skill with which the story is retold makes it all the more amusing and intriguing: setting out in the "dead of night," being in the presence of "good-for-nothing youths"; shaking down fruit and "carrying off great loads," casting most of it "to pigs"; and all this despite having access to "plenty of better fruit."[2] Put simply, it is unsurprising that this episode has frequently captured the attention of many patristic scholars, especially since Augustine's participation in the theft was, by his own admission, fueled by doing that which was forbidden.[3]

Despite the reader's first instincts, the most significant aspect of Augustine's pear theft is perhaps its practical theological relevance. The first *humorous* reading of the episode is really the reader's initial experience of its literal implications. Absorbing the meaning of the words, the reader constructs a literal scene in which the imagery of a boyish group conveys a literal, or *actual*, loss of innocence. Yet it is this literal loss of innocence that provides practical insights into how the reader views their natural human selves. In this way, Augustine's pear theft is not dissimilar to Terrence Malick's experimental film *The Tree of Life* where a young Jack O'Brien breaks into a female neighbour's house to steal her nightwear before shamefully discarding it in a nearby river.[4] Or, to consider a Latter-day Saint example, a remarkable comparison is found in Kenneth Johnson's autobiographical retelling of stealing apples with friends from a local schoolteacher's garden, before partially consuming and then discarding them in nearby bushes.[5] Contained across these episodes is the imagery of a child becoming aware of their natural human selves in relation to a looming moral order; a story describing a palpable and harrowing loss of childhood innocence. Only the digestive process, where the reader turns to cast their amused eyes upon themselves, begins to transform a once humorous response into an Augustinian soberness of conscience.[6]

The reflection Augustine offers, that of literally digesting the imagery of a human scene and discovering human nature as a loss of innocence, is practically invaluable for readers of scripture. For instance, when readers of the Book of Mormon find the patriarchal character, Lehi, describing his vision to his family in the eighth chapter of 1 Nephi, they are first confronted with a practically relevant human scene.[7] And even before the vision introduces the imagery of trees, fruit, or rivers, Lehi describes seeing a person in white inviting him to follow (vv. 5–6). Yet, as Lehi attempts to follow, he declares: "I beheld myself that I was in a dark and dreary waste"—a state of darkness that continues, in the vision, for "many hours" (vv. 7–8). From its outset, and even on a literal level, Lehi's vision describes human self-consciousness in such a way that its human readers can readily relate to the imagery of darkness and despair.

The contrast of following a person in white and unblemished clothing, only to become lost in a dark and dreary wasteland, is striking. In part this is due to the relatively large amount of time Lehi spends in visionary darkness, despite textual brevity.[8] But as a moment of spiritual introspection, Lehi's use of the reflexive pronoun in the phrase "*I beheld myself*,"[9] and doing so in darkness, contrasts his own human nature with the unblemished nature of the person he attempts to follow. In this sense, Lehi describes a contrast of ontology, or an ontological distinction.[10] If the person Lehi sees in vision and attempts to follow is God, and his beholding of himself in relation to God causes him to consciously awaken to his human self (with all that entails), then Lehi may too be describing a loss of innocence in relation to the moral order.[11] To turn back to Augustine, a loss of innocence akin to Lehi's experience is eloquently foreshadowed at the very beginning of book two of the *Confessions* (a few paragraphs prior to the pear-theft episode). Despite the omnipresence of God's love and mercy, Augustine here declares: "You were silent then, and I wandered far, so far, from you, toward more and more sterile seeds, whose only fruit was grief."[12]

POLARISED TREES

In Augustine's *Confessions*, as in scripture, it is difficult for the reader to determine what is literal, and what is not merely literal.[13] However, one indication that a passage may contain a deeper figurative or spiritual meaning is found in the choice and arrangement of its imagery. This is something noted by Harmless, who comments that Augustine's pear-theft narrative is a reworking of the Edenic arboreal imagery of the fall.[14] For instance, Augustine locates the pear tree within the vicinity of his own vineyard amidst plenty of sanctioned fruit; the tree of knowledge is located in the Garden of Eden over which Eve and Adam have stewardship, amidst plenty of sanctioned fruit.[15] The fruit Augustine seeks is forbidden, and he takes it with companions; the fruit of the tree of knowledge is forbidden, and Eve and Adam take it in each other's companionship.[16] After taking the fruit, Augustine realises a loss of innocence in relation to God, and continually reflects upon this throughout his confessional narratives; when Eve is enticed to take the forbidden fruit, the serpent causes Eve to behold her own nature in relation to God—"*you shall become as the gods*"—which prompts a loss of innocence, and which is continually revisited throughout Christian scripture.[17] In both narratives, therefore, human fallenness is described through the imagery of fruit, trees, and gardens in such a way that the essential elements are not easily forgotten and readily anticipate readerly application.

Before turning back to Lehi's vision, it is worth considering another especially compelling hermeneutic on Augustine's pear-theft episode. Penned by Ferrari in the 1970s, "The Pear-Theft in Augustine's *Confessions*" considers the way polarising arboreal imagery is arranged throughout the broader narrative episodes of the *Confessions*.[18] Essentially, it is not just the Edenic arboreal imagery that captures Ferrari's attention, but the way Augustine's later conversion in a Milan garden polarises this Edenic arboreal imagery.[19] In the pivotal eighth book of the *Confessions*, Augustine's continued experience of turmoil when reflecting on his human fallenness (potently calling back to his loss of innocence in the pear-theft episode) is revisited, this time at the foot of a fig tree, where he pleads to the Lord through bitter tears. To quote Augustine directly:

> Somehow or other I cast myself upon the ground beneath a fig tree, and I gave free rein to my tears and they flowed in torrents from my eyes, an acceptable sacrifice to you. I spoke to you at length, not in these actual words, but along these lines, "As for you, how long, Lord? Lord, how long will you be angry, for ever? Do not remember our sins any more." For I felt that I was in their grip. I sobbed out my pitiful cries, "How long? How long must it be 'tomorrow' and 'tomorrow'? Why not 'now'? Why not end my degradation from this very moment?"[20]

Following his pleading with the Lord for mercy, and still under the gracious shade of the fig tree, Augustine hears the Latin phrase uttered by innocent children playing in a neighbouring garden: "tolle lege, tolle lege" meaning "take up and read, take up and read."[21] Perhaps it is the innocence of the children playing that draws Augustine back to his own childhood innocence prior to consciously awakening to the self through forbidden pear theft. Whatever the intention of the phrase, Augustine takes this audible sound to prompt a reading of sacred scripture where he finds the Pauline passage "clothe yourself in the Lord Jesus Christ and make no provision for the flesh concerning its physical desires."[22] At the reception of these words at the foot of the fig tree, Augustine experiences an infusion of God's grace into his heart, and writes: "I neither wanted nor needed to read further. Immediately, the end of the sentence was like a light of sanctuary poured into my heart; every shadow of doubt melted away." In the depths of darkness and despair, and in the very moment he cries to the Lord for help, Augustine realises the omnipresent love and mercy of God; a remedy to his previous loss of human innocence. Rhetorically, the contrast between darkness and light is mirrored by the contrast between figs and forbidden fruit. But more importantly, through polarised arboreal imagery, Augustine's conversion takes him back into the Garden of God—perhaps to the very tree which first initiated human fallenness.

In Book of Mormon terms, Augustine's conversion bears striking resemblance to that of Alma the Younger, where the Lord declares that all people must be "changed from their fallen and carnal state, to a state of righteousness, being born of God" (Mosiah 27:25). In Alma's own words, a personal loss of innocence is contrasted with a rather Augustinian description of God's light: "I was in the darkest abyss; but now I behold the marvelous light of God" (Mosiah 27:29). And it is the same contrast we find in Lehi's vision, where the darkness of human fallenness juxtaposes the light of God, this time at the foot of the tree of life. To quote Lehi's experience directly:

> And after I had travelled for the space of many hours in darkness, I began to pray unto the Lord that he would have mercy upon me, according to the multitude of his tender mercies. And it came to pass after I had prayed unto the Lord I beheld a large and spacious field. And it came to pass that I beheld a tree, whose fruit was desirable to make one happy. And it came to pass that I did go forth and partake of the fruit thereof; and I beheld that it was most sweet, above all that I had ever before tasted. Yea, and I beheld that the fruit thereof was white, to exceed all the whiteness that I had ever seen. And as I partook of the fruit thereof it filled my soul with exceedingly great joy (vv. 8–12).

In comparable fashion to Augustine's own conversion, the reader of Lehi's vision finds a human in a state of darkness making their way to the foot of a fruit tree and receiving the light and mercy of divine grace. Just as the audible phrase "tolle lege" prompts Augustine's memory of childhood innocence in the Garden of God; so too does the visual whiteness of Lehi's fruit and the sweetness of its taste in a visionary garden hark back to Lehi's association with a person clothed in white before becoming conscious to the self.[23] In both accounts, as the purity of divine fruit contrasts with the fruit of Eden, so the light of God provides a remedy for the dark and dreary state of human fallenness. Therefore, as Lehi makes visionary progress toward the light of a fruit tree in a field—*a garden*—he does so from the dark and dreary world that emerges after human experience in the Garden of Eden.

Another important feature of the above passage from Lehi is found in both the location and description of the arboreal imagery Lehi sees. Textually, "a large and spacious field" is situated between Lehi's travels in the darkness and his encounter with the tree (vv. 9–10). And, at the very least, there is an implication that the tree which comes into Lehi's field of vision stands somewhere within this "large and spacious field."[24] Add to this that the tree's determinative pronoun is "whose" (and not "of which"), and an interesting image begins to emerge. To interrogate Lehi's phrase precisely, it is within a large and spacious field that he states: "I beheld a tree, *whose* fruit was desirable to make one happy" (v. 10). Whilst the Book of Mormon is not entirely consistent in this regard, in this instance the choice of determinative pronoun "whose" appears to indicate the personification of an otherwise nonhuman object, correlating with at least two other instances of a tree's fruit or branches in 1 Nephi.[25] Given the context afforded by the Edenic scene (which is aided by reading Lehi's vision in parallel with Augustine's *Confessions*), the presence of subtle grammatical encoding potentially brings the vision into dialogue with the recognised rhetorical techniques of personification and projection in linguistic allegory.[26] This consideration strengthens an argument that Lehi's visionary tree allegorically signifies a person inhabiting a great open space. Any light or joy experienced at the foot of the tree in the vast garden that holds it is therefore describing the light and joy experienced at the foot of a *person* who resides in a vast dark and dreary landscape.

Across Christian scripture, the person of Jesus is conveyed through various forms of imagery, not least the arboreal representation of Jesus as "the true vine" in the gospel of John (John 15:1–11). Since the arboreal imagery of John, that of vines, branches, and fruit, figuratively indicates the relationship between Jesus and humans, it is entirely conceivable that the tree Lehi describes is not really a tree at all, but a way of articulating the presence of Jesus in the vastness of the world.[27] Interpreting the tree of Lehi's vision as the person of Jesus in the world is not only consistent with the imagery of the New Testament but is further supported by Nephi's later expositions in dialogue with the "Spirit of the Lord" (1 Ne. 11:1). At the very point in scripture where Nephi explains how the reader may have "the mysteries of God . . . unfolded unto them" (that is, God himself revealed to humans), the Spirit of the Lord carries him away in his own vision, declaring: "behold this thing [the tree seen by Lehi] shall be given unto thee for a sign" (1 Ne. 10:19; 11:7). The potential signification of the tree weighs heavily enough on Nephi's mind as to inform his response to the question "What desirest thou?" (1 Ne. 11:2). But importantly, this question is asked after Nephi is shown the tree of his father's vision, presumably because (despite seeing the tree himself) any adequate interpretation remains unclear. Thus, when Nephi audibly confirms his unresolved desire "to know the interpretation" of the tree, despite seeing it for himself, Nephi is awakening the reader to the greater textual importance of the vision that follows: seeing the great condescension of God in the world through the virgin birth.[28] It is only when Nephi sees the actual image of Jesus in the world that he begins to fully appreciate the *significance* of the tree Lehi had seen. Or, to add a slightly different emphasis, it is only when Nephi sees the actual image of Jesus in the world that he realises that Lehi's vision is not primarily about trees at all.[29] Providing a hermeneutical remedy for readers equally perplexed with scriptural ambiguity,

Nephi exposes the tree as "a sign"—a sign of a God who resides in the dark and dreary world to redeem the humans of Eden (1 Ne. 11:7).

FIGURATIVE FIGS AND NARROW PATHS

The polarised arboreal imagery of the Old Testament inspires much of the figurative language of the New Testament. In the latter part of the Sermon on the Mount, for instance, the reader finds Jesus using the imagery of "good" and "evil" trees, with both implicit and explicit links to Eden. Naturally, the forbidden and sanctioned trees of Eden are represented by the tree of knowledge on one hand, and the tree of life (amidst other sanctioned trees of paradise) on the other (Gen. 2:15–17).[30] At least implicitly, this division correlates rather neatly with Matthew 7:17: "Even so every good tree bringeth forth good fruit, and the evil tree bringeth forth evil fruit." In the Latin Vulgate, the subtle difference between "omnis arbor bona," and "mala . . . arbor" (the distinction between "every good tree" and "the evil tree") may suggest a plurality of good trees compared to one "evil tree" or *the forbidden tree* (Matt. 7:17).[31] However compelling the contrast, the distinction made here between the forbidden and the sanctioned ought not to dismiss the complex nature of the ethical dilemma humans face in Eden, which is beautifully articulated by the medieval philosopher and theologian Peter Abelard.[32] But more to the point, the critical observation here is that, if only implicitly, the contrasting nature of Edenic arboreal imagery becomes a central feature of Jesus' discussion of good and evil; a discussion of practical relevance for the complexity of human experience.

Looking at the preceding verse in Matthew 7:16, the reader finds the more explicitly polarised imagery of Eden in terms of figs (which were present within the paradise of Eden), and thistles (which were present in the dark and dreary world, beyond Eden). To this end, when Jesus rhetorically asks: "Do men gather grapes of thorns or figs of thistles?" he is in fact using contrasting imagery associated with both the pre- and post-lapsarian human condition (Matt 7:16).[33] It is not that figs or grapes necessarily correlate with the sanctioned fruit of Eden or even with the discussion of "good trees" of Eden (prior to the introduction of thorns and thistles). As Abelard speculates in his hexameral treatise (combining both his own and Jewish exegetical thought) the tree of knowledge may in fact have been either a fig tree or a grapevine.[34] Rather, the point being made here is connected to whether or not humans, experiencing a loss of innocence which characterises the essential nature of the post-lapsarian world, will adopt a right relationship with the creative order despite the seeming omnipresence of the fruits of evil.[35]

Given that a few verses prior to this familiar imagery of the fall of Eve and Adam, Jesus directs his readers and listeners to consider the strait and narrow "way that leadeth to life," it could be argued that the thistle and fig, or thorn and grape, are being placed at either end of human existence.[36] With the strait and narrow path figuratively leading humans away from the thistles and thorns (resulting from the forbidden) and toward a rightly-ordered use of grapes and figs, Jesus is in fact laying out the remedy for human loss of innocence in Eden. Only the "evil tree," whether a fig tree, pear tree, or grapevine, vanishes to the imagery of thistles and thorns, and in its place a polarised tree emerges as the way to life.[37] The very fact that both the forbidden and sanctioned may be represented through the same arboreal imagery speaks to the idea found in both Lehi and Augustine that the way to life is found by returning to the Garden of God via "his narrow gate."[38] In fact, in the very context of being renewed in God following a loss of human innocence in Eden, Augustine again invokes the phrase "narrow gate" in his De doctrina christiana (On Christian Teaching). This time, Augustine uses the imagery of a serpent shedding its skin to posit that humans must imitate the "astuteness" of the serpent of Eden in putting off the old man, in order to make way for the new:

> And the fact that a snake confined in its narrow lair puts off its old garment and is said to take on new strength chimes in excellently with the idea of imitating the serpent's astuteness and putting off the old man (to use the words of the apostle) in order to put on the new, and also with that of doing so in a confined place, for the Lord said "enter by the narrow gate."[39]

Given the context of his other writings, Augustine again demonstrates how the natural imagery of the Old and New Testaments are intertwined, and how each—whether of fruit trees, vines, paths, gates, or even serpents—can be used to articulate the meaning of both human fall and restoration. Just as the serpent's astuteness may indicate both the calamity of the fall as well as its remedy, so too can the fruit of Eden invite humans back to the garden of God for human restoration.

With the above considered, it is of little wonder that the sacramental nature of the last supper again uses the imagery of trees, where the symbolic consumption of grapes—that is to say, "the fruit of the vine"—signifies the way to life, the very evening before a crown of thorns brings about death.[40] In a profound way the person of Jesus, as the true vine, invites humans back into Eden to consume fruit and provides a remedy for their palpable and harrowing loss of personal innocence. Once again, Augustine phrases it so perfectly moments before his conversion beneath the fig tree in Milan: "I knew I was an evil creature and I had no idea how good a creature I might become a short while later. So I withdrew into the garden . . ."[41]

The above reading of Matthew is not one where human actors perpetually eat the forbidden fruit of Eden in a literal sense, but where humans consider the redemptive path away from their own nature through the figurative, even sacramental, imagery of strait paths, figs, and grapes. Taking into account the positioning of the imagery of a "strait . . . and narrow . . . way that leadeth to life"—leading away from the thistles of evil and toward the redemptive nature of figs—such a reading parallels Lehi's dream quite remarkably. For instance, after Lehi describes the tree and his desire for his family to eat its fruit, he sees a rod of iron, running alongside a path, leading to the tree and its fruit:

> And I beheld a rod of iron, and it extended along the bank of the river, and led to the tree by which I stood. And I beheld a strait and narrow path, which came along by the rod of iron, even to the tree by which I stood; and it also led by the head of the fountain, unto a large and spacious field, as if it had been a world (vv.19–20).

Mirroring the imagery of both the Old and New Testaments, and especially the imagery of Matthew, Lehi's vision too depicts a "strait and narrow path" cutting through the great and spacious field (which imminently becomes enveloped in a mist of darkness), and toward the tree of life and its fruit. Most remarkably, just as the biblical imagery of the forbidden tree of Eden fades to the imagery of thistles and thorns, so too does the dark and dreary waste of Lehi's dream signify all that precedes human consumption of the redemptive fruit.[42] Therefore, in Lehi's vision as in wider scriptural and patristic narratives, the tree that rightly orders humans who have navigated the path, or way, back to God is calling them back to Eden. Yet practically, this call back to the Garden of God is necessitated by the very loss of innocence that defines the dark and dreary world to which God, himself, condescends.[43]

RECONSIDERING SCRIPTURE

At this point in the vision, it is worth considering the lateral arrangement of Lehi's imagery. Potentially the vision may be viewed as a coherent narrative, one that paints a series of seamless scenes that can be observed in their entirety as if from a distance. However, once other elements and actors are introduced into the picture, it may be more beneficial to rethink each scene as another aspect, or version, of what the vision broadly signifies. For instance, since the rod and path feature later in the vision, there is no mention of Lehi, or his family, having to navigate either of them (vv. 14–16).[44] Furthermore, though one reading may see the rod and path connecting (at either end) the tree to the large and spacious field, earlier verses imply the tree is situated within the large and spacious field, and not away from it.[45] The mists of darkness arise even further in the vision's narrative, distorting the experience severely for later human actors, compared to earlier ones, though admittedly calling back to Lehi's own description of a "dark and dreary waste" (vv. 7–11, 22–24). And at one point in Lehi's vision, Nephi's editorial voice interrupts the narrative to suggest there was greater complexity in an original version, presumably relating to the differing ways in which multitudes of people interact with the vision's ever evolving and altering imagery (vv. 29–38).[46]

Viewing the vision as fluid or shifting versions of a broadly similar narrative expands its textual relevance, and even its interconnectedness, across the small plates of Nephi. Until this point, the chapter's above expositions have been mostly contained to the arboreal imagery of Augustine, the Bible, and that contained within the parameters of Lehi's vision. Naturally, they have not been extended to the extra-visionary imagery of the Book of Mormon's surrounding narrative episodes. However, when one exposits the more obviously figurative imagery of Lehi and Nephi's visionary accounts, a new way of reading and interpreting the book's less-obviously figurative imagery emerges. Just as Augustine's open encounter with Ambrose and his learning of the Alexandrian tradition of reading scripture initiated by Origen affects the way in which the reader interprets his confessional narratives, so too does a figurative exposition of imagery already present in Lehi's vision provide a helpful way of reading the extra-visionary narratives of the small plates of Nephi (the very narratives in which Lehi and Nephi's visions are situated).[47] However, before an adequate exposition of the visionary and extra-visionary narratives of Lehi and Nephi can be conducted, it is first needful to perform a close reading of the Book of Mormon. In particular, considering the way narrative episodes are structured within the text of the Book of Mormon, especially in the small plates of Nephi, may indicate a less obvious layer of meaning at play within the text.

In the exegetical practice of late antiquity and the Middle Ages, initiated by Origen and taken up by Ambrose and Augustine (the latter of whom enjoyed a generous reception across the High Middle Ages), there is much discussion around the "senses" of scripture.[48] Common across these authors is the agreement that scriptural meaning may either be literal or figurative—what is often described as the "letter" and the "spirit."[49] And in each author, the "literal" sense of scripture is always the first reading and refers to the obvious meaning of a text.[50] In medieval Latin, present in the exegetical work of the twelfth-century Augustinian Canon Regular, Hugh of St Victor, the "literal" is referenced by the term *historia*, which can be translated as the "historical" sense of scripture.[51] Put simply, this incorporates the obvious sense of the words on a page, a reading of words in order. It is *historia* that sets a scriptural scene, identifies place and character, and draws out a basic and coherent narrative.[52] But that does not mean *historia* always refers to the historical, especially when a passage of scripture is obviously allegorical.[53] For instance, applied to the Book of Mormon, *historia* sets the literal scene of the family of Lehi travelling through the very setting where Lehi experiences a remarkable vision. And, understanding the vision as a vision, *historia* is also able to distinguish the visionary realm from the actual world in which the vision's dreamer lives, breathes, and experiences.

The second "spiritual" exegetical sense may include several Latin terms, including *allegoria* (the allegorical sense) and *tropologia* (the tropological, or the moral, sense). But without being drawn into the complexity of these distinctions (which may be slightly different according to the exegetical approach adopted), this second sense can be communicated through the Latin term *figura*, that is to say, the "figurative" sense of a passage.[54] Thus, when a reader proposes an allegorical or tropological sense of scripture or speaks of the use of metaphor, type, or trope, they are broadly invoking the "figurative" sense as their guiding interpretation. An example of this is where a passage contains a coherent literal/historical narrative (*historia*), such as the travels of Lehi and his family in the wilderness, but where the deeper intention at play exists beyond *historia*. A similar phenomenon is witnessed in Augustine's extensive commentaries on Genesis, where Augustine demonstrates how both trees and rivers in Eden are both literal and figurative at the same time.[55] Therefore, this approach to the text accepts the first literal/historical reading as the basis for discovering deeper figurative meanings. Yet it is also an approach that begins to propose a figurative reading in narrative episodes beyond Lehi's vision; one that extends to the extra-visionary (and historical) narrative episodes of the small plates of Nephi by seeing or reading *figura* within *historia*.

Intriguingly, in the chapter immediately following Lehi's vision, Nephi editorially inserts a textual note on the nature of the small plates of Nephi. This note speaks to the idea that what he writes may perform both a historical and figurative function. Distinguishing the nature of the small plates (from the large plates) as "not the plates upon which I make a full account *of the history of my people*," Nephi suggests the small plates have their own "special purpose"

(1 Ne. 9:2–3). As Nephi goes on to say, whether or not one is "particular to give a full account of all the things of my father" is unimportant (1 Ne. 6:3). Rather, what matters most to Nephi is that "the mysteries of God" are discovered by those who read (1 Ne. 10:19). In terms of interpretation, the distinction Nephi makes between the small plates of Nephi and the large plates of Nephi has far-reaching implications. For in view of the readings presented in this chapter, the "special purpose" may in fact refer to the allegorical potential of the literal narrative Nephi provides.

Further to the above, Nephi's textual note in the ninth chapter of 1 Nephi appears between the first account of Lehi's vision and Nephi's obvious figurative exposition of it. This means it is situated prior to Nephi's conscious personal struggle to make sense of the imagery of his father's visually rich narratives.[56] In terms of meaning and signification, Nephi's note prompts the reader to reconsider the potential interpretative senses of the broader narrative episodes of the small plates of Nephi. The presence of Nephi's later exposition of the visual imagery of his father's vision provides a lesson in reading that transcends the narrative of the vision and extends into extra-historical considerations of the book's extra-visionary narratives. In this respect, Nephi's exposition may in fact intentionally provide the reader with a hermeneutical mode of reading: an exemplary lesson in the fundamentals not only of how to read, but of how to read the deeper figurative imagery of scripture *he is writing*.[57]

LEAVING THE GARDEN

Prior to Lehi's vision, the small plates of Nephi contain a number of narrative episodes that detail Lehi leaving one Jerusalem in search of another and momentarily dwelling in the wilderness.[58] Figuratively, the fact that Lehi leaves a once-holy city to journey through a wilderness landscape correlates neatly with Eve and Adam leaving Eden to journey through the dark and dreary world. Of course, in line with the contrast between the two trees of life and knowledge in Eden, it is the subsequent contrast between figs and thistles that demarcate the garden boundaries, providing a way of visually locating human mortality in the world. In Lehi's narratives, however, the visual boundaries that demarcate entry into a dark and dreary landscape are perhaps less obvious but no less significant. For instance, as the dark and dreary wasteland of Lehi's vision parallels his tent-dwelling wilderness narrative, the very setting in which the vision occurs, so too does Lehi's visual experience with the person in white parallel his previous life and visions in the holy city.[59] Whatever occurs within the walls of Jerusalem in the extra-visionary narrative episodes of Lehi's family, therefore, is potentially relevant to comprehending precisely what occurs within Lehi's vision itself, for they form the very narratives that precede entry into the dark and dreary wasteland in which Lehi's family reside in both a visionary and extra-visionary sense. In other words, the obviously figurative nature of the Edenic imagery of Lehi's vision may also provide a way of interpreting the less-obviously figurative extra-visionary narratives that textually precede the vision. When considered together, there emerges an overarching theological narrative that again speaks practically about God's nature and being in relation to human experience.[60]

Viewing the extra-visionary activities of Lehi and his family members within the walls of Jerusalem as a parallel to Eden is compelling for the following reason. The final departure from Jerusalem's walls into the dark and dreary wilderness landscape happens immediately prior to Lehi's vision and is done so by Lehi's sons in the company of Ishmael's daughters (1 Ne. 16:4–7). Such an entrance into the dark and dreary world before becoming parents of a new nation mirrors Eve and Adam's parenthood at the beginning of human mortality in a comparable landscape (Gen. 3:23–24; 4:1–2). In light of this, both narratives capture the vulnerability of human existence in the wake of a loss of innocence and, more precisely, the imposing presence of death in a dark and dreary world. Any visionary narrative that follows this new mortal phase of human life and offers a way back to the Garden of God thus becomes a welcome and necessary remedy to the new human status quo.

RETURNING TO THE GARDEN TREE

Reading Lehi's vision through the lens of Augustine's confessional narratives, as well as through the exegetical practice of reading that informs them (and later medieval treatises), speaks practically about God's nature and being in relation to human experience. Common across the above readings of Augustine's pear-theft, Lehi's vision, and other relevant biblical episodes, is the idea that God awaits figurative exposition in a world rich with imagery and meaning. In terms of practical human experience, it is not really the imaginary world that contains God's presence, but the actual human world.[61] And so, in each of the above readings, God awaits discovery in the seemingly ordinary; the dark and dreary realities in which humans find themselves; the moral anguish, pain, and torment those realities entail. The success of biblical authors in capturing the complexity of human fallenness through narratives comprised of arboreal imagery—of consuming fruit from garden trees—is found in the endless interpretations and discussions these narratives have provoked. And so, as readers immerse themselves in these same narratives, appreciating the dimension and texture of paper, pen, and ink, their task is not to retreat to the imaginary or otherworldly scenes immediately signified by the letter but to ever search for the deeper, even hidden, meaning of the spirit. To the human readers of scripture, such meaning is discovered beneath the letter, *beneath historia*, and points to discovering God's boundless nature in the actual imagery of the world in which they themselves live.

That Augustine, Lehi, and Nephi each draw upon Edenic arboreal imagery in their own narratives, demonstrates their understanding of, first, how to read scripture figuratively and, second, how to textually incorporate this imagery into figurative narratives in order to render them practically significant. Augustine's success in this regard, in deftly making a forbidden act practically relevant to his human readers, is partly found in the array of scholarly readers who have since joined the discussion.[62] Even if a reader responds through laughter, the delightful nature of Augustine's imagery is such that the narrative is remembered and retold, as if it had actually occurred. Readers place themselves at the garden scene, join in the act of pear theft, and muse and reflect on the meaning of it all, only to discover their own personal loss of innocence in relation to their own personal God. When this imagery reappears at the point of Augustine's conversion in the Milan garden, the reader is then able to apprehend the omnipresence of God's love and mercy, recognising that he has necessarily condescended to the dark and dreary realities of the human world, as much for them as for Augustine.

In a similar way, the arboreal imagery of Lehi's dream speaks not to a world beyond human reach, but to the one in which humans live. The strait and narrow path, the mists of darkness, the great and spacious field, the rod of iron, the life of the fruit tree, *the true vine*—all convey the omnipresence of God who has condescended to human life. Whilst this may not be immediately obvious to the reader, as demonstrated in Nephi's own search for interpretative meaning, it appears as though it is obvious to Lehi's "visionary" mind. Drawing upon familiar imagery, available not only from the five books of Moses contained in the plates of brass but in the wilderness landscape in which he lives, Lehi recreates a garden scene in which God awaits *rediscovery*. And it is within this polarised Edenic garden scene that humans live and are, too, able to recognise the mysteries of God within the created world.

Responding to the actions of Eve, Lehi's polarised imagery of Eden invites humans to return to the very garden scene of God and *rediscover* the omnipresent Creator who ever reaches out to human creatures in love. In Abelardian terms, the God who emerges throughout the text of Lehi's vision is the God who sees the necessity of human life despite its inevitable and harrowing loss of innocence: "seeking humans through himself and redeeming humans by his own death, and by showing us so great a love, that as he himself says: *Greater love has no man.*"[63] Put simply, the God who emerges through Lehi's figurative imagery, is a God of love awaiting *rediscovery* in and through the rightly ordered use of all useful things.

PLATE 8. Annie Poon, *The Dark and Dreary Waste*, photographic print of mixed media (clay, tape, wire, paper, fabric), 2021.

Artwork:

The Dark and Dreary Waste

ANNIE POON

WHILE WE CELEBRATE LEHI'S DREAM FOR THE BEAUTIFUL IMAGERY of the tree, I am often preoccupied with verses 7 and 8 of 1 Nephi 8 in which Lehi must first pass through a dark and dreary waste. My heart breaks when I read that he walked for hours before starting to "pray unto the Lord that he would have mercy on me." It reminds me of my own struggle with being afraid of the dark.

From my childhood until just a few years ago, I had hallucinations each night of jagged black ghosts as shards from the shadows in the corners of my bedroom. They danced and flickered and made tiny rustling sounds to prevent me from falling asleep. Like Lehi, Joseph Smith, Alma the Younger, and so many women I have spoken with, sometimes we cannot see the deliverance that waits just around the corner. Instead, we feel forever trapped in the darkness. At times, even the Holy Ghost seems to have left our side. Lehi's dream teaches us that despite this, a celestial being is always present and guiding us on our long and difficult journey, even when we cannot focus our minds enough to see him there.

I decided not only to make Lehi's environment spooky, but also to make him look like a phantom himself. His form reflects the torment I once felt each night: disoriented, hyper-alert, vulnerable, and traumatized. For Lehi's eyes I used "safety eyes," which are regularly used in stuffed animals. They bulge as he struggles to see, like a mole in the dark groping along. To create the puppet of Lehi I used a very crude armature of wire, tape, paper, and clay. I tried to heighten the feeling of trauma by leaving the wires and tape exposed in many places. Even his naked chest lacks the protection of his clothing. I omitted ears and hair to make Lehi starker and more skeletal. For the black ghosts I hung paper cutouts on wires and shook them so they danced for the camera.

The Tree of Life:
Cacophony, Risk, and Discernment

TERRYL GIVENS

MANY OF THE MOMENTOUS RELIGIOUS INNOVATIONS IN CHRISTIAN history occurred because of spiritual anxiety. Early Christians for the most part understood salvation as a cooperative affair. Pelagius, now recognized to be more orthodox than heterodox in his views,[1] taught that "We always stand in need of God's help," but he gives to us the gift of moral agency: "man always is in a state that he may sin, or may not sin, so as to know ourselves always to be of a free-will."[2] Augustine's animosity toward Pelagian views may have been motivated in part by his fear that they left too little room for Christ's grace. However, it is not difficult to detect in Augustine's reinvention of Christianity an escape from the terrifying specter that we are, after all, the unreliable architects of our own eternal destiny. And so, in his *De praedestinatione sanctorum* (*On the Predestination of the Saints*), Augustine writes that "the grace given by God does not simply allow one to believe, but that it makes one believe."[3] In that logic, as subsequent authorities like Fulgentius wrote, predestination "was the only reasonable conclusion to the Christian doctrine of salvation by grace."⁴ Our fate does not lie uncertainly in the balance at every moment; God has disposed of our future before we took our first breath.

Martin Luther's rediscovery of this principle was the catalyst for the entire project of Reformation. Indeed, his acknowledged personal anxiety set the stage and the Augustinian path provided the comforting resolution. "My situation was that, although an impeccable monk, I stood before God as a sinner troubled in conscience, and I had no assurance that my merit would assuage him."⁵ He lived with "the most anxious possible conscience," in the words of his biographer. It was his reading of Romans that convinced him that we are passive recipients of grace, not fretful strivers toward righteousness. "I felt myself absolutely reborn," he wrote, his anxiety replaced by certitude of Christ's righteousness.⁶ Indeed, the Westminster Confession that grounded most Protestant denominations addresses explicitly this incertitude and its Augustinian/Lutheran resolution as a core tenet: "such as truly believe in the Lord Jesus, and love him in sincerity, endeavoring to walk in all good conscience before him, may in this life be certainly assured that they are in a state of grace."⁷

John Wesley's conversion followed a similar trajectory, caught up as he was with millions of contemporaries in the hellfire terrors of eighteenth-century revivalism. His converting epiphany transpired, and suddenly he found that "I did trust in Christ, Christ alone for salvation, and an assurance was given me, that he had taken away my sins, even mine, and saved me from the law of sin and death."⁸ And so, not coincidentally, did Joseph Smith live out this same pattern—but only to a point. The cause of his prayerful quest was—as the case with countless others before and since—spiritual unease. "I [had] become convicted of my sins," he recorded of his early adolescence, "therefore I cried unto the Lord for mercy for there was none else to whom I could go." (His later words, spoken out of personal experience, tie him even more closely to the pattern of Protestant terror about one's prospects of salvation: "There is no pain so awful as the pain of suspense."⁹) Oliver Cowdery confirmed this spiritual impetus: claiming Smith's assistance for his 1834 narrative, he wrote that Smith hungered for "that *assurance* which the Lord Jesus has so freely offered."¹⁰ In the theophany to which Smith's 1820 search for assurance led him, he heard the words that place him within the tradition of the Protestant conversion narrative: "Joseph my son thy sins are forgiven thee."¹¹

The sentiment of religious anxiety goes to the very foundations of the religious impulse. Not just because the fear of death and its aftermath is a virtually universal phenomenon, but because the manner of making sense of that anxiety and systematically addressing it might itself be considered the essence of religious construction. For instance, in simplified terms, in Catholic soteriology, assurance of salvation can only come when an imperfect faith is supplemented, as Adolf von Harnack long ago characterized the principle, "by the doctrinal authority of the Church on the one side and by the Sacramental Church institution on the other, and yet in such a way that it is obtained only approximately."[12] In other words, salvation from a default condition of condemnation and hellfire comes from belonging to the true church and receiving its sacraments from authorized administrators. Those conditions provide a degree of assurance that may fall short of absolute certitude but is as close to a guarantee as is possible in this world. Providing such assurance was a conspicuous function of the church.

Protestantism, broadly speaking, removes both priesthood authority and qualifying righteousness from the equation, redefines sacraments as edifying and supportive channels of grace, and relies upon personal, experiential witness of God's redemptive power for assurance of a happy judgment. The Latter-day Saint resolution to the question of how religion addresses the anxiety surrounding the human predicament will be the task of Joseph Smith's theological project, which culminates in Nauvoo in the months before his death. However, we may find in the Book of Mormon's most extensive visionary account a précis of that formidable religious task. Lehi's vision gives us a picture of the universal quest for relief from spiritual anxiety and confusion—and a prophet's insight into how challenging the quest for clarity and certainty can be. Lehi introduces his visionary experience in language that places the perils of the spiritual journey—like his own quest for a promised land—front and center. Unlike the common conversion narrative common in Christian history, the tree of life vision anticipates the Restoration's reconstruction of salvation into a communal enterprise. Thus Lehi reframes his religious quest and associated anxieties as familial rather than personal. Augustine's religious quest was not only famously personal, it served as a template for the very genre of religious autobiography (his *Confessions*). Luther, as we saw, begins his conversion narrative as a deeply troubled monk, and Wesley—and even Joseph—as young men in a kind of existential crisis. Lehi, by striking contrast, opens this religious narrative with salvational concern as a family affair. "I have reason to rejoice . . . because of Nephi and also . . . Sam. . . . But behold, Laman and Lemuel, I fear exceedingly because of you" (vv. 3–4).[13] That anxiety frames the narrative to follow. His emotional register constitutes the question, the dilemma, to which the vision will be a response, a template. We begin with a concern, beautifully rendered by Graham Greene's priest beholding the young girl in *The Power and the Glory*: "He was aware of an immense responsibility; it was indistinguishable from love. This, he thought, must be what all parents feel: ordinary men go through life like this crossing their fingers, praying against pain, afraid."[14] The general question that follows is this: as a human connected to other humans I love and for whom I feel a responsibility, how do I find meaning, safety, and security? How do I shepherd my little flock to a happy, harmonious, and shared existence?

We might pause here to contrast this mythic framework of the tree of life vision with the Genesis narrative. Adam and Eve find themselves in a concrete setting, entrusted with each other's care, confronting a future of uncertain unfolding. The story they fashion, whether historical and literal or not, captures the most essential features of the human predicament universally applicable to us all. Whereas the creation, the flood, and Babel's tower all serve as particular etiologies—How did we originate? Whence came the rainbow? Why the disparity of languages?—the conundrum of the Tree is the greatest, most substantive and important etiology of them all; what is the source of our human predicament, caught as we are in a maelstrom of competing demands, unable to address all the moral imperatives that challenge and define our moral nature? How can we find a serene existence, as limited and fragile beings unable to respond to infinite needs, yearnings, and duties?

This of course is the LDS version of the Edenic etiology, a vastly more authentically tragic account of human life than the simplistic Good v. Evil diorama of past dispensations. The power of our tradition's revision is in the vastly nearer similitude and relevance of Eve's dilemma to that essential drama of real life as we know it: The most pertinent question is not how do we avoid Evil but, rather, how do we negotiate the omnipresent competing demands that infiltrate every moment of our earthly existence? How do we arbitrate equally valid but incommensurate appeals to our time, energies, and devotions?

Eve's intrepid choice to brave pain, death, and exile leads to no Fall, but an ascent into the angelic, even divine realms of holy tears, where our heart must stretch wide as eternity to encompass the infinite pain of a heart that cannot escape the infinite tragedy of either/or. Eve and Adam foreshadow for us the inevitability—and necessity—of the kind of cognitive dissonance, contending imperatives, and oppositional alternatives that constitute the essence of our mortal sojourn. No coincidence, this, that the New World Bible similarly begins with an allegory, an etiology, that provides a cosmic template for human existence, in which a Tree will prove pivotal.

"Methought I saw in my dream, a dark and dreary wilderness" (v. 4). We are not, at this point of commencement, even in the world of human habitation (that comes later). We are nowhere. Perhaps we are at this moment in that Noplace Lehi later describes, before reality becomes articulated, when all

The Tree of Life: Cacophony, Risk, and Discernment

potentiality is only "a compound in one; wherefore, if it should be one body it must needs remain as dead, having no life neither death, nor corruption nor incorruption, happiness nor misery, neither sense nor insensibility" (2 Ne. 2:11). Lehi's cosmology, like the Bible's, begins in a pre-creation state, where meaning is not yet mapped.

Suddenly, "a man appears," who presents himself as a guide, an interpreter. "He spake unto me, and bade me follow him" (v. 6). At this transitional point in the narration, Lehi becomes participant in rather than observer of a vision. Earlier, he "saw" in a dream the featureless "wilderness." Now, suddenly, he "beheld [him]self that [he] was *in* that same "dark and dreary waste" (v. 7). (One notes here the resonance with Robert Alter's pre-creation rendering: "the earth then was welter and waste and darkness," Gen. 1:1). This transition to Lehi's intensely personal *experience* of the template rather than distant *observation* of it is intensified by a description that pushes the boundaries of dream-vision. "After I had traveled for the space of many hours . . ." (v. 8). Most would agree that dreams are experienced generally as highly compressed affairs, with little to no cognizance of time passing. The markedly, strikingly prolonged immersion in a vacuous time certainly tempts, if it does not require, an interpretation of premortal eons that precede our actual engagement as embodied beings on the field of mortality. That reading comports with the long-awaited culmination of Lehi's transit, which is a distant "large and spacious field," identified subsequently as "a world" (vv. 9, 20). Lehi, like Eve and Adam, is a sojourner, a pilgrim whose field of action is the expansive world. (I note here the Old-World counterparts to this cosmic plot: Philo of Alexandria, Origen, and Didymus the Blind, all read God's clothing of Eve and Adam in coats of skin as allegorical language for the transition from premortality to incarnation).

Curiously, it is not the mysterious messenger who delivers Lehi to the field/world. Most readers assume that this personage, called only "a man" in the text, is an angel. This is ultimately unclear, however. In fact, one can interpret the text as suggesting that Lehi prays for deliverance *from* that messenger, pleading for "mercy" after being led by the figure into darkness (v. 8). I have noted that the first and most theologically distinctive element in Lehi's framing of his vision is his familial concern. It seems striking that we are now made aware of the fact that Lehi's dream was personally traumatic—though it is described with typical classical understatement. But his dream was initially a nightmare—experienced as hours long in duration, while immersed in darkness, and ignorant of setting or the destination. It would have been entirely reasonable and natural for Lehi to frame his entire experience as a personal ordeal and personal salvation narrative. And yet, he never makes his own deliverance the focus of his attention. This is a conspicuous and portentous echo of the salvation narratives of Luther and Wesley, as well as from those of Joseph Smith and Enos. The difference is that Lehi's self-preoccupation is the most fleeting, shifting almost immediately from the personal to the communal.

The deliverance he finds, at this stage, is entirely ambiguous. Who delivers Lehi? It is possible that the messenger intended this destination all along. However, in such a case his pleadings to the Lord would have been redundant. And the textual juxtaposition of his sight of the spacious field, immediately after his expressed reliance—not upon the messenger—but upon "[the Lord's] tender mercies," again suggests the possibility that we see these two figures (the messenger and the Lord) as oppositional. As we will see, that reading comports perfectly with the dominant theme that unfolds from this point on.

This reading is also in parallel with an early Christian text that is strikingly similar in structure—*The Shepherd of Hermas*. That figure describes how he, too, experiences a dream, follows a dubious messenger, and prays for deliverance, whereupon he finds an ample vision unfolding: "I fell into a trance as I walked. And a spirit seized me and carried me through a pathless region where no man could make his way, because it was steep and broken into ridges by the waters. So, when I had crossed that river and came to level ground, I knelt down and began praying to the Lord and confessing my sins. During my prayers I saw the heavens open. . . ."[15]

Yet for Lehi, his prayer will be the first—and the last—mention of the Lord (or any appellation of God) in the entire vision. Both he and the messenger disappear forever. Simultaneous with that disappearance is the sudden sight of the beautiful tree, "whose fruit was desirable to make one happy" (v. 10). The desirable tree suggests that the Lord has responded to his prayer with deliverance, but that reading is problematic. For after his prayer, he does not find escape or respite or reward. On the contrary, he finds himself on neutral ground. Actually, the "large and spacious field" where he finds himself, later identified with "a world," is an arena of contestation, danger, and most significantly, a field of competing voices.

One could venture at this point an interpretation of the vision in its most crucial dimensions: Lehi's vision does work parallel to that of (the Restoration's) Eden story. We begin in a pre-created—or uncreated realm. We then see a world of concrete actuality and transition *into* that world. The temporal prolongation of the vision ("many hours") and the move from "I saw" to "I beheld myself . . . in" emphasize the drama of an experiential immersion. Eve's and Adam's transition into existence, like Lehi's, *precedes* any eating of a tree's fruit; in both cases, we are witness to an etiology of the human condition as a baptism from potentiality into a domain of opportunity and experience. Eve and Adam are presented with one set of options, Lehi with many.

In fact, the world into which Lehi has entered is characterized as a maelstrom of possibilities and paths, with competing counsels and instructions, providing confusion, anxiety, and uncertainty. He had framed his account of this vision by indicating the "exceeding fear" it produced. And the first human emotion he experiences within that vision was his own fear, causing him to pray for mercy. Now, the first human emotion he sees outside himself is confusion and uncertainty: "Sariah and Sam and Nephi . . . stood as if they knew not whither they should go" (v. 14). Lehi had himself arrived at the field in spite of, rather than because of, the messenger who "bade [Lehi to] follow" him (v. 6). There is a path leading to the tree where Lehi stands, and he beckons his family "with a loud voice" to come, which they do (15). His sons Laman and Lemuel ignore his entreaties (v. 18). Other "concourses" of people are trying "to obtain the path," succeeding in doing so, only to lose their way in darkness (vv. 22–23). Others persevere successfully. Across the river, people in a great and spacious building in turn add their voices to the scene of confusion (paths, mists, concourses, separated families, perilous waters), "mocking and pointing" and "scoffing" (vv. 27–28). In a scene that is the most unsettling of all, those who had successfully secured the prize of the tree's fruit, "fell away" and "were lost" (v. 28).

By this time, anxiety pervades the dream like a nightmare, resisting any possibility of assurance or peace or resolution. Lehi begins with a guide of unknown standing. He is consumed with anxiety. He prays to the Lord, but with an ambiguous response. He sees his family lost and anxious, his sons resistant to his pained entreaties. And worst of all, even those who negotiate the hazards of this arena of mysterious personages, silent Lord, malignant voices, enshrouding mists of darkness and various paths, find whatever safety they manage to secure is precarious and fragile. Even after securing the prize, their continuing vulnerability results in their fall from happiness and enlightenment. Those who negotiated the paths successfully to a place of presumed salvation, having "tasted of the fruit," subsequently "fell away into forbidden paths and were lost" (v. 28).

We might venture the moral of Eden as follows: life will present us with few simple choices. Good will compete for our loyalty against other Goods; it will be impossible to honor all virtuous commitments to which we are devoted. Even a life of righteous choosing will precipitate pain, suffering, disaster, and tragedy. They are part of the process—inevitable, unavoidable, and (as Moses and 2 Nephi affirm), ultimately educative and edifying. The moral of 1 Nephi 8 is similar in tone, though, as befits a prophet on the cusp of Zion-building, more communitarian in its dynamic. God sets us upon a field of possibilities, where our challenge is to negotiate our way to the fulness that is in Christ through a minefield of hazards. We rely upon each other to get there. In this human family, we find empathy, concern, and good counsel. We also find hostility, deception, and malice. Our responsibility is to help and not hinder each other in finding and securing the path. Most disconcerting of all, that assurance sought by Augustine, by Luther, by Wesley—and by Joseph Smith—is totally absent from the soteriology intimated by Lehi's vision.

Whether secured by Christ's dispensation of grace or by duly authorized sacraments, salvation has no fixed, stable status in Lehi's vision. He reaffirms at the vision's conclusion that he is left with "exceeding fear" (v. 37). For Laman and Lemuel, particularly. And yet, his hope for his other family is born of personal faith in their character, not in sacramental efficacy or God's grace. What we get here is a picture of a soteriological cosmos that is radically unstable, in flux. This is entirely in keeping with that conception of a dynamic hereafter expounded by Christianity's first systematic theologian. Origen wrote that "in those *unseen and eternal* ages, . . . every rational being is able, passing from one order to another, to go from each order to all and from all to each, while it continues, through its faculty of free will, susceptible of promotions and demotions according to its own actions and efforts."[16] The closest parallel may be Hyrum Smith's interpretation of Joseph's quasi-universalism. Hyrum saw Joseph as teaching that no salvific state was static: "Hiram said Aug 1st. Those of the Terrestrial Glory either advance to the Celestial or recede to the Telestial or else the moon would not be a type, [because] it 'waxes & wanes.'"[17]

The caveat to the above, of course, is the presence and role of the "rod of iron." Even before we encounter Nephi's exegesis in subsequent chapters, we can infer this rod to be the word of God. The reason is that all the variables in this allegory are voices. A messenger's, Lehi's to his family, concourses of humans beckoning to one another. We are not confronted with attributes or actions: we are not told that Laman and Lemuel are rebellious, or that Sam is steadfast, that the wanderers are weak or sinful, or that those who secure the fruit are virtuous or obedient. Those who fall into mists or deathly waters listen to the wrong voices. Those who secure the fruit listen to Lehi—or follow the rod of iron. The rod of iron, as the word of God, is often assumed by Latter-day Saints to be scripture or prophetic utterance. This is possible, but the subsequent details of the vision prompt us to seek a richer explanation. How do we know when we have secured God's word? What if Lehi mistook a false messenger for a true one? What of Nephi's later words about the corruption of "plain and precious things" (1 Ne. 13:28–29) in the Bible? What

The Tree of Life: Cacophony, Risk, and Discernment

of Joseph's own early experience that "the same passages of scripture" can be understood "so differently as to destroy all confidence in settling the question by an appeal to the Bible" (JS-H 12). What of our own encounters with scriptures that seem problematic, historically inaccurate, or bafflingly contradictory? The pattern of the whole vision and the various responses of the vision's characters point us to a deeper understanding of the iron rod. It is God's word, yes; but God's word must be personally heard and discerned for it to be efficacious in our own alignment with the covenant path. The challenge for Lehi, his family and the throngs in his vision, as for us today, is the capacity for spiritual *discernment* of God's voice.

Following the pathways in the world of Lehi's vision is relatively simple. The problem that confronts the inhabitants of Lehi's dreamworld is discerning what guides to follow. So, too, did the Restoration begin with Joseph Smith's recognition of the unreliability of preachers and the Bible alike as sufficient guides.[18] Thus Joseph Smith's own experience, and the many pronouncements of himself and modern prophet alike, give priority to our responsibility to personally discern the "word of God." Assuming that phrase to have a simple one-to-one correspondence with the printed words of a canon does not comport with the world of Lehi's vision, the experience of Joseph Smith, or the teachings of modern prophets.[19] We are not let off the hook so easily; the task of searching out the divine voice is ongoing and endless. That is an unsettling realization, but it goes to the roots of the Christian tradition. The earliest document of Christian instruction—the *Didache*—makes discernment in the midst of an earthly cacophony of voices a primary principle of successful discipleship. More than half a dozen keys are given whereby a saint may know the true from the false prophet, those one should heed and those one should reject.[20] Of course Paul, as well as Joseph Smith, made such discernment a spiritual gift (1 Cor. 12:10; D&C 46:23). For Adam and Eve, it might be said, discernment was the first spiritual challenge they faced; it is more than coincidence that, textually speaking, one of the first great divisions between conventional and Restoration narratives is the belief of the Saints that Eve and Adam discerned correctly.

THE TREE OF LIFE AND THE NATURE OF GOD

A most striking revelation about God to come from Lehi's vision is the reciprocity of trust between God and the human that it implies. The world is a labyrinth, a perilous realm of terrors. Neither the pre-Restoration accounts of Creation, nor Lehi's vision, tell us *why* God would subject us to the myriad trials of life. Christian Gnostics felt justifiable revulsion for those readings that saw the Edenic setting as a simple test of obedience rather than an occasion for growth and spiritual education, an occasion to invite and then rebuff humanity's aspirations to godlike freedom.

> What kind of God is this? First, he envied Adam that he should eat from the tree of knowledge. . . . And secondly he said, "Adam, where are you?" And God does not have foreknowledge, since he did not know this from the beginning. And afterwards, he said, "Let us cast him [out] of this place lest he eat of the tree of life and live forever." Surely he has shown himself to be a malicious envier. And what kind of God is this?[21]

At first glance, this reading does not seem too terribly removed from the scenario described in the Book of Abraham:

> And there stood one among them that was like unto God, and he said unto those who were with him: We will go down, for there is space there, and we will take of these materials, and we will make an earth whereon these may dwell; And we will prove them herewith, to see if they will do all things whatsoever the Lord their God shall command them; And they who keep their first estate shall be added upon; and they who keep not their first estate shall not have glory in the same kingdom with those who keep their first estate; and they who keep their second estate shall have glory added upon their heads for ever and ever (3:24–26).

However, the 1828 Webster's dictionary suggests a magnificent alternative to that interpretation of Abraham 3:25. "Prove," the term's very first entry explains, means "to ascertain *some unknown quality* . . . by an experiment." Webster elaborates: "to experience . . . to gain certain knowledge by the operation of something on ourselves."[22]

Life, in other words, is a process of creative exposition. God's creative work is ongoing and proceeds hand in hand with our own. Lehi's vision tells us the end is no foregone conclusion. Latter-day Saints take rather more literally than most the Healer's words that he "will have all men to be saved" (1 Tim. 2:4). However, in utter contradistinction from the Protestant creeds,[23] which insist that everything that God wills comes to pass, the Book of Moses conveys a God of more limited sovereignty. That Enoch finds the God of "all eternity to all eternity" weeping is proof dispositive that what this God wills, and what unfolds in an agent-laden universe, are not in perfect sync (Moses 7). Together the two texts, Moses 7 and 1 Nephi 8, present us with a God who presides over a risky universe. However, it is risk in which both the humans and the God who anticipates so hopefully their companionship, together share.

PLATE 9. Kathleen Peterson, *A Father and Two Sons*, oil on mahogany wood panel, 12 × 39 inches, 2020.

Artwork:

A Father and Two Sons

KATHLEEN PETERSON

DURING HIS MARVELOUS VISION, LEHI PARTAKES OF THE BEAUTIFUL white fruit of the tree of life and is filled with exquisite joy. When he invites his family to also partake of the fruit and share in his joy, only Sariah, Sam, and Nephi respond, and Lehi finds to his sorrow that Laman and Laman will not. This painting depicts the passion of a loving father pleading with his sons to open themselves to the light and love of God. Lehi was trying to convey to his sons the importance of holding to truth and loving God and each other. Laman and Lemuel are typical young people trying to find their own voice and independence. They do not really want to be told what to do. It is possible Lehi did not have skills of persuasion, but it is very clear he loved his family and wanted what was best for them. The tree of life with its white fruit is represented in the background as the love of God, and the fruit on the sides represent life and growth. I have painted other depictions of Lehi's dream but this one was focused on the particular personal nature of father and sons and love.

A Father and Two Sons

Contributors

Jennifer Champoux is the director of the Book of Mormon Art Catalog and a scholar of the visual culture of The Church of Jesus Christ of Latter-day Saints. She previously taught art history as adjunct faculty at Northeastern University and various colleges. Her scholarship on religious art can be found in several articles in *BYU Studies* and she is currently writing a book on pioneer artist C. C. A. Christensen. She lives in Colorado with her husband and three children.

Caitlin Connolly is an artist, writer, and creative enthusiast. Since graduating in 2009 from the University of Utah with a BFA in Painting and Drawing, she has passionately pursued and cultivated her creative path. Driven by a curiosity of femininity, her work explores the visual and conceptual contradiction of softness and strength in a variety of mediums and themes. Born and raised in Utah, the only girl with three brothers, Caitlin grew up coloring the walls of the home of a flute-teaching mother and tool-savvy father. She currently works and lives in Provo, Utah, with her musician husband and twin boys. You can learn more about her at http://caitlinconnolly.com/.

D.C. native and Virginia-raised artist **Rose Datoc Dall** is a Filipina-American contemporary figurative painter known for her bold, unconventional colors, unique compositions, and linear graphic quality. While her figurative work is metaphorical and spiritual in a general way, her most iconic works are her devotional pieces on the life of the Savior. She is a three-time Purchase Award Winner of the International Art Competition held by The Church of Jesus Christ of Latter-day Saints. Several of her works are part of the permanent collections at the Church History Museum, Brigham Young University, and Southern Virginia University. Her work graces church buildings and meetinghouses worldwide, church publications, books, and magazines. Rose earned her BFA in Art History and Fine Art Studio in 1990 from Virginia Commonwealth University (VCUArts) in Richmond. Rose and her husband, Tim, raised their four children in Virginia but left their Virginia roots in 2019 and moved to Utah to live closer to their adult kids and three grandchildren. You can learn more about her work at https://www.rosedatocdall.com/.

José de Faria is a Portuguese painter who has been passionately dedicated to painting since his youth. His art reflects his overcoming of the suffering caused by intense chronic headaches that have plagued him for decades. It is in a profound spirituality that he finds the strength and motivation to celebrate God and His Creation. His work is a hymn to the greatness of the universe and the big achievements of humanity, including the epic of the Portuguese discoveries of new worlds. His work has been exhibited internationally and distinguished with several awards, the most recent of which were a gold medal of creativity at the 10th Carrousel Exhibition of the Louvre, the Giuliano Ottaviani Trophy for the city of Rome, the first prize at the contemporary art exhibition in Venice and, in October 2022, the silver medal awarded by the French Academy of Arts-Sciences-Lettres in Paris for his body of work. Most of his works belong to museums and private collections in Portugal and abroad.

Timothy Farrant is a Fellow in Religion at BYU. He completed his DPhil in Theology and Religion at the University of Oxford, and has interests in medieval and practical theology.

Megan Knobloch Geilman is a dedicated artist, freelance graphic designer, and stay-at-home mom currently residing in Provo, Utah. She studied art at the

California College of the Arts and Brigham Young University. She uses art historical references and symbolic objects to explore doctrine, history, and social issues within The Church of Jesus Christ of Latter-day Saints. Her current work can be seen at https://meganknoblochgeilman.com/ or on Instagram @ megan.knobloch.geilman.

Terryl Givens is a Neal A. Maxwell Senior Research Fellow. He formerly held the Jabez A. Bostwick Chair of English and was Professor of Literature and Religion at the University of Richmond. He is the author of many books about Latter-day Saint history and culture, including *Wrestling the Angel: The Foundations of Mormon Thought, Feeding the Flock: The Foundations of Mormon Practice*, and *By the Hand of Mormon: The American Scripture That Launched a New World Religion*, each with Oxford University Press. He is also co-author, with Fiona Givens, of *The God Who Weeps, The Crucible of Doubt, The Christ Who Heals*, and *All Things New: Rethinking Sin, Salvation and Everything in Between*.

Benjamin Keogh is a PhD candidate in Systematic and Historical Theology at the University of St Andrews. A native of Scotland, he lives in St Andrews with his wife and three children.

Kimberly Matheson is a Research Fellow at the Neal A. Maxwell Institute for Religious Scholarship. She received a PhD in theology from Loyola University Chicago and an MTS in philosophy of religion from Harvard Divinity School. She serves on the boards of the Latter-day Saint Theology Seminar and the Book of Mormon Studies Association, and is the author most recently of *Helaman: A Brief Theological Introduction* (Maxwell Institute, 2020).

Hildebrando de Melo was born in Angola, in the midst of civil war. He grew up mostly in Portugal, but later returned to the Angolan capital city of Luanda in 2000 where he established his studio at the headquarters of the Angolan National Union of Plastic Artists. Through his painting and sculpture, de Melo explores forms of expression, tests the limits of art, and reinvents folklore and popular culture. Crossing boundaries between figuration and abstraction, de Melo's work is often imbued with an original rawness that opposes the superfluous and disposable nature of the contemporary world. In a fusion of urbanity and elements of tribal African ritual and sculpture, de Melo's drawing expresses a state of mutability. In a metaphysical search for transformation through art, de Melo invents hybrids of living organisms and mythological creatures. His work explores the human condition, with a focus on lived materiality as well as the search for God and the spiritual. De Melo's work is eminently political in nature, drawing on Angolan history and his personal experience. In a rhizomatic exercise of returning order to chaos and reviving the still, Hildebrando de Melo's work converges the realms of the spiritual, the political, and the autobiographical.

Joy Nevada is a Scottish illustrator inspired by nature and the people around her. Whilst studying Design, she found her passion lay in drawing and she has since been commissioned to produce works for many private and commercial clients and institutions such as Historic Royal Palaces, MIT, and The National Gallery of Art in Washington, D.C. You can find out more about her work at joynevada.com and on Instagram @joynevada

Born in Provo, Utah, **Kathleen B. Peterson** received a BA in commercial art from Brigham Young University and continued her artistic studies at the University of Hawaii and Snow College. Her work has been displayed in galleries throughout Utah as well as in Malaysia, Hawaii, and Jackson Hole, Wyoming. She paints landscapes, architecture, and people, using oils, water-colors, pastels, and batik. Kathy also enjoys illustrating books and publications, including *A World of Faith* (by Peggy Fletcher Stack, featuring 28 world religions), *Stones of the Temple* (by Fred Voros about the building of the Salt Lake Temple), seven books of fables (by Carol Lynn Pearson including *The Lesson*, *What Love Is*, *Will You Still Be My Daughter*, *A Strong Man*, *Girlfriend*, *The Gift*, and *Sisters*), *Koa's Seed: Pele and Poliahu, A Tale of Fire and Ice* (a Hawaiian legend by Carolyn Han), *Girls Who Choose God* (Book 1: *Women in the Bible*, Book 2: *Women in the Book of Mormon*, and Book 3: *Women in Church History* by McArthur Krishna and Bethany Brady Spalding). You can learn more about her work at https://www.kathleenpetersonart.com.

Annie Poon is a profilic multimeadia artist, animator, printmaker, author, and musician. When she was growing up in the woods Connecticut as the middle child in a family of nine, her mother used to take her out of elementary school to explore the Metropolitan Museum of Art in New York. Later, she earned a BFA in drawing and painting from the School of Visual Arts in Manhattan, where she still lives and works. Her animation *The Runaway Bathtub* is included in the permanent collection of the Museum of Modern Art. Over the last decade she has illustrated hundreds of chapters of the standard works and published several books, including the recent *Color Your Way through The New*

Testament: A Come Follow Me Companion. Follow her work at www.anniepoon. com and on social media @anniepoon.

Joseph M. Spencer is a philosopher and an associate professor of ancient scripture at Brigham Young University. He is the author or editor of many books on the Book of Mormon, and the author of dozens of essays on philosophy, theology, and scripture. He served for six years as the editor of the *Journal of Book of Mormon Studies,* and he serves currently as the associate director of the Latter-day Saint Theology Seminar and in the leadership of the Book of Mormon Studies Association.

The **Revd. Dr. Andrew R. Teal** has been in public ministry in the Church of England since 1988, the last twenty years of which have been in the academy. He is Fellow, Chaplain, and tutor in Patristic and Modern Theology in Pembroke College in Oxford University, where he has served since 2008. In November 2018, he hosted and accommodated the visit of Elder Jeffrey R. Holland to Oxford to participate in lectures and panel presentations with leading Anglican, Catholic, Orthodox, and Methodist scholars in an event called Inspiring Service. This led to a delightful, lively, and committed relationship with The Church of Jesus Christ of Latter-day Saints, with a desire to heal schism and promote understanding and mutual advocacy. He has visited Utah for General Conferences and was a visiting resident affiliate scholar at the Neal A. Maxwell Institute of Brigham Young University in Provo in 2021. He is married to Rachel, a stroke researcher at Oxford University Hospitals Trust. Together they have two children.

Kylie Nielson Turley is an adjunct faculty member in BYU's Department of Ancient Scripture and in BYU's English Department. She teaches writing and rhetoric courses, Book of Mormon courses, and a course on the "Literature of the LDS People." She is the author of *Alma 1–29: A Brief Theological Introduction* and has published academic articles on topics ranging from Alma and Book of Mormon studies to settlement-era Utah politics and LDS women's death poetry. She also writes creatively and has published numerous creative nonfiction essays.

Rosalynde Frandsen Welch is a research fellow at Brigham Young University's Neal A. Maxwell Institute for Religious Scholarship. She holds a PhD in early modern English literature from the University of California at San Diego. She is the author of *Ether: A Brief Theological Introduction* and, with Adam Miller,

Seven Gospels: The Many Lives of Christ in the Book of Mormon. Her work has also appeared in *BYU Studies, Element, Journal of Book of Mormon Studies, Mormon Studies Review,* and numerous edited volumes. Her research focuses on literature, scripture, and theology. She lives in Provo, Utah, with her family.

Sarah Winegar is a printmaker and painter who creates in the after hours of her full-time work, which is raising her kids. She and her husband live in Utah where she paints from the kitchen table and prints at Saltgrass Printmakers. Her work is about being at home and the complex simplicity of day to day living. Her work can be viewed at https://www.sarahwinegar.com/ or on Instagram @sarah_winegar_art.

Notes

Introduction

BENJAMIN KEOGH

1. Gerhard Lohfink, *Jesus of Nazareth: What He Wanted, Who He Was*, Linda M. Maloney, trans., (Collegeville: Liturgical Press, 2011), 11.
2. Lohfink, *Jesus of Nazareth*, 12.
3. Lohfink, *Jesus of Nazareth*, 13.
4. Lohfink, *Jesus of Nazareth*, 11.
5. See Paula Fredriksen, *From Jesus to Christ: The Origins of the New Testament Images of Jesus* (New Haven: Yale University Press, 2000), 18–61.
6. Donald M. Baillie, *God Was in Christ*, (London: Faber and Faber, 1961), 188.
7. The variety of accounts include ransom, substitution, satisfaction, and victory. For an accessible introduction to the variety of atonement accounts see Oliver

Crisp, *Approaching Atonement: The Reconciling Work of Christ* (Downers Grove: InterVarsity Press, 2020).

8. Ben Pugh, *Pictures of Atonement: A New Testament Study* (Eugene: Cascade Books, 2020).

9. Theodore Vial, *Schleiermacher: A Guide for the Perplexed* (London: Bloomsbury, 2013), 83.

10. Lawrence Kushner, *God Was in This Place & I, i Did Not Know: Finding Self, Spirituality and Ultimate Meaning* (Woodstock: Jewish Lights Publishing, 2010), 12.

11. Kushner, *God Was in This Place*, 11–12.

12. Terence E. Fretheim, *The Suffering of God: An Old Testament Perspective* (Philadelphia: Fortress Press, 1984), 1 (emphasis in original).

13. Terence E. Fretheim and Karlfried Froelich, *The Bible as Word of God: In a Postmodern Age* (Eugene: Wipf and Stock, 2001), 89–90.

14. There are two stylistic notes readers should be aware of: first, three of our essayists—Benjamin Keogh, the Rev'd Dr. Andrew Teal, and Timothy Farrant—are from the UK. In an effort to maintain the authenticity of their voices British spelling has been retained in their essays, and in this Introduction; second, throughout the volume references to verses with no specified chapter or book of scripture will apply strictly to 1 Nephi 8.

Wandering in Strange Roads: Interpretations of Lehi's Dream

JOSEPH M. SPENCER

1. I follow here the textual reconstruction in Royal Skousen, ed., *The Book of Mormon: The Earliest Text* (New Haven: Yale University Press, 2009), although I take the liberty of reworking Skousen's proposed punctuation of the text. This includes italicizing words within the text.

2. This approach to this text is something Kylie Turley addresses in her contribution to this volume.

3. Others have sketched the history of how leaders of The Church of Jesus Christ of Latter-day Saints have interpreted the dream. See Mary Jane Woodger and Michelle Vanegas Brodrick, "Lehi's Dream and Nephi's Vision as Used by Church Leaders," in *The Things Which My Father Saw: Approaches to Lehi's Dream and Nephi's Vision*, eds. Daniel L. Belnap, Gaye Streathearn, and Stanley A. Johnson (Salt Lake City and Provo, UT: Deseret Book and BYU Religious Studies Center, 2011), 374–92. In addition, of course, the history of artistic portrayals of the dream is the subject of Jenny Champoux's essay in the present volume.

4. On Pratt's editorial work on the Book of Mormon (in which he offered, through the footnotes he introduced into the text, various interpretations of the dream of the tree of life), see Richard E. Turley Jr. and William W. Slaughter, *How We Got the Book of Mormon* (Salt Lake City: Deseret Book, 2011), 80–91; and Paul Gutjahr, "Orson Pratt's Enduring Influence on *The Book of Mormon*," in *Americanist Approaches to The Book of Mormon*, eds. Elizabeth Fenton and Jared Hickman (New York: Oxford University Press, 2019), 83–104.

5. Reynolds's and Sjodahl's most interesting comments were gathered into a running commentary on the text in George Reynolds and Jane M. Sjodahl, *Commentary on the Book of Mormon*, 7 vols., ed. Philip C. Reynolds (Salt Lake City: Deseret Book, 1955). Roberts's most important works on the Book of Mormon are B. H. Roberts, *New Witnesses for God*, 3 vols. (Salt Lake City: George Q. Cannon & Sons, 1909); and B. H. Roberts, *Studies of the Book of Mormon*, ed. Brigham D. Madsen (Urbana and Chicago: University of Illinois Press, 1985).

6. For important recent studies of these crucial forefathers of Book of Mormon studies, see Amy Easton-Flake, "Knowing the Book Better: Orson Pratt, George Reynolds, and Janne M. Sjödahl on the Book of Mormon," *Journal of Book of Mormon Studies* 30 (2021): 41–61; and Matthew Bowman, "Biblical Criticism, the Book of Mormon, and the Meanings of Civilization," *Journal of Book of Mormon Studies* 30 (2021): 62–89.

7. Sidney B. Sperry, *Our Book of Mormon* (Salt Lake City: Bookcraft, 1947), 83.

8. Sperry, *Our Book of Mormon*, 127.

9. Sperry, *Our Book of Mormon*, 128.

10. Sperry would reprint his 1940s interpretation of the dream more or less without alteration in his last major work on the Book of Mormon in the 1960s. See Sidney B. Sperry, *Book of Mormon Compendium* (Salt Lake City: Bookcraft, 1968), 112–14.

11. Hugh Nibley, "Lehi in the Desert, Part III," *The Improvement Era* 53, no. 3 (March 1950): 200.

12. Nibley, "Lehi in the Desert," 200.

13. Nibley, "Lehi in the Desert," 200.

14. Nibley, "Lehi in the Desert," 200.

15. See Hugh Nibley, *Lehi in the Desert and the World of the Jaredites* (Salt Lake City: Bookcraft, 1952), 47–51.

16. See Eldin Ricks, *Book of Mormon Commentary*, vol. 1: *Comprising the Complete Text of the First Book of Nephi with Explanatory Notes* (Salt Lake City: Deseret News Press, 1953), 96–106.

17. See Boyd Jay Petersen, *Hugh Nibley: A Consecrated Life* (Salt Lake City: Greg Kofford Books, 2002), 249–52.

18. See Hugh Nibley, *An Approach to the Book of Mormon* (Salt Lake City: The Council of the Twelve Apostles of The Church of Jesus Christ of Latter-day Saints, 1957), 217–28.

19. Nibley, *An Approach to the Book of Mormon*, 366.

20. Nibley, *An Approach to the Book of Mormon*, 1.

21. See M. Wells Jakeman, "An Unusual Tree-of-Life Sculpture from Ancient Central America," *Bulletin of the University Archaeological Society* 4 (1953): 26–49.

22. All this history is covered well and in great detail—along with detailed bibliographical information for relevant publications—in Stewart W. Brewer, "The History of an Idea: The Scene on Stela 5 from Izapa, Mexico, as a Representation of Lehi's Vision of the Tree of Life," *Journal of Book of Mormon Studies* 8, no. 1 (1999): 12–21, 77.

23. Jakeman, "An Unusual Tree-of-Life Sculpture," 35.

24. Jakeman, "An Unusual Tree-of-Life Sculpture," 48–49.

25. See Brewer, "The History of an Idea," 17–18.

26. See M. Wells Jakeman, *The Complex "Tree-of-Life" Carving on Izapa Stela 5: A Reanalysis and Partial Interpretation* (Provo, UT: Brigham Young University, 1958), 34–47.

27. M. Wells Jakeman, *Stela 5, Izapa, Chiapas, Mexico: A Major Archaeological Discovery of the New World, Detailed Commentary on the Carving* (Provo, UT: Brigham Young University, 1958), 8.

28. V. Garth Norman, *Izapa Sculpture, Part 2: Text* (Provo, UT: Brigham Young University, 1976), 167.

29. Brewer, "The History of an Idea," 77.

30. See V. Garth Norman, "I Have a Question: What Is the Current Status of Research Concerning the 'Tree of Life' Carving from Chiapas, Mexico?" *Ensign* 15 (June 1985): 54–55.

31. For a further endorsement of this view from the later 1980s, see Alan K. Parrish, "Stela 5, Izapa: A Layman's Consideration of the Tree of Life Stone," in *First Nephi, The Doctrinal Foundation*, eds. Monte S. Nyman and Charles D. Tate, Jr. (Provo, UT: BYU Religious Studies Center, 1988), 125–50.

32. For a light-hearted lampooning of the continued devotion expressed toward Izapa Stela 5, see Avi Steinberg, *The Lost Book of Mormon: A Journey through the Mythic Lands of Nephi, Zarahemla, and Kansas City, Missouri* (New York: Doubleday, 2014), 143–47.

33. Davis Bitton, ed., *Mormons, Scripture, and the Ancient World: Studies in Honor of John L. Sorenson* (Provo, UT: FARMS, 1998), xviii.

34. See especially John L. Sorenson, "Ancient America and the Book of Mormon Revisited," *Dialogue: A Journal of Mormon Thought* 4, no. 3 (Summer 1969):

80–94; and John L. Sorenson, "The 'Brass Plates' and Biblical Scholarship," *Dialogue: A Journal of Mormon Thought* 10, no. 4 (Autumn 1977): 31–39.

35. See John L. Sorenson, *An Ancient American Setting for the Book of Mormon* (Salt Lake City and Provo, UT: Deseret Book and FARMS, 1985). Brant Gardner sees a slight allusion to the monument in Sorenson's comments on the name "Lehi." See Brant A. Gardner, *Second Witness: Analytical and Contextual Commentary on the Book of Mormon*, 6 vols. (Salt Lake City: Greg Kofford Books, 2007), 1:166.

36. See John W. Welch, "Connections between the Visions of Lehi and Nephi," in *Pressing Forward with the Book of Mormon* (Provo, UT: FARMS, 1999), 49–53.

37. See John W. Welch and Donald W. Parry, eds., *The Tree of Life: From Eden to Eternity* (Salt Lake City and Provo, UT: Deseret Book and Neal A. Maxwell Institute, 2011).

38. See Sperry, *Our Book of Mormon*, 82. In almost the same year, Fawn Brodie wrote that "the prose style" of the Book of Mormon "was unfortunate," its sentences "loose-jointed, like an earthworm hacked into segments that crawl away alive and whole." Fawn M. Brodie, *No Man Knows My History: The Life of Joseph Smith, the Mormon Prophet*, 2nd ed. (New York: Vintage Books, 1995), 63.

39. See John W. Welch, "Chiasmus in the Book of Mormon," *BYU Studies Quarterly* 10, no. 1 (1969): 1–15. A half-century after Welch's initial publication, interest in chiasmus remains strong. See, for instance, the essays and perhaps especially the selected bibliography in the 2020 supplementary issue of *BYU Studies Quarterly* (volume 59), jointly edited by John W. Welch and Donald W. Parry.

40. See Robert E. Nichols, Jr., "Beowulf and Nephi: A Literary View of the Book of Mormon," *Dialogue: A Journal of Mormon Thought* 4, no. 3 (Autumn 1969): 40–47; and Douglas Wilson, "Prospects for the Study of the Book of Mormon as a Work of American Literature," *Dialogue: A Journal of Mormon Thought* 3, no. 1 (Spring 1968): 29–41.

41. See Robert K. Thomas, "A Literary Critical Looks at the Book of Mormon," in *To the Glory of God: Mormon Essays on Great Issues*, no ed. (Salt Lake City: Deseret Book, 1972), 147–61.

42. Nichols, "Beowulf and Nephi," 43.

43. See Wilson, "Prospects for the Study of the Book of Mormon as a Work of American Literature," 38. Often cited but apparently impossible to find today is another late-1970s essay on Lehi's dream by a BYU student: Courtney J. Lassetter, "Lehi's Dream and Nephi's Vision: A Look at Structure and Theme in the Book of Mormon," *Perspective: A Journal of Critical Inquiry* (Winter 1976): 50–54.

44. Bruce W. Jorgensen, "The Dark Way to the Tree: Typological Unity in the Book of Mormon," in *Literature of Belief: Sacred Scripture and Religious Experience*, ed.

Neal E. Lambert (Provo, UT: BYU Religious Studies Center, 1981), 221. This essay was originally published in *Encyclia* 54, no. 2 (1977): 16–24.

45. Jorgensen, "The Dark Way to the Tree," 222.

46. Jorgensen, "The Dark Way to the Tree," 226.

47. See especially George S. Tate, "The Typology of the Exodus Pattern in the Book of Mormon," in *Literature of Belief*, 245–62; and Steven P. Sondrup, "The Psalm of Nephi: A Lyric Reading," *BYU Studies Quarterly* 21, no. 3 (1981): 357–72.

48. See Richard Dilworth Rust, *Feasting on the Word: The Literary Testimony of the Book of Mormon* (Salt Lake City and Provo, UT: Deseret Book and FARMS, 1997), 54, 172, 179–81.

49. For a celebration of all these developments—with a mention also of Noel Reynolds's early work on a possible structure for 1 Nephi—see Eugene England, "A Second Witness for the *Logos*: The Book of Mormon and Contemporary Literary Criticism," in *By Study and Also By Faith*, vol. 2, *Essays in Honor of Hugh W. Nibley on the Occasion of His Eightieth Birthday, 27 March 1990* (Salt Lake City and Provo, UT: Deseret Book and FARMS, 1990), 91–100.

50. Mark Thomas, "Lehi's Dream: An American Apocalypse," in *Proceedings of the Symposia of the Association for Mormon Letters, 1979–82* (Salt Lake City: Association for Mormon Letters, 1983), 93. Thomas's strong focus on genre with respect to apocalyptic literature is very much in tune with literary biblical studies in the 1970s, during which decade the literary genre of the apocalyptic received intense interest. See the helpful overview in John J. Collins, "What Is Apocalyptic Literature?" in *The Oxford Handbook of Apocalyptic Literature*, ed. John J. Collins (New York: Oxford University Press, 2014), 1–16. It might be noted that subsequent readers have certainly agreed that Nephi's vision fits the apocalyptic genre well. See, for example, Stephen E. Robinson, "Early Christianity and 1 Nephi 13–14," in *First Nephi, the Doctrinal Foundation*, 177–91; and Shon D. Hopkin, "Seeing Eye to Eye: Nephi's and John's Intertwining Visions of the Tree of Life," in *Apocalypse: Reading Revelation 21–22*, ed. Julie M. Smith (Provo, UT: Neal A. Maxwell Institute, 2016), 66–84.

51. Thomas, "Lehi's Dream," 92–93.

52. Thomas, "Lehi's Dream," 96.

53. Mark D. Thomas, *Digging in Cumorah: Reclaiming Book of Mormon Narratives* (Salt Lake City: Signature Books, 1999), 107.

54. Thomas, *Digging in Cumorah*, 108.

55. Thomas, *Digging in Cumorah*, 109.

56. Jorgensen, "The Dark Way to the Tree," 227.

57. Rust's project would eventually appear as the sole-authored *Feasting on the Word* in 1997, and Jorgensen would explain why his project had never materialized in Bruce W. Jorgensen, "Alma's Wisdom-Poem to Helaman (Alma 37:35–37)," in

Perspectives on Mormon Theology: Scriptural Theology, eds. James E. Faulconer and Joseph M. Spencer (Salt Lake City: Greg Kofford Books, 2015), 97–99.

58. For a helpful review of a whole variety of converging events in the late 1970s and early 1980s regarding questions of the Book of Mormon's spiritual value, see John-Charles Duffy, "Mapping Book of Mormon Historicity Debates—Part 1: A Guide for the Overwhelmed," *Sunstone: Mormon Experience, Scholarship, Issues, and Art* 151 (October 2008): 41–42. See also, more generally, Massimo Introvigne, "The Book of Mormon Wars: A Non-Mormon Perspective," *Journal of Book of Mormon Studies* 5, no. 2 (1996): 1–25.

59. See, for instance, Anthony A. Hutchinson, "The Word of God Is Enough: The Book of Mormon as Nineteenth-Century Scripture," in *New Approaches to the Book of Mormon: Explorations in Critical Methodology*, ed. Brent Lee Metcalfe (Salt Lake City: Signature Books, 1993), 1–52; and Robert M. Price, "Joseph Smith: Inspired Author of the Book of Mormon," in *American Apocrypha: Essays on the Book of Mormon*, eds. Dan Vogel and Brent Lee Metcalfe (Salt Lake City: Signature Books, 2002), 321–66.

60. For some discussion, see Terryl L. Givens, *By the Hand of Mormon: The American Scripture that Launched a New World Religion* (New York: Oxford University Press, 2002), 240–46.

61. See Julie Adams Maddox, "Lehi's Vision of the Tree of Life: An Anagogic Interpretation" (M.A. Thesis, Brigham Young University, 1986). This thesis deserves much more attention than it has received.

62. See Bruce R. McConkie, *Doctrinal New Testament Commentary*, 3 vols. (Salt Lake City: Bookcraft, 1965–73).

63. One potential exception—although it never dwells on the details of the dream, only on Nephi's quotation and then abridgment of Lehi's original source—is S. Kent Brown, "Lehi's Personal Record: Quest for a Missing Source," *BYU Studies Quarterly* 24, no. 1 (1984): 19–42.

64. Kent P. Jackson, "The Tree of Life and the Ministry of Christ," in *Studies in Scripture*, vol. 7: *1 Nephi to Alma 29*, ed. Kent P. Jackson (Salt Lake City: Deseret Book, 1987), 35.

65. Susan Easton Black, "'Behold, I Have Dreamed a Dream,'" in *The Book of Mormon: First Nephi, the Doctrinal Foundation*, eds. Monte S. Nyman and Charles D. Tate, Jr. (Provo, UT: BYU Religious Studies Center, 1988), 117–18.

66. Joseph Fielding McConkie and Robert L. Millet, *Doctrinal Commentary on the Book of Mormon*, vol. 1—*First and Second Nephi* (Salt Lake City: Bookcraft, 1987), 55.

67. McConkie and Millet, *Doctrinal Commentary*, 56.

68. McConkie and Millet, *Doctrinal Commentary*, 58. For examples of others working from a variety of distinct interpretive perspectives who nonetheless draw on

this interpretation, see Raymond C. Treat, "The Four Levels," in *Recent Book of Mormon Development: Articles from the Zarahemla Record*, vol. 1 (Independence, MO: Zarahemla Research Foundation, 1992), 148–53; Jeffrey R. Holland, *Christ and the New Covenant: The Messianic Message of the Book of Mormon* (Salt Lake City: Deseret Book, 1997), 161–62; John A. Tvedtnes, *The Most Correct Book* (Salt Lake City and Phoenix: Cornerstone, 1999), 113–15; and Jana Riess, ed., *The Book of Mormon: Selections Annotated and Explained* (Woodstock, VT: Skylight Paths, 2005), 20–21.

69. Louis Midgley, "Prophetic Messages or Dogmatic Theology? Commenting on the Book of Mormon: A Review Essay," *Review of Books on the Book of Mormon* 1, no. 1 (1989): 104.

70. Hugh W. Nibley, *Teachings of the Book of Mormon, Semester 1: Transcripts of Lectures Presented to an Honors Book of Mormon Class at Brigham Young University, 1988–1990* (Provo, UT: FARMS, 1993), 174.

71. Kevin Christensen, "'Nigh unto Death': NDS Research and the Book of Mormon," *Journal of Book of Mormon Studies* 2, no. 1 (Spring 1993): 15.

72. Jeanette W. Miller, "The Tree of Life, a Personification of Jesus Christ," *Journal of Book of Mormon Studies* 2, no. 1 (Spring 1993): 102–3.

73. Corbin T. Volluz, "Lehi's Dream of the Tree of Life: Springboard to Prophecy," *Journal of Book of Mormon Studies* 2, no. 2 (Fall 1993): 37–38.

74. See Alan Goff, "Boats, Beginnings, and Repetitions," *Journal of Book of Mormon Studies* 1, no. 1 (1992): 67–84.

75. See, again, Rust, *Feasting on the Word*, 54, 172, 179–81.

76. See Marilyn Arnold, "Unlocking the Sacred Text," in *Expressions of Faith: Testimonies of Latter-day Saint Scholars*, ed. Susan Easton Black (Salt Lake City and Provo, UT: Deseret Book and FARMS, 1996), 193–200. FARMS would publish this essay again in a 1999 issue of the *Journal of Book of Mormon Studies*.

77. Marilyn Arnold, *Sweet Is the Word: Reflections on the Book of Mormon: Its Narrative, Teachings, and People* (American Fork, UT: Covenant Communications, 1996), 12.

78. Marilyn Arnold, *Sweet Is the Word*, 13.

79. See issue 6, no. 1 (1994) throughout. Further responses appeared in issues 7, no. 1 (1995), 7, no. 2 (1995), and 8.1 (1996) of the same journal. Thomas has an essay in the book that spurred such strong responses, deepening the impression made by his decision to publish *Digging in Cumorah* with Signature Books.

80. Thomas, *Digging in Cumorah*, ix.

81. Alan Goff, "Scratching the Surface of Book of Mormon Narratives," *FARMS Review of Books* 12, no. 2 (2000): 51–52.

82. Grant Hardy, "Speaking So That All May Be Edified," *FARMS Review of Books* 12, no. 2 (2000): 85.

83. Hardy, "Speaking So That All May Be Edified," 94.

84. He gives just two pages—but two incisive pages—to it; see Grant Hardy, *Understanding the Book of Mormon: A Reader's Guide* (New York: Oxford University Press, 2010), 53–55.

85. Grant Hardy, "Prophetic Perspectives: How Lehi and Nephi Applied the Lessons of Lehi's Dream," in *The Things Which My Father Saw*, 201.

86. Hardy, "Prophetic Perspectives, 202–3.

87. Hardy, "Prophetic Perspectives, 204.

88. Hardy, "Prophetic Perspectives, 207.

89. Daniel L. Belnap, "'Even as Our Father Lehi Saw': Lehi's Dream as Nephite Cultural Narrative," in *The Things Which My Father Saw*, 233. In many ways, so does Matthew L. Bowen, "Not Partaking of the Fruit: Its Generational Consequences and Its Remedy," in *The Things Which My Father Saw*, 240–63.

90. A somewhat similar thesis appears in the brief treatment of Lehi's dream and Nephi's vision in Steven L. Olsen, "Prophecy and History: Structuring the Abridgment of the Nephite Records," *Journal of Book of Mormon Studies* 15, no. 1 (2006): 24–27.

91. See Jared M. Halverson, "Lehi's Dream and Nephi's Vision as Apocalyptic Literature," in *The Things Which My Father Saw*, 53–69.

92. See Heather Hardy, "The Double Nature of God's Saving Work: The Plan of Salvation and Salvation History," in *The Things Which My Father Saw*, 17.

93. See Jared T. Parker, "The Doctrine of Christ in 2 Nephi 31–32 as an Approach to the Vision of the Tree of Life," in *The Things Which My Father Saw*, 161–78.

94. Amy Easton-Flake, "Lehi's Dream as a Template for Understanding Each Act of Nephi's Vision," in *The Things Which My Father Saw*, 183.

95. Easton-Flake, "Lehi's Dream as a Template," 186.

96. Easton-Flake, "Lehi's Dream as a Template," 188.

97. Easton-Flake, "Lehi's Dream as a Template," 190.

98. Easton-Flake, "Lehi's Dream as a Template," 194.

99. Charles L. Swift, "'I Have Dreamed a Dream': Typological Images of Teaching and Learning in the Vision of the Tree of Life" (PhD dissertation, Brigham Young University, 2003), 41. The experiential dimension of the literary is also the focus of Swift's contribution to the Sperry Symposium of 2011; see Charles Swift, "'It Filled My Soul with Exceedingly Great Joy': Lehi's Vision of Teaching and Learning," in *The Things Which My Father Saw*, 347–73. The archetypal dimension of the dream is the focus of another of Swift's later essays; see Charles Swift, "'I Have Dreamed a Dream': Lehi's Archetypal Vision of the Tree of Life," in *The Tree of Life: From Eden to Eternity*, 129–49.

100. See Swift, "'I Have Dreamed a Dream': Typological Images of Teaching and Learning in the Vision of the Tree of Life," 111–12.

101. Swift, "'I Have Dreamed a Dream,'" 140. This might be compared with the more (Carl) Jungian interpretation of the same elemental opposition in Maddox, "Lehi's Vision of the Tree of Life," 24–29—as well as with one of Swift's subsequent published essays: Charles Swift, "Lehi's Vision of the Tree of Life: Understanding the Dream as Visionary Literature," *Journal of Book of Mormon Studies* 14, no. 2 (2005): 55–56.

102. Swift, "'I Have Dreamed a Dream': Typological Images of Teaching and Learning in the Vision of the Tree of Life," 141.

103. Swift, "'I Have Dreamed a Dream,'" 145.

104. Swift, "'I Have Dreamed a Dream,'" 147.

105. See Gardner, *Second Witness*, 152–81.

106. See S. Kent Brown, "New Light from Arabia on Lehi's Trail," in *Echoes and Evidences of the Book of Mormon*, ed. Donald W. Parry, Daniel C. Peterson, and John W. Welch (Provo, UT: FARMS, 2002), 64–69.

107. See Dana M. Pike, "Lehi Dreamed a Dream: The Report of Lehi's Dream in Its Biblical Context," in *The Things Which My Father Saw*, 92–118.

108. See especially Aaron Schade, "The Strait and Narrow Path: The Covenant Path of Discipleship Leading to the Tree of Life," in *The Things Which My Father Saw*, 135–60; and C. Robert Line, "Bitter and Sweet: Dual Dimensions of the Tree of Life," in *The Things Which My Father Saw*, 318–29. For a slightly earlier and classically doctrinal study, see Matthew O. Richardson, "Vision, Voice, Path, and Rod: Coming to Partake of the Fulness," in *The Fulness of the Gospel: Foundational Teachings from the Book of Mormon*, eds. Camille Fronk Olson, Brian M. Hauglid, Patty Smith, and Thomas A. Wayment (Salt Lake City and Provo, UT: Deseret Book and BYU Religious Studies Center, 2003), 26–38.

109. See Monte S. Nyman, *I Nephi Wrote This Record: Book of Mormon Commentary* (Orem, UT: Granite Press, 2004), 96–109, 114–17; and, often more practical than doctrinal in orientation but within the same interpretive tradition, D. Kelly Ogden and Andrew C. Skinner, *Verse by Verse: The Book of Mormon*, 2 vols. (Salt Lake City: Deseret Book, 2011), 1:37–42.

110. Givens, *By the Hand of Mormon*, 63–64.

111. See the manifesto of sorts that opens the first volume of the Seminar's proceedings: Adam S. Miller, ed., *An Experiment on the Word: Reading Alma 32* (Salem, OR: Salt Press, 2011), 1–8.

112. Note that, in the decade that followed, important works of a theological interpretation of the Book of Mormon curiously lack any treatment of Lehi's dream. See, for example, James E. Faulconer, *The Book of Mormon Made Harder: Scripture Study Questions* (Provo, UT: Neal A. Maxwell Institute, 2014); Joseph M. Spencer, *An Other Testament: On Typology*, 2nd ed. (Provo, UT: Neal A. Maxwell Institute, 2016); and John Christopher Thomas, *A Pentecostal Reads the*

Book of Mormon: A Literary and Theological Introduction (Cleveland, TN: CPT Press, 2016).

113. Already in By the Hand of Mormon itself, Givens moderates this position by providing some theological readings of texts scattered throughout the volume. See especially Givens, By the Hand of Mormon, 185–239.

114. Terryl L. Givens, The Book of Mormon: A Very Short Introduction (New York: Oxford University Press, 2009), 20.

115. Givens, The Book of Mormon, 18.

116. Givens, The Book of Mormon, 19.

117. Joseph M. Spencer, 1st Nephi: A Brief Theological Introduction (Provo, UT: Neal A. Maxwell Institute, 2020), 28.

118. Spencer, 1st Nephi, 29.

119. For the larger theological framework assumed in my study of Lehi's dream, see Joseph M. Spencer, The Vision of All: Twenty-five Lectures on Isaiah in Nephi's Record (Salt Lake City: Greg Kofford Books, 2016), 1–11, 37–117.

120. See Bradley J. Kramer, Beholding the Tree of Life: A Rabbinic Approach to the Book of Mormon (Salt Lake City: Greg Kofford Books, 2014), 3–21.

121. Robert L. Millet and James C. Christensen, Lehi's Dream (Salt Lake City: Deseret Book, 2011), 30.

122. Millet and Christensen, Lehi's Dream, 48.

123. See Matthew Scott Stenson, "Lehi's Dream and Nephi's Vision: Apocalyptic Revelations in Narrative Context," BYU Studies Quarterly 51, no. 4 (2012): 159–65.

124. David Calabro, "Lehi's Dream and the Garden of Eden," Interpreter: A Journal of Mormon Scripture 26 (2017): 271.

125. Calabro, "Lehi's Dream and the Garden of Eden," 296.

126. Michael Austin, Buried Treasures: Reading the Book of Mormon Again for the First Time (Salt Lake City: BCC Press, 2017), 15.

127. See Daniel C. Peterson, "Nephi and His Asherah," Journal of Book of Mormon Studies 9, no. 2 (2000): 16–25, 80–81; as well as Brant A. Gardner, Second Witness: Analytical and Contextual Commentary on the Book of Mormon, 6 vols. (Salt Lake City: Greg Kofford Books, 2007), 1:153–60; and John S. Thompson, "The Lady at the Horizon: Egyptian Tree Goddess Iconography and Sacred Trees in Israelite Scripture and Temple Theology," Interpreter: A Journal of Latter-day Saint Faith and Scholarship 38 (2020): 153–78.

128. Daniel C. Peterson, "Nephi and His Asherah: A Note on 1 Nephi 11:8–23," in Mormons, Scripture, and the Ancient World: Studies in Honor of John L. Sorenson, ed. Davis Bitton (Provo, UT: FARMS, 1998), 218.

129. Among Barker's writings, see especially Margaret Barker, The Mother of Lord, vol. 1, The Lady in the Temple (New York: Bloomsbury T&T Clark, 2012). For a

systematic exposition of Barker's writings—now somewhat dated—in terms of their potential relevance to Latter-day Saints, see Kevin Christensen, *Paradigms Regained: A Survey of Margaret Barker's Scholarship and Its Significance for Mormon Studies* (Provo, UT: FARMS, 2001); for a provocative Latter-day Saint review of Barker's *The Mother of Lord*, see Zina Petersen, "Where Shall Wisdom Be Found?" *Interpreter: A Journal of Latter-day Saint Faith and Scholarship* 7 (2013): 71–112.

130. See Alyson Skabelund Von Feldt, "Does God Have a Wife," *FARMS Review* 19, no. 1 (2007): 81–118; Kevin L. Barney, "How to Worship Our Mother in Heaven (Without Getting Excommunicated)," *Dialogue: A Journal of Mormon Thought* 41, no. 4 (2008): 121–46; and Val Larsen, "Hidden in Plain View: Mother in Heaven in Scripture," *SquareTwo* 8, no. 2 (Summer 2015), http://squaretwo.org/Sq2ArticleLarsenHeavenlyMother.html. For such an interpretation even in a more strictly devotional and more obviously traditional treatment, see Heather Farrell, *Walking with the Women of the Book of Mormon* (Springville, UT: CFI, 2019), 22–23.

131. This tradition of interpretation begins, in a somewhat critical vein, with Carol Lynn Pearson, "Could Feminism Have Saved the Nephites?" *Sunstone Magazine* 19, no. 1 (March 1996): 32–40.

132. See, to take one example, Kathryn Knight Sonntag, *The Tree at the Center* (Salt Lake City: BCC Press, 2019). It seems important to note that this connection is either overlooked or deliberately rejected in the strongly political commentary offered in Fatimah Salleh and Margaret Olsen Hemming, *The Book of Mormon for the Least of These: 1 Nephi–Words of Mormon* (Salt Lake City: BCC Press, 2020), 18–21.

133. Hugh Nibley, *An Approach to the Book of Mormon*, 3rd ed., ed. John W. Welch (Salt Lake City and Provo, UT: Deseret Book and FARMS, 1988), 255.

134. Welch and Parry, *The Tree of Life*, xiii.

135. Jaime Lara, "The Tree of Life in the Catholic Religious and Liturgical Imagination," in *The Tree of Life*, 171.

136. See Richard Oman, "The Tree of Life: A Cross-Cultural Perspective in Mormon Art," in *The Tree of Life*, 241–60.

The Thing Which I Have Seen: A History of Lehi's Dream in Visual Art

JENNIFER CHAMPOUX

1. Richard Bushman, "Art & Vision," Center for Latter-day Saint Arts keynote address (Zoom), July 26, 2020, available at https://youtu.be/wdxgtastkco.

2. The Book of Mormon Art Catalog, http://bookofmormonartcatalog.org.

3. George M. Ottinger, Journal, 1872, 197–98, Special Collections, Marriott Library, University of Utah, as quoted in Noel A. Carmack, "'A Picturesque and Dramatic History': George Reynolds's *Story of the Book of Mormon*," *BYU Studies Quarterly* 47, no. 2 (2008): 120.

4. See John Christopher Thomas, *A Pentecostal Reads the Book of Mormon: A Literary and Theological Introduction* (Cleveland, TN: CPT Press 2016), 329–32.

5. John W. Welch and Doris R. Dant, *The Book of Mormon Paintings of Minerva Teichert* (Provo, UT: BYU Studies, 1997), 60.

6. Now renamed the Church History Museum.

7. Richard G. Oman, "Lehi's Vision of the Tree of Life: A Cross-Cultural Perspective in Contemporary Latter-day Saint Art," *BYU Studies Quarterly* 32, no. 4 (1992): 19.

8. George Q. Cannon, "To the Artists of Utah," *Deseret Weekly* 40, no. 11 (March 8, 1890): 367.

9. Vern G. Swanson and Micah J. Christensen, *Arnold Friberg: The Book of Mormon Drawings* (Salt Lake City, UT: Anthony's Fine Art & Antiques, 2015), 13.

10. Vern Swanson, "The Book of Mormon Art of Arnold Friberg: Painter of Scripture," *Journal of Book of Mormon Studies* 10, no. 1 (2001): 29.

11. The numbers of Lehi's dream artworks in this essay are based on a list of 245 artworks found at The Book of Mormon Art Catalog, http://bookofmormonartcatalog.org. These artworks come from a variety of sources including the Church History Museum collection, online exhibitions by the Church (including the International Art Competitions), Church magazines and manuals, the Brigham Young University Museum of Art, the Springville Museum of Art, the Book of Mormon Central (now renamed Scripture Central) Art Contest online exhibitions, and the private collections of artists and individuals. While some images were likely not included in this compilation, the points of this essay are based on the overall trajectory of the art as seen in this robust sampling of Lehi's dream images, including the images most seen by Church members. I'm grateful to Laura Paulsen Howe and Carrie Snow for assistance in locating artworks in the Church History Museum collection.

12. Anthony Sweat, "Visualizing the Vision: The History and Future of First Vision Art," *BYU Studies Quarterly* 59, no. 2 (2020): 227, 230.

13. "LDS General Conference Corpus," https://lds-general-conference.org.

14. Oman, *Lehi's Vision of the Tree of Life*, 5.

15. The other two are "Lehi's Dream" by James C. Christensen and "The Tree of Life" by Jorge Cocco Santángelo. https://deseretbook.

com/p/17x28-tree-of-life-lehis-dream-framed-textured-paper?ref=Grid%20
%7C%20Search-2&variant_id=143163-framed.

16. Johan H. Benthin, as quoted in Oman, *Lehi's Vision of the Tree of Life*, 9.

17. It appeared on the cover of the *Ensign* and *Liahona* in August 2010; was featured in "The Tree of Life," *Ensign* June 1996 and "Tree of Life," *Liahona* September 1996; appeared on the back cover of *BYU Studies* in 1992; and is included in the Church History Museum online exhibition "The Vision of the Tree of Life," https://history.churchofjesuschrist.org/exhibit/tree-of-life?lang=eng#mv10.

18. Oman, *Lehi's Vision of the Tree of Life*, 30.

19. Oman, *Lehi's Vision of the Tree of Life*, 31.

20. "Family: A Proclamation to the World," *Ensign* 25 (November 1995), 102.

21. See Oman, *Lehi's Vision of the Tree of Life*; Sarah Jane Weaver, "A Shared Vision: Lehi's Dream of the Tree of Life," *Church News*, February 3, 1996, https://www.thechurchnews.com/archives/1996-02-03/a-shared-vision-lehis-dream-of-the-tree-of-life-134662; "Tree of Life: Lehi's Dream—A Shared Vision," *Liahona*, September 1996, https://www.churchofjesuschrist.org/study/liahona/1996/09/tree-of-life-lehis-dream-a-shared-vision?lang=eng; "The Tree of Life: Art Depicting Lehi's Dream and the Tree of Life," *Ensign*, June 1996, https://www.churchofjesuschrist.org/study/ensign/1996/06/the-tree-of-life-art-depicting-lehis-dream-and-the-tree-of-life?lang=eng.

22. Richard Oman, interview by author, June 29, 2021.

23. Richard Oman, email to author, July 1, 2021.

24. "I Beheld a Tree," *Ensign* January 2004, https://www.churchofjesuschrist.org/study/ensign/2004/01/i-beheld-a-tree?lang=eng.

25. "Our Heritage of Faith: Seventh International Art Competition," *Ensign*, August 2006, https://www.churchofjesuschrist.org/study/ensign/2006/08/our-heritage-of-faith?lang=eng.

26. Elder Daniel L. Johnson, "Hold Fast to the Rod," *Ensign*, February 2016, https://www.churchofjesuschrist.org/study/ensign/2016/02/hold-fast-to-the-rod?lang=eng.

27. Symbolic images are becoming more prominent in the Community of Christ too. The Community of Christ Temple in Independence, Missouri features a metal wall sculpture of a tree made by Turkish-American artist Suat Gurtan about 2005. This sculpture, however, does not allude to Lehi's dream and is instead representative of various scriptural references to God as a tree or vine. See "Independence Temple Self-guided Tour," Community of Christ, https://cofchrist.org/temple-tour/.

28. Alonzo L. Gaskill, *The Lost Language of Symbolism: An Essential Guide for Recognizing and Interpreting Symbols of the Gospel* (Salt Lake City, UT: Deseret Book, 2003), 7–8.

29. Matthew R. Brown and Paul Thomas Smith, *Symbols in Stone: Symbolism on the Early Temples of the Restoration* (American Fork, UT: Covenant Communications, 1997), 105.

30. Joseph M. Spencer, "How to Write Up a Revelation: Some Advice from Nephi," (unpublished manuscript, 2020).

31. See https://www.caseyjexsmith.com/2010.

32. "Tree of Life," Moeller Studios, https://www.moellerstudios.org/portfolio/tree-of-life/; Camille West, "New Tree of Life App Lets You Explore and Teach Lehi's Vision," *Church News*, January 8, 2020, https://www.churchofjesuschrist.org/church/news/new-tree-of-life-app-lets-you-explore-and-teach-lehis-vision?lang=eng.

33. Richard Oman, email to author, July 1, 2021.

34. Walter Rane, email to author, June 25, 2021.

35. Charles Swift, "Lehi's Vision of the Tree of Life: Understanding the Dream as Visionary Literature," *Journal of Book of Mormon Studies* 14, no. 2 (2005): 59.

36. Swift, "Lehi's Vision of the Tree of Life," 61.

37. Joseph M. Spencer, *1st Nephi: A Brief Theological Introduction* (Provo, UT: Neal A. Maxwell Institute, 2020), 27–29.

38. Swift, "Lehi's Vision of the Tree of Life," 56.

39. Rosalynde Welch, "How to Do Things with Doubt," *Journal of Book of Mormon Studies* 28 (2019): 238.

40. Jennifer Champoux, "Wise or Foolish: Women in Mormon Biblical Narrative Art," *BYU Studies Quarterly* 57, no. 2 (2018): 89.

41. Church History Museum online exhibition "The Vision of the Tree of Life," https://history.churchofjesuschrist.org/exhibit/tree-of-life.

42. Nan Shepherd, *The Living Mountain* (Canongate Books, 2008), Loc 514, Kindle.

43. Shepherd, *The Living Mountain*, Loc 1533.

44. James C. Christensen, "Artist's Notes," in Robert L. Millet and James C. Christensen, *Lehi's Dream* (Salt Lake City, Utah: Deseret Book, 2011), 69.

A Father's Plea

ROSE DATOC DALL

1. In each artist comment throughout this book, references to verses with no specified chapter or book of scripture will apply strictly to 1 Nephi 8.

Lehi and His Dream: A Relational Reading

BENJAMIN KEOGH

1. On Lehi's prayer as one of repentance, see Adam S. Miller, "Burnt Offerings: Favor, Afflictions, and the Mystery of God," in *A Dream, a Rock, and a Pillar of Fire: Reading 1 Nephi 1*, ed. Adam S. Miller (Provo: Neal A. Maxwell Institute, 2017), 17–23; on Lehi's quaking and trembling as evidence for his need for repentance, see Kylie Nielson Turley's "Symbolic Seeds and Separated Seeds: Unity and Division in Lehi's Dream" in this volume.
2. The interplay between disrelation and shame deserves more space than it can be given here. For a treatment of the interplay in the narrative of Genesis 3, see Simon Cozens and Christoph Ochs, "'Have You No Shame?' An Overlooked Theological Category as Interpretive Key in Genesis 3," *Journal of Theological Interpretation*, 13, no. 2 (2019): 186–199.
3. Thanks to my mother-in-law, Lorna Hale, for this insight.
4. On this, see Jesus' teachings in the Sermon on the Mount contained in Matthew 5:21–48, particularly verses 23–24.

Lehi's Parable of the Fruitful Tree

ROSALYNDE FRANDSEN WELCH

1. Royal Skousen tentatively identifies Christian Whitmer as the "Scribe 3" in whose handwriting the text of 1 Nephi 8 was written. See https://interpreter-foundation.org/publication-of-part-6-of-volume-3-of-the-critical-text-of-the-book-of-mormon. On the speculative dating of the translation, see John Welch, "Days Never to be Forgotten," *BYU Studies Quarterly* 57, no. 4 (2018).
2. Richard Bushman and Jed Woodworth, *Joseph Smith: Rough Stone Rolling* (New York: Alfred A. Knopf), 76.
3. On the Whitmer wheat fields, see "Lucy Mack Smith, History, 1844–1845, p. [8], bk. 8," p. [8], bk. 8, The Joseph Smith Papers, https://www.josephsmith-papers.org/paper-summary/lucy-mack-smith-history-1844-1845/100.
4. See Samuel Morris Brown, "Seeing the Voice of God: The Book of Mormon on Its Own Translation," in *Producing Ancient Scripture: Joseph Smith's Translation Projects in the Development of Mormon Christianity*, eds. Michael Hubbard MacKay, Mark Ashurst-McGee, Brian M. Hauglid (Salt Lake City: The University of Utah Press, 2020). Brant A. Gardner summarizes alternate models of the translation of the Book of Mormon in Brant A. Gardner, *The Gift and Power: Translating the Book of Mormon* (Salt Lake City: Greg Kofford Books, 2011), 147–56. It is premature to name any scholarly consensus on the precise cognitive and sensory mode of Joseph Smith's translation "by the gift and power of God."

5. Linguists refer to *lexical* or *semantic fields* in similar ways.

6. http://webstersdictionary1828.com/Dictionary/Wilderness.

7. An ancient Near Eastern historical context for Lehi's dream has been amply explored by scholars. See, for instance, Hugh Nibley, "Ezekiel 37:15–23 as Evidence for the Book of Mormon," in *An Approach to the Book of Mormon*, ed. John W. Welch, 3rd ed. (Salt Lake City: Deseret Book; Provo, UT: FARMS, 1988), 311–28. See also C. Wilford Griggs, "The Book of Mormon as an Ancient Book," in *Book of Mormon Authorship: New Light on Ancient Origins*, ed. Noel B. Reynolds (Provo, UT: FARMS, 1982), 75–101; Daniel C. Peterson, "Nephi and His Asherah" (2000), *Journal of Book of Mormon Studies* 9, no. 2; Dana Pike, "Lehi Dreamed a Dream: The Report of Lehi's Dream in Its Biblical Context," in *The Things Which My Father Saw: Approaches to Lehi's Dream and Nephi's Vision* (2011 Sperry Symposium), eds. Daniel L. Belnap, Gaye Strathearn, and Stanley A. Johnson (Provo, UT: Religious Studies Center, Brigham Young University; Salt Lake City: Deseret Book, 2011), 92–118.

8. In an effort to clarify my thesis, this formulation frames the division between biblical and antebellum American lexical worlds much too starkly. Even if it is the case, as I argue, that Joseph Smith draws on the lexical world of the early American farm to supply the semantic content of the words used to express Lehi's dream, there is no doubt that Smith's dictated language in 1 Nephi 8 continues to make frequent recourse to biblical words, phrases, and quotations.

9. For an example of an historical contextualization of Lehi's dream as an ancient Near Eastern text, see S. Kent Brown, "New Light from Arabia on Lehi's Trail," in *Echoes and Evidences of the Book of Mormon*, eds. Donald W. Parry, Daniel C. Peterson, and John W. Welch (Provo, UT: FARMS, 2002), 64. For an example of historical contextualization of the dream as an early American artifact, see Rick Grunder, "The Dream of the Iron Rod," PDF file taken from Entry 350, "Reynolds Arcade (Rochester, New York)," in *Mormon Parallels: A Bibliographic Source*, 2nd ed. (Lafayette, NY: Rick Grunder Books, 2014), 1367–1431; available at http://www.rickgrunder.com/parallels/mp350.pdf. Note that my essay employs an entirely different method of inquiry than these historicizing treatments.

10. Philip Barlow, *Mormons and the Bible: The Place of the Latter-day Saints in American Religion* (New York: Oxford University Press, 1991), 15.

11. For instance, 1 Nephi 8:8 quotes Psalm 51:1 (and Psalm 69:16), "according to the multitude of [thy] tender mercies." For more on this, see Kimberly Matheson's contribution to this volume.

12. See Webster's 1828 "Desert": http://webstersdictionary1828.com/Dictionary/desert.

13. Roderick Nash, *Wilderness and the American Mind*, 5th ed. (New Haven, CT: Yale University Press, 2014), 14.

14. Leland Ryken, James C. Wilhoit, and Tremper Longman III, *Dictionary of Biblical Imagery* (Intervarsity Press, 1998), 950.

15. Charles Swift, "Lehi's Vision of the Tree of Life: Understanding the Dream as Visionary Literature," *Journal of Book of Mormon Studies* 14, no. 2 (2005): 52–63.

16. Bruce W. Jorgensen, "The Dark Way to the Tree: Typological Unity in the Book of Mormon," in *Literature and Belief: Sacred Scripture and Religious Experience*, ed. Neal A. Lambert (Provo, UT: Religious Studies Center, Brigham Young University, 1981), 217–31. Available at https://rsc-legacy.byu.edu/archived/literature-belief-sacred-scripture-and-religious-experience/11-dark-way-tree-typological.

17. The most extensive exploration of the biblical context of Lehi's dream is Hugh W. Nibley, *Lehi in the Desert, The World of the Jaredites, There Were Jaredites*, eds. John W. Welch, Darrell L. Matthews, and Stephen R. Callister, vol. 5 in *The Collected Works of Hugh Nibley* (Salt Lake City: Deseret Book and FARMS, 1988).

18. See Hugh Nibley, *Lehi in the Desert* (Salt Lake City: Deseret Book and FARMS, 1988), 43–44.

19. It should be noted that the idea of a dark wilderness is not entirely absent in the Old Testament but is very unusual. Jeremiah 2:31 combines images of wilderness and darkness in close proximity: "O generation, see ye the word of the Lord. Have I been a wilderness unto Israel? a land of darkness? wherefore say my people, We are lords; we will come no more unto thee?"

20. Hugh Nibley suggests the iron rod is a staff or weapon. See Hugh Nibley, "Ezekiel 37:15–23 as Evidence for the Book of Mormon," in *An Approach to the Book of Mormon*, ed. John W. Welch, 3rd ed. (Salt Lake City: Deseret Book; Provo, UT: FARMS, 1988), 311–28. John Tvedtnes follows Nibley's suggestion. See John A. Tvedtnes, "Rod and Sword as the Word of God," *Journal of Book of Mormon Studies* 5, no. 2 (1996): 148–55. Daniel Peterson sees a connection between the rod of iron and the biblical injunction to "lay hold" on Wisdom in the book of Proverbs. See Daniel C. Peterson "Nephi and His Asherah," *Journal of Book of Mormon Studies* 9, no. 2 (2000), 24. https://scholarsarchive.byu.edu/jbms/vol9/iss2/4.

21. See Donald L. Enders, "The Joseph Smith, Sr., Family: Farmers of the Genesee," in *Joseph Smith: The Prophet, The Man*, eds. Susan Easton Black and Charles D. Tate Jr. (Provo, UT: Religious Studies Center, Brigham Young University, 1993), 213–225.

22. Shawna Norton, "Land as Regenerative Space in The Book of Mormon," *Journal of Book of Mormon Studies* 27 (2018): 190.

23. See Brian Donahue, *The Great Meadow: Farmers and the Land in Colonial Concord* (New Haven, CT: Yale University Press, 2007), 12.

24. Donahue, 15.

25. Nash, 146.

26. Nash, 24.

27. Nash, 45.

28. Donahue, 18–19.

29. "Landscape History of Central New England," Harvard Forest website, https://harvardforest.fas.harvard.edu/diorama-series/landscape-history-central-new-england.

30. Isaac Weld, *Travels Through the States of North America: And the Provinces of . . .*, vol. 1, 40–41. Accessed at https://books.google.com/books?id=iiQwAAA AYAAJ&lpg=PA39&ots=EF2yjyUt7t&dq=%2522unconquerable%2520avers ion%2520to%2520trees%2522&pg=PA39#v=onepage&q=%2522unconquera ble%2520aversion%2520to%2520trees%2522&f=false.

31. Lucy Mack Smith, *Biographical Sketches of Joseph Smith the Prophet, and his progenitors for many generations*, digital publication (Provo, UT: Brigham Young University Digital Collections, 2004), 70. Available at https://contentdm.lib.byu.edu/digital/collection/NCMP1820-1846/id/17401/.

32. Donahue, 20.

33. Quoted in Nash, 230.

34. Timothy Sweet, "American Pastoralism and the Marketplace: Eighteenth-Century Ideologies of Farming," *Early American Literature* 29, no. 1 (1994): 76.

35. See William Kerrigan, *Johnny Appleseed and the American Orchard: A Cultural History* (Baltimore, MD: John Hopkins University Press, 2012), 6.

36. Kerrigan, 10.

37. See Enders, question 4. See also Richard Lloyd Anderson, "The Whitmers: A Family that Nourished the Church," *Ensign*, August 1979. Accessed at https://www.churchofjesuschrist.org/study/ensign/1979/08/the-whitmers-a-family-that-nourished-the-church?lang=eng.

38. Kerrigan, 4.

39. Kerrigan, 82.

40. "Perspective: Surveying Land," *Nova Cæsarea: A Cartographic Record of the Garden State, 1666–1888*, Princeton University Library, Historic Maps Collection. Available at https://library.princeton.edu/njmaps/perspective.html.

41. Recently T. J. Uriona has suggested that the rod of iron should be historicized within the ancient near East as a shepherd's staff. See T. J. Uriona, "Rethinking the Rod of Iron," *BYU Studies Quarterly* 61, no, 3 (2022): 141–163.

42. Royal Skousen, *Analysis of Textual Variants of the Book of Mormon*, pt. 1, 1 Nephi 1–2 Nephi 10, 174–181.

43. Leland Ryken, *How to Read the Bible as Literature* (Grand Rapids, MI: Zondervan, 1984), 165.

44. See, for instance, Isaiah's parable of the Vineyard in Isaiah 5, the source of the agricultural imagery so prominent in biblical parables. On fathers and sons, see, of course, Luke 15, the parable of the Prodigal Son. On rich and poor, see Luke 16, the parable of the Rich Man and Lazarus. On houses and lands, see Luke 12, the parable of the Rich Fool.

45. N.T. Wright, *Jesus and the Victory of God* (Minneapolis, MN: Fortress Press, 1992), 180–181.

46. See Mark Wrathall, *Alma 30–63: A Brief Theological Introduction* (Provo, UT: Maxwell Institute, 2020).

47. Parable is related to allegory inasmuch as both genres employ figurative language to convey a partially or entirely concealed spiritual meaning. Allegory, however, is typically more schematic than parable, more formalized, and places greater importance on the referent behind its symbolic objects, often providing a key for the reader to decipher its veiled message. Nephi's vision of his father's dream, in 1 Nephi 11–15, is a typical allegory, as is his brother Jacob's allegory of the vineyard in Jacob 6. Considered on its own, by contrast, Lehi's dream contains no explanatory key to historical meaning and emphasizes the experiential, rather than symbolic, value of the narrative.

48. Botanical parables include the parables of the Sower (Matthew 13:1–23), the Hidden Treasure (Matthew 13:44), the Growing Seed (Mark 4:26–29), the Mustard Seed (Matthew 13:31–32), the Tares (Matthew 13:24–43), the Wicked Husbandmen (Matthew 21:33–46), and the Budding (Matthew 24:32–35) and Barren (Luke 13:6–9) Fig Trees. For a perceptive reflection on the relation between Lehi's dream and the parable of the Sower, see Jeffrey R. Holland, *Christ and the New Covenant* (Salt Lake City: Deseret Book, 1997), 161–62.

49. For a fascinating, if obscure, suggestion that the coming of the Day of the Lord may be contingent on timebound events, see Doctrine & Covenants 130:14–17.

50. Prophetic throne theophanies include Micaiah's (1 Kings 22:19), Isaiah's (Isaiah 6), and Ezekiel's (Ezekiel 1:26).

51. N.T. Wright, *Jesus and the Victory of God* (Minneapolis, MN: Fortress Press, 1992), 176.

52. Rosalynde Welch, "How to Do Things with Doubt," *Journal of Book of Mormon Studies* 28 (2019): 237–249.

53. See, for instance, Stephen H. Webb, "Mormonism Obsessed with Christ," *First Things*, February 2012.

Lehi's Dream: Desire for God and Endless Progress

REV'D DR. ANDREW R. TEAL

1. Of the many examples, consider God or angels coming to people in dreams (e.g., Gen. 20:3; 31:10; 37:5f; 40:5f; 41:7f; 42:9; Dan. 2; Joel 2:28).

2. Cf. especially Matthew's infancy account, and throughout his gospel: Matt. 1:20; 2:12–13; 2:19; 2:22; 27:19.

3. My own perspective, as an outsider-reader of this text, is as that of a priest and scholar from within the Church of England, nurtured by ancient and contemporary spiritual writings from the Eastern Orthodox and Western Catholic traditions as well as Anglican, Protestant, and Restored traditions. If this sounds rather a confused blend, it must be admitted that in many ways that is the case! Despite the Thirty-Nine Articles of Religion of the Book of Common Prayer, the Church of England has historically had no distinctive doctrines of its own, preferring the rule of prayer and therefore having a conciliatory identity. But— like all Christian denominations—it is marked by conflicts within a spectrum of perspectives and choices. It is in the interests of full disclosure, rather than defensiveness or apologetic, that this perspective is voiced, in the conviction that an ecumenical engagement with 1 Nephi 8 can illuminate the power and direction of this scripture and help Christian communities travel to authentic reconciliation.

4. Compare also the repeated motif of emissaries or spies in, for example, Mosiah 10:7, etc.

5. John H. Eaton, *The Psalms: A Historical and Spiritual Commentary with an Introduction and New Translation* (London & New York: Continuum, 2003), 132. For more on *hesed*, in addition to Eaton's magisterial and devotional 2003 work, see also his earlier, *Psalms* (London: SCM, 1967) Cf. Artur Weiser, *The Psalms* (London: SCM, 1962).

6. Cf. Richard Lyman Bushman, *Mormonism. A Very Short Introduction* (Oxford: Oxford University Press, 2008), 9; and see James 1:5.

7. Winston S. Churchill, *Hansard*, HC Deb., vol. 360, col. 1502, 13 May 1940.

8. Cf. St. Benedict of Nursia, *Rule*, ch.4:72, "finally, never despair of the mercy of God," trans. Patrick Barry OSB (Ampleforth, York: Ampleforth Abbey Press, 1997), 15.

9. Cf., for example, the excellent example of this genre, Christian Wiman, *My Bright Abyss: Meditation of a Modern Believer* (New York: Farrar, Strauss and Giroux, 2013).

10. An excellent example of a series of novels which eschews one-off encounters or disconnected soundbites is the series by Marilynne Robinson, especially her

Gilead, which like few other novels enables a graceful and sustained exploration of baptism, for example. *Gilead* (London: Virago, 2004).

11. Cf. Michael W. Holmes, *The Apostolic Fathers: Greek Texts and English Translations* (Grand Rapids, Michigan: Baker Academic, 2007), 3–20.

12. Cf. Julius Wellhausen, *Prolegomena to the History of Israel* (1878, 1883) e-text version Project Gutenberg at https://www.gutenberg.org/ebooks/4732. New Testament study reflected this academic pressure to move from evaluation of *theological* content into speculation about sources, for example, B. H. Streeter, *The Four Gospels: A Study in Origins* (London: MacMillan, 1927); and especially Rudolf Bultmann, *The History of the Synoptic Tradition*, trans. John Marsh (Oxford: Basil Blackwell, 1972); and *The Gospel of John*, trans. G. R. Beasley-Murray (Oxford: Basil Blackwell, 1971). There has, it is a relief to admit, been a significant shift to studies that are more respectful of the literary integrity of texts in this century.

13. Cf., for example, David Friedrich Strauss, *The Life of Jesus Critically Examined*, trans. G. Eliot, ed. P.C. Hodgson (London: SCM Press, 1973), especially "Introduction," §§1–16, and "Concluding Dissertation," §§144–52.

14. Cf. the discussion in Seán Burke, *The Death and Return of the Author: Criticism and Subjectivity in Barthes, Foucault, and Derrida* (Edinburgh: Edinburgh University Press, 2010).

15. Note, Friedrich Schleiermacher's pertinent observations and critique of this tyranny in his 1799 lectures, (ET) *On Religion: Speeches to Its Cultured Despisers*, trans. John Oman (New York: Harper Torchbooks, 1958).

16. Invented by Paul Ricœur, a hermeneutic of suspicion refers to one's reading a text skeptically for the purpose of its debunking or exposing.

17. Cf. the Norse Yggdrasil, an immense sacred tree at the heart of the universe, around which all else exists, in the Icelandic *Edda* poems. Cf. Jackson Crawford, ed., *The Poetic Edda: Stories of the Norse Gods and Heroes* (Indianapolis: Hackett Publishing, 2015).

18. Cf. the books *Bahir* and *Zohar*. Cf. John Woodland Welch and Donald W. Parry, *The Tree of Life: From Eden to Eternity* (Salt Lake City: Deseret Books & Provo, UT: Neal A. Maxwell Institute, BYU, 2011).

19. Frances M. Young, *Construing the Cross: Type, Sign, Symbol, Word, Action* (Eugene, Oregon: Cascade, 2015), 48. Augustine, also, accepts typological "spiritual" readings of the tree in Genesis, without abandoning its historical reality.

20. Frances M. Young, 48. Emphasis my own.

21. St. Ephrem the Syrian, *Hymns on Paradise*, trans. Sebastian Brock (Crestwood, New York: St. Vladimir's Seminary Press, 1990), 7:15.

22. St. Ephrem the Syrian, 7:17, emphasis my own.

23. Cf. Matt. 26:47–56 and parallels.

24. E.g., Ps. 2:9; Jere. 28:14; Rev. 2:27; 12:5; 19:15.
25. "Targum Pseudo-Jonathan" in Gary A. Anderson, *The Genesis of Perfection: Adam and Eve in Jewish and Christian Imagination* (Louisville: Westminster John Knox, 2001), 180.
26. Contrast, for example, Paul's epistle to the Galatians with the epistle of James.
27. Aaron Milavec, *The Didache: Text, Translation, Analysis, and Commentary* (Collegeville, Minnesota: Liturgical Press / Michael Glazier Book, 2003). The text was discovered in 1873 in a Greek convent in Istanbul by Archbishop Philotheos Bryennios (now Codex Hierosolymitanus 54). The *Didachē* seems to have much in common with the theological emphasis of Matthew's gospel but seems to have been "composed independently of any known gospel" (xiv) comparable to the Epistle to the Hebrews and representing "preserved oral tradition whereby mid-first-century house churches detailed the step-by-step transformation by which gentile converts were to be prepared for full active participation in their assemblies" (ix).
28. St. Irenaeus of Lyons, *On the Apostolic Preaching*, trans. John Behr (Crestwood, New York: St Vladimir Seminary Press, 1997). Referenced in Eusebius' *Ecclesiastical History* 5:36, the text was rediscovered in an Armenian version in 1904, by Archimandrite Karapet Ter-Mekerttschian in Erevan (ms 3710).
29. I am very pleased to be informed that the *Didachē's* doctrine of two paths is very familiar to the Latter-day Saint community through the work of Hugh Nibley and his intellectual heirs. *Didachē* 1:1, Greek text (own translation) in Milavec, 2.
30. *Didachē* 1:1–2:7, Greek text (own translation) in Milavec, 2–6.
31. *Didachē* 2:7, Greek text (own translation) in Milavec, 6.
32. *Didachē* 3:2, Greek text (own translation) in Milavec, 8.
33. Cf. *Didachē* 3, Greek text (own translation) in Milavec, 8f.
34. Cf. St. Irenaeus of Lyons, *On the Apostolic Preaching*, trans. John Behr (Crestwood, New York: St Vladimir's Seminary Press, 1997), introduction, 1–26.
35. St. Irenaeus of Lyons, 48.
36. St. Irenaeus of Lyons, 39–40.
37. St. Irenaeus of Lyons, 41.
38. John Bunyan, *The Pilgrim's Progress* (Pennsylvania: Franklin Library, 1976). Facsimile of the 1678 London edition of Nath. Ponder; reprint from the text edited Edmund Venables & Mable Peacock, permission of the Clarendon Press, Oxford.
39. Bunyan, 33.
40. Bunyan, 17.
41. Bunyan, 240.
42. Bunyan, 81.
43. Bunyan, 97.

44. Bunyan, 145.
45. Bunyan, 176.
46. Bunyan, 363.
47. Facsimile title page of the 1678 edition, Bunyan, 1.
48. Sarah Coakley, "Introduction—Gender, Trinitarian Analogies, and the Pedagogy of *The Song*" in *Re-Thinking Gregory of Nyssa*, ed. Sarah Coakley (Oxford: Blackwell, 2003), 1–13.
49. See especially Hans Boersma, *Heavenly Participation: The Weaving of a Sacramental Tapestry* (Grand Rapids, Michigan: Eerdmans, 2011), and Hans Urs von Balthasar, *Presence and Thought: An Essay on the Religious Philosophy of Gregory of Nyssa* (San Francisco, California: Ignatius Press—Communio Books, 1995).
50. Cf. G. W. H. Lampe, *A Patristic Greek Lexicon* (Oxford: Clarendon Press, 1978), 1077.
51. Cf. Boersma. Compare this project also with Mark Julian Edwards, *Origen against Plato* (London: Routledge, 2017).
52. Gregory of Nyssa, *Contra Eunomium* 8; II, 797 A, in von Balthasar, 38.
53. Gregory of Nyssa, *de Hominis Opificio* 13; I, 165 AC, in von Balthasar, 39.
54. Gregory of Nyssa, *de Hominis Opificio* 1; I, 128 C–129B, von Balthasar, 40.
55. Gregory of Nyssa, *Homily on Ecclesiastes* 1; I, 628 C, in von Balthasar, 43.
56. Gregory of Nyssa, *de Vita Mosis*, I, 301 C, in von Balthasar, 44–45.
57. Cf. Gregory of Nyssa, *On the Psalms*, 3; I, 444 ABC.
58. von Balthasar, 45, citing Gregory of Nyssa's *Homily on the Song of Songs*, 6 (I, 892).
59. Cf. William Blake, *The Marriage of Heaven and Hell: A Facsimile in Full Color* (Garden City, New York: Dover Fine Art, 1999).
60. W. H. Auden, "For the Time Being," in *Collected Poems*, ed. Edward Mendelson (London: Faber & Faber, 1994), 390.
61. W. H. Auden, 400.

The Tree of Knowledge and the Pedagogy of Lehi's Dream

KIMBERLY MATHESON

1. Grant Hardy, *Understanding the Book of Mormon: A Reader's Guide* (New York: Oxford University Press, 2010), 54.
2. By "pedagogy," I refer simply to the method and practice of teaching. Lehi's dream betrays anxieties about his success in teaching his sons and, in the end, shows readers something about how God teaches each of us.
3. John Hilton has also argued for a connection between 1 Nephi 8:8 and the book of Psalms although, curiously, he overlooks the tight link between this verse and

Psalm 51:1 and prefers instead to associate it with the looser parallel in Psalm 69:16. See John Hilton III, "Old Testament Psalms in the Book of Mormon," in *Ascending the Mountain of the Lord: Temple, Praise, and Worship in the Old Testament*, eds. David Rolph Seely, Jeffrey R. Chadwick, Matthew J. Grey (Provo, UT: Religious Studies Center, Brigham Young University, 2013), 291–311. For an excellent discussion of the phrase "tender mercies" in particular (including its appearance in Psalm 51:1), see Miranda Wilcox, "*Tender Mercies* in English Scriptural Idiom and in Nephi's Record," in *A Dream, A Rock, and a Pillar of Fire: Reading 1 Nephi 1*, ed. Adam S. Miller (Provo, UT: Neal A. Maxwell Institute, 2017), 75–110.

4. For the classic essay on the sin-significance of these sacrifices, see S. Kent Brown, "What Were Those Sacrifices Offered by Lehi?" in *From Jerusalem to Zarahemla: Literary and Historical Studies of the Book of Mormon* (Provo, UT: Religious Studies Center, Brigham Young University, 1998), 1–8.

5. For an especially thorough treatment of this resonance, see Matthew L. Bowen, "Not Partaking of the Fruit: Its Generational Consequences and Its Remedy," in *The Things Which My Father Saw: Approaches to Lehi's Dream and Nephi's Vision*, eds. Daniel L. Belnap, Gaye Strathearn, and Stanley A. Johnson (Provo, UT: Religious Studies Center, Brigham Young University, 2011), 240–63.

6. Charles Swift has written a dissertation on pedagogy and Lehi's dream. Though his intentions are more pragmatically oriented toward classroom instruction, his study is a unique and thorough treatment of 1 Nephi 8 in conjunction with pedagogical questions. See Charles L. Swift, "'I Have Dreamed a Dream:' Typological Images of Teaching and Learning in the Vision of the Tree of Life," PhD diss. (Brigham Young University, 2003). See also Swift, "'It Filled My Soul with Exceedingly Great Joy': Lehi's Vision of Teaching and Learning," in *The Things Which My Father Saw: Approaches to Lehi's Dream and Nephi's Vision*, eds. Daniel L. Belnap, Gaye Strathearn, and Stanley A. Johnson (Provo, UT: Religious Studies Center, Brigham Young University, 2011), 347–73.

7. In this light, it may be best to understand the discrepancy between Nephi's response to his father's dream and that of his brothers' in terms of two different *kinds* of desire, since Nephi also presents his relationship to the dream in terms of desire (1 Ne. 10:17; 11:2–3). The point of recounting Laman and Lemuel's discussion in 1 Nephi 15 may thus be to demonstrate that they lack the specific kind of desire that would motivate them to seek out a vision themselves, as Nephi had done.

8. This pedagogical difference between Nephi and Lehi may stem from a much more substantive difference in how each encounters revelation and the divine word. For a truly exceptional essay on these differences as reflected in each character's encounter with the Liahona, see Rosalynde Welch, "Lehi's Brass Ball:

Astonishment and Inscription," *Journal of Book of Mormon Studies* 29 (2020): 20–49.

9. Or, too, dreamscapes as places to work through our anxieties. See Joseph M. Spencer's essay on the dreamscape invoked by Jacob 7:26, "Weeping for Zion," in *Christ and Antichrist: Reading Jacob 7*, eds. Adam S. Miller and Joseph M. Spencer (Provo, UT: Neal A. Maxwell Institute, 2018), 81–110.

Symbolic Seeds and Separated Sons: Understanding Lehi's Dream as a Setting for Unity and Division

KYLIE NIELSON TURLEY

1. Sidney B. Sperry, *Book of Mormon Compendium* (Salt Lake City: Bookcraft, 1968), 113.

2. Sperry, *Book of Mormon Compendium*, 113.

3. See Genesis 1 and Genesis 6–8. See also Stephen G. Dempster, *Dominion and Dynasty: A Theology of the Hebrew Bible* (Downers Grove: IVP Academic, 2003).

4. Noel Reynolds, "Nephi's Outline," *BYU Studies Quarterly* 20:2 (1980): 140. Reynolds argues that the seeds in chapters 8 and 18 constitute one parallelism in a holistic chiasm encompassing 1 and 2 Nephi. While the seeds in 1 Nephi 18:24 are absolutely the seeds "which we had brought from the land of Jerusalem," the repetition "of every kind" is a tighter parallel with the creation.

5. Lehi's vision in 1 Nephi 8 and Nephi's vision in 1 Nephi 11–14.

6. Lehi's further visionary exhortations are found in 1 Nephi 10, and Nephi's explanation of Lehi's vision is found in 1 Nephi 15.

7. In 1 Nephi 9, Nephi interrupts the narrative to discuss writing (see 1 Nephi 9), and in 1 Nephi 16:10 the family is surprised to find the Liahona.

8. Charles Swift, "'It Filled My Soul with Exceedingly Great Joy': Lehi's Vision of Teaching and Learning," in *The Things Which My Father Saw: Approaches to Lehi's Dream and Nephi's Vision*, eds. Daniel L. Belnap, Gaye Strathearn, and Stanley A. Johnson (Salt Lake City and Provo, UT: Deseret Book and BYU Religious Studies Center, 2011), 358.

9. Richard Dilworth Rust, "Taste and Feast: Images of Eating and Drinking in the Book of Mormon," *BYU Studies Quarterly* 33:4 (1993): 744.

10. See 2 Nephi 3:11. Lehi tells Joseph that a seer will be born to the "*fruit* of thy loins" and have power to "bring forth [the Lord's] word unto the *seed* of thy loins."

11. Dana M. Pike, "Lehi Dreamed a Dream," in *The Things Which My Father Saw: Approaches to Lehi's Dream and Nephi's Vision*, eds. Daniel L. Belnap, Gaye Strathearn, and Stanley A. Johnson (Salt Lake City and Provo, UT: Deseret Book and BYU Religious Studies Center, 2011), 92–118.

12. *American Dictionary of the English Language*, s.v. "seed,"
    http://webstersdictionary1828.com/Dictionary/seed.

13. *American Dictionary of the English Language*, s.v. "fruit,"
    http://webstersdictionary1828.com/Dictionary/fruit.

14. Oddly, Lehi never refers to Jacob's seed. This may be because Lehi's words
    to Jacob change about halfway through his speech and begin referring to his
    "sons" rather than Jacob in particular. Indeed, this discussion seemingly merges
    back into the discussion with Laman and Lemuel and the sons of Ishmael in
    2 Nephi 1, which notably does not end with "Amen," as the other blessings /
    sermons do. In any case, Jacob "is redeemed," which insinuates his personal
    partaking of the fruit. Moreover, he has "beheld that in the fullness of time [the
    Redeemer] comes to bring salvation unto me," possibly an indication that Jacob
    has had a visionary experience similar to the tree of life vision (2 Ne. 2:3).

15. See Jacob 3:5–7, 10.

16. James T. Duke, "Word Pairs and Distinctive Combinations in the Book of
    Mormon," *Journal of Book of Mormon Studies* 12:2 (2003): 33.

17. Leland Ryken, *Words of Delight: A Literary Introduction to the Bible* (Grand
    Rapids: Baker Books, 1993), 180–181.

18. Duke, "Word Pairs and Distinctive Combinations in the Book of Mormon," 33.

19. Lexical study was found by English and Hebrew definitions. Syntactic study
    consisted of categorizing grammatical parts of speech, and semantical study was
    categorization as one of three choices: synonyms, antonyms, or complements.
    Complementary pairs are "words that have distinct yet reciprocal meanings, such
    as kings and queens, silver and gold, or bows and arrows." See Cynthia L. Hallen
    with Josh Sorenson and ELANG 324 students, "What's in a Word: Pairs and
    Merisms in 3 Nephi," *Journal of Book of Mormon Studies* 13:1–2 (2004): 152.

20. Hallen and Sorenson, "What's in a Word," 153.

21. See tables below.

22. Intriguingly, Jacob alludes to Lehi's dream but creates his own word pair, stating
    "our lives passed away like as it were unto us a dream, we being a *lonesome and
    solemn* people, wanderers, cast out from Jerusalem, born in tribulation, in a wil-
    derness . . ." (Jacob 7:26).

23. Noel B. Reynolds, "The Language of Repentance in the Book of Mormon,"
    Journal of Book of Mormon Studies 29 (2020): 197.

24. *American Dictionary of the English Language*, s.v. "come,"
    http://webstersdictionary1828.com/Dictionary/come.

25. *American Dictionary of the English Language*, s.v. "forth,"
    http://webstersdictionary1828.com/Dictionary/forth.

26. *American Dictionary of the English Language*, s.v. "partake,"
    http://webstersdictionary1828.com/Dictionary/partake.

27. Hallen and Sorenson, "What's in a Word," 153.

28. See Mosiah 12:23; 15:30; 3 Nephi 16:19, and 3 Nephi 20:34. See also Isaiah 52:9.

29. Adam Miller explores these verses in great depth, arguing that Lehi is offering a sacrifice in the desert outside of Jerusalem for some of the same reasons. See Adam S. Miller, "Burnt Offerings: Favor, Afflictions, and the Mysteries of God," *A Dream, a Rock, and a Pillar of Fire: Reading 1 Nephi 1*, ed. Adam S. Miller (Provo, UT: Neal A. Maxwell Institute, 2017), 17–29.

30. For example, Nephi speaks of a "land of their inheritance" in his vision in 1 Nephi 10:3, 13:15, and 13:30, and Lehi speaks of that land in 2 Nephi 1:5, 8 and 9.

31. See 2 Nephi 5:1–5.

32. For example, Lehi is uncertain whether he experienced a dream or a vision (1 Ne. 8:2), and Laman and Lemuel are not sure whether symbols are temporal or spiritual or both (1 Ne. 15:31).

33. Miller, "Burnt Offerings," 23.

34. Michaël Ulrich, "Joining the Heavenly Chorus," in *A Dream, a Rock, and a Pillar of Fire: Reading 1 Nephi 1*, ed. Adam S. Miller (Provo, UT: Neal A. Maxwell Institute, 2017), 112.

35. Parallels clearly exist, such as the following: Lehi finishes his vision telling Laman and Lemuel that Jerusalem "should be destroyed" and the inhabitants "carried away captive into Babylon" (1 Ne. 10:3), quoting his second vision verbatim (1 Ne. 1:13). In one vision, a man in a white robe "came and stood" before Lehi and then "spake and bade" him to follow (1 Ne. 8:5, 6), and in the other vision, a man with a "luster" brighter than the "sun at noon-day" (1 Ne. 1:9) "came and stood before" Lehi and "bade him that he should read" a book (1 Ne. 1:11). Both visions have "numberless concourses" in them (1 Ne. 1:8; 8:21), rare phrasing that Ulrich finds particularly meaningful.

36. Nephi's vision of his father's vision also has many parallels and is also incomplete. See 1 Nephi 14:28.

37. See 1 Nephi 2:6, 15; 3:1; 4:38; 5:7; 7:5, 21, 22 (2); 9:1; 10:16; 15:1; 16:6, 10, 12.

38. Swift, "Lehi's Vision," 58.

39. Swift, "Lehi's Vision," 59.

40. Joseph Spencer, *1st Nephi: A Brief Theological Introduction* (Provo, UT: Neal A. Maxwell Institute, 2020), 29.

41. Enos (Enos 1:21) and Limhi (Mosiah 7:22) refer to grain in wording that lightly echoes the seed sentence, and there are a number of straightforward references to literal grain in the Book of Mormon.

Notes

42. This title is taken from 2 Nephi 3:14, which includes commas to separate *Lord* from *of the fruit of my loins*. That punctuation makes sense, although removing the commas also makes sense, introducing readers to a new name for Christ.

43. Everything on this list is something described "as every kind" in the Book of Mormon: Seeds (1 Ne. 8:1), beasts in the forests (1 Ne. 18:25), animals (2 Ne. 5:11), sin (Jacob 3:12), cattle (Enos 1:21), tools (Jarom 1:8), riches (Mosiah 4:19), grain (Mosiah 7:22; Alma 11:7; 3 Ne. 6:2), ruins of buildings (Mosiah 8:8), weapons of war (Mosiah 10:1; Alma 2:12, 14; Alma 60:2; 3 Nephi 3:26), fruit (Mosiah 10:4), cloth (Mosiah 10:5; Hel. 6:13), fatlings (Alma 1:29), diseases (Alma 9:22), wild animals (Alma 22:31), trials and troubles (Alma 36:27), afflictions (Alma 56:16; Alma 60:3), flocks and herds (Alma 62:29; 3 Ne. 4:4), shields (Hel. 1:14), many books and many records (Hel. 3:15), precious ore (Hel. 6:11), precious things (Hel. 12:2). Jaredites, too, gather seeds of every kind for this journey (Ether 1:41, 2:3), and they like Noah also gather "flocks, both male and female, of every kind" (Ether 1:41). Christ suffers "pains and afflictions and temptations of every kind" (Alma 7:11).

44. This name-title is only used once in the Book of Mormon. See Alma 26:7.

45. Although I have argued that there are substantially more word pairs in Lehi's vision than those found by Hallen's students, this first chart shows intra- and intertextual usage of the six word pairs found by Hallen's students. See Hallen, "Pairs and Merisms," 153. (The data making up this chart, beyond the identification of the pairs themselves, are my own findings.)

46. Here I add new word pairs to those found by Hallen's students, as well as add inter- and intratextual data.

Returning to the Garden: *Augustine, Lehi, and the Arboreal Imagery of Eden*
TIMOTHY FARRANT

1. Augustine, *Confessions*, vol. 1, trans. C. Hammond (Cambridge, MA: Harvard University Press, 2014), bk. 2, 4(9), 72–75. Hereafter, cited as *Conf.*

2. *Conf.* bk. 2, 4(9) & 6(12), 72–73, 78–79. First Augustine states: "For I stole what I had already in plenty, and of far better quality." Later he reinforces this point by again saying: "I had plenty of better fruit."

3. *Conf.* bk. 2, 6(12) 78–79. Here Augustine states: "I plucked these only for the sake of thieving."

   An indication of the amount of scholarly attention provoked by the pear theft episode can be seen in the following articles: William Mann, "The Theft of the Pears," *Apeiron* 12, no. 1 (1978): 51–59; Leo Ferrari, "The Pear-Theft in

Augustine's 'Confessions,'" *Revue d'Etudes Augustiniennes Et Patristiques* 16, nos. 3–4 (1970): 233–242; Hans Schmid, "The Guise of the Bad in Augustine's Pear Theft," *Ethical Theory and Moral Practice* 21, no. 1 (2017): 71–89; Brooke Hopkins, "St. Augustine's 'Confessions': The Pear-Stealing Episode," *American Imago* 38, no. 1 (1981): 97–104; Mateusz Stróżyński, "The Fall of the Soul in Book Two of Augustine's Confessions," *Vigiliae Christianae* 70, no. 1 (2016): 77–100; Danuta Shanzer, "Pears before Swine: Augustine, Confessions 2.4.9," *Revue d'Etudes Augustiniennes Et Patristiques* 42, no. 1 (1996): 45–55; William Harmless, *Augustine in His Own Words* (Washington, D.C.: Catholic University America Press, 2010), 7; William Mallard, *Language and Love: Introducing Augustine's Religious Thought through the Confessions Story* (University Park, PA: Pennsylvania State University Press, 1994), 29–31; Gillian Evans, *Augustine on Evil* (Cambridge: Cambridge University Press, 1992), 3. It should be noted that Evans references Augustine's attitude to the pear theft in an introductory discussion on the nature of "evil." Whilst Evans does not expound on the episode further, she does demonstrate its centrality in Augustine's writings.

4. Terrence Malick, dir., *The Tree of Life*, 2011; Los Angeles: Cottonwood Pictures, River Road Entertainment, & Fox Searchlight Pictures.

5. Kenneth Johnson, "Yielding to the Enticings of the Holy Spirit," *Ensign* (November 2002): 89–91.

6. Johnson, 89–90. Whilst Kenneth Johnson nowhere cites Augustine's pear theft, his own act of theft from the apple orchard contains striking parallels to Augustine's. This is especially so when considering the *moral*, rather than merely physical, implications of eating what he describes as "unripe" fruit: "As I sat regretting what I had done, I realized that a feeling within me was producing even more discomfort than the unripe apples. The greater discomfort resulted from the realization that what I had done was wrong."

7. Whilst the vision itself does not *immediately* open with imagery-rich descriptions of the landscape, it is notable that the very verses that precede the vision describe humans living in a wilderness and gathering the seeds of grain and fruit. Moreover, a few chapters earlier, Lehi uses the imagery of valleys and rivers as a way to provide moral instruction for his sons. See 1 Nephi 8:1; 2:5–11.

8. What I mean here is that the amount of text used to convey the "dark and dreary" part of the vision in 1 Nephi 8:7–8 may not correlate with its prominence in the wider visionary narrative. The notion put forward by Lehi is that he is entirely consumed by darkness and travels in that state of darkness for many hours. Whilst this is described in only a few words, the actual experience of travelling for hours in darkness transcends the textual brevity as it appears on the printed page.

9. The emphasis is mine, unless indicated otherwise.

Notes

10. In a basic sense, ontology deals with defining "what is." When defining "what is" in relation to beings, such as humans and God, to state there is an ontological distinction is to state a fundamental difference in their mode of being. It is noteworthy that the very opening paragraph of Book 1 of Augustine's *Confessions* begins by drawing an ontological distinction between the Creator and his human creatures. In medieval theology, this contrast of ontology would later be taken up by Boethius in his assertion (consistent with Augustine's thought) that God exists beyond categorical distinctions, as well as in Avicenna's thought on "necessary existence" vs. "possible existence." The basic notion of a contrast of ontology would also form the very basis of Anslem's ontological argument which, too, posits God's unique nature in terms of "necessary existence," and one to which Anselm appeals when responding to the contemporary critique of Gaunilo of Marmoutiers. See *Conf.* bk. 1, 1(1), 1; Boethius, *The Theological Tractates and the Consolation of Philosophy*, trans. H.F. Stewart, Wilfred Mustard, and Edward Rand (London: W. Heinemann, 2003), 16–17; Avicenna, "Proof of the Necessary of Existence," *Basic Issues in Medieval Philosophy: Selected Readings Presenting the Interactive Discourses among the Major Figures*, ed. Richard Bosley and Martin Tweedale (Ontario: Broadview Press, 1997), 14–15; Anselm of Canterbury, "Reply to Gaunilo," *Anselm of Canterbury: The Major Works*, trans. G.R. Evans (Oxford: Oxford University Press, 2008), 101–122.

11. The imagery of a person calling others to follow is seen in the New Testament, where the person of Jesus begins to preach repentance by asking fishermen to forsake their maritime vocations, calling them with the words "follow me." See Matthew 4:17–24.

12. *Conf.* bk. 2, 2(2), 62–63.

13. This is a problem Augustine himself identifies in his *De doctrina christiana* where he states: " . . . ambiguity in scripture resides in either literal or metaphorical usages." See Augustine, *On Christian Teaching*, trans. R. Green (Oxford: Oxford University Press, 2008), bk. 3, 2, 68.

14. Harmless, *Augustine in His Own Words*, 7.

15. Compare *Conf.* bk. 2, 4(9), 72–73; Genesis 2:15–7.

16. Compare *Conf.* bk. 2, 4(9), 72–73; Genesis 2:15–7; 3:1–3. It is also noteworthy that a little earlier in Augustine's narrative, he references his adolescent companions, stating: "Looking what kind of companions I had as I journeyed over the wide roads of Babylon." *Conf.* bk. 2, 8, 70–71.

17. Compare: *Conf.* bk. 2, 6(12), 76–79; Genesis 3:4–5.

18. Leo Ferrari, "The Pear-Theft in Augustine's *Confessions*" in *Revue d'études augustiniennes et patristiques* 16, nos. 3–4 (January 1970): 233–4; 237–9. Here, Ferrari makes his approach clear: "The aim of the present study is to show that the pear-tree episode is much more significant than has been recognized. Indeed, it will

be argued that its sources lie very deep, both in Augustine's youthful past, and in his re-examined experience, particularly as interpreted in the light of his studies of the Scriptures; studies which intervened between the pear-stealing and the recount of it in the *Confessions*." And later in the same article, Ferrari expounds by stating: "It remains therefore that the Scriptures are polarized between two epochal events: the fall of mankind in Eden on the one hand, and on the other, the Recall of mankind to salvation through the death of Christ on the Cross. Significantly too, both events feature an important Tree—the former, the Tree of Knowledge of Good and Evil; the latter, the Tree of Life. What is of interest to present considerations is that the *Confessions* also contains two principal focal points. As a work of art, it is polarized between two powerful climaxes—the first is the domination of Sin as expressed in the strange episode of the theft of the pears; the second is the triumph of Grace which occurs at the memorable moment of Augustine's conversion in the garden."

19. Ferrari, "The Pear-Theft in Augustine's *Confessions*," 239–242.
20. *Conf.* bk. 8, 12(28), 408–409.
21. See both: *Conf.* bk. 8, 12(29), 408–409; and Ferrari, "The Pear-Theft in Augustine's *Confessions*," 239.
22. *Conf.* bk. 8, 12(30), 410–411.
23. Compare 1 Nephi 8:5; 8:11. Strikingly, in verse 5 the person is "dressed in a white robe," whereas in verse 11 the fruit of the tree is "white, to exceed all the whiteness that I had ever seen." See also: *Conf.* bk. 8, 12(29), 408–409.
24. In Eden, the forbidden tree is located in paradise, that is, the Garden of Eden. Since Augustine fashions his account after Eden, the forbidden pear tree is placed within the vicinity of what Augustine describes as "our vineyard." Likewise, Lehi's tree is located within a field of considerable dimensions. In addition to the Edenic imagery of the scene, the size of the field may indicate the presence of other unmentioned trees across this natural landscape. See Genesis 2:8–9; *Conf.* bk. 2, 4(9), 72–73; 1 Nephi 8:9–10.
25. Elsewhere in the 1 Nephi, the determinative pronoun "whose" is used with reference to both the branches of an olive tree: " . . . they should be compared like unto an olive tree, *whose* branches . . ."; and again the tree of life: " . . . that tree of life, *whose* fruit. . . ." See 1 Nephi 10:12; 15:36.
26. A detailed discussion of methods in linguistic allegory, in light of recent scholarship, is presented in a compelling article by Jacqueline Cordell, who traces their use in medieval literature. Here, the cognitive effort of the reader in discerning allegory is aided by the priming function of both grammatical encoding and context. See Jacqueline Cordell, "Priming Text Function in Personification Allegory: A Corpus-Assisted Approach," *Language and Literature* 27, no. 3 (2018): 219–220.

27. This point speaks to the theology of David Jenkins, who describes God in terms of divine transcendence within the very fabric of the world in which humans live: "He is a being-with and suffering-through God who again and again produces miracles of collaboration and transcendence, all in the midst of our suffering, struggling, and oddly glorious world." See David Jenkins, *God, Miracle and the Church of England* (London: SCM Press, 1987), 6–7.

28. It is important that after Nephi is shown the tree, and acknowledges the visual beauty of it, he then asks how to interpret this imagery. This eventually results in the Spirit speaking in dialogue about the Incarnation (which Nephi has little understanding of), and showing, in vision, the events of the virgin birth and the ministry of Jesus, declaring "Look and behold the condescension of God!" See 1 Nephi 11:9–28.

29. This is seen most clearly when Nephi is able to see the love of God in the humanity of Jesus, rather than understanding it as an abstract concept. Compare 1 Nephi 11:16–7 with 26–34.

30. This neatly corresponds to the earlier observation about the symmetry between the location of the pear tree in Augustine's *Confessions* and the forbidden fruit tree in Eden. See above.

31. Whilst Latin has neither a definite nor indefinite article, the inclusion of "omnis" before "good tree," and absence of "omnis" before "evil tree" may be drawing upon the fact that only one tree in the midst of Eden was forbidden: "Of the fruit of the trees that are in paradise we do eat, but of the fruit of the tree which is in the midst of paradise, God hath commanded us that we should not eat and that we should not touch it, lest perhaps we die." See also Genesis 3:2–3. For a usable and modern edition of the Vulgate, together with a facing English translation (mostly inspired by Challoner's revision of the Douay-Rheims Version), see Angela Kinney, ed., *The Vulgate Bible: Dumbarton Oaks Medieval Library*, vols. 1–4 (Cambridge, MA: Harvard University Press, 2013).

32. Peter Abelard, *An Exposition on the Six-Day Work*, trans. W. Zemler-Cizewski (Turnhout: Brepols Publishers, 2011), lines 428–460, 108–114.

33. Author's note: I have sometimes seen "postlapsarian" erroneously interpreted as the period following the biblical flood of Noah. For precision, the term actually denotes the period following, and characterised by, the fall of Eve and Adam as presented in the Bible.

34. Abelard, *An Exposition on the Six-Day Work*, 103–4.

35. For further insights on right relationships and the creative order, see the fascinating contribution by Benjamin Keogh in this volume.

36. Matthew 7:14. It is in the context of the paths that lead to destruction and the paths that lead to life that Jesus speaks about trees and fruit. Here, there are

striking parallels with Lehi's strait and narrow path and the Tree of Life. On this, see the discussion below.

37. There is some discussion around the words "straight" and "strait" in the Book of Mormon. In Augustine, however, the adjective *angusta, -us, -um* is used convey the "narrow" gate and, in Matthew 7 of the Vulgate, both the adjectives *angusta, -us, -um* and *arta, -us, -um* are used to describe the "narrow" gate and "strait" path. Curiously, *angusta* and *arta* can each be translated as "strait." Whilst Noel Reynolds and Royal Skousen trace the etymology of "strait" back to the Latin term *strictus*, it is not this term that appears in Matthew 7 of the Vulgate. Further, in his *De doctrina christiana*, Augustine favours the phrase *angustam portam* when referring to the "narrow gate," with no citation of either *arta* or *stricta* in relation to paths. See Matthew 7:14 (of the Vulgate); *Conf.* bk. 8, 1(1), 354–355; Augustine, *De doctrina christiana*, trans. Roger Green (Oxford: Oxford University Press, 1996), bk. 2, 24(60), 84. See also Noel Reynolds and Royal Skousen, "Was the Path Nephi Saw 'Strait and Narrow' or 'Straight and Narrow,'" *BYU Faculty Publications* (2001), 1487.

38. This point in Augustine is strengthened by the observation that book 2 of the *Confessions*, which contains the pear theft episode, has allusions to the fall through the imagery of thorns. For instance, when Augustine describes his sixteenth year, he declares: "Thorny growths of sexual immorality sprouted up higher than my head, and there was no hand to uproot them." Later in book 8, when Augustine writes how God "delivered me from the chains of sexual desire," he does so by invoking the imagery of "pass[ing] through his narrow gate," and entering the Milan garden with his friend, Alypius: "There was a little garden at our lodgings. . . . So I withdrew into the garden, and Alypius followed in my footsteps." See *Conf.* bk. 2, 3(6), 66–67; bk. 8, 1(1), 354–355; 6(13), 378–379; 8(19), 390–393.

It is also noteworthy that the idea of returning to the garden, present in Lehi, has been put forward by Corbin Volluz, who asserts: "The Play ends where it begins—the Garden of Eden and the tree of life." See Corbin Volluz, "Lehi's Dream of the Tree of Life: Springboard to Prophecy," *Journal of Book of Mormon Studies* 2, no. 2 (July 1993): 36.

39. Augustine, *De doctrina christiana*, bk. 2, 24(60), 84–85.

40. See Matthew 26:17–29; 27:29. It is quite significant that after the bread is broken, and wine is drunk, Jesus says to his disciples in verse 29: "I will not drink from henceforth of this *fruit of the vine* until that day when *I shall drink it new with you in the kingdom of my Father.*"

41. *Conf.* bk. 8, 8(19), 390–393.

42. Before Lehi eats of the fruit of the tree, he becomes aware of his dark and dreary state. It is striking that this same pattern follows others who eat, with Lehi first

reporting: " . . . there arose a mist of darkness" moments before he reports: " . . . I beheld others pressing forward . . . even until they did come forth and partake of the fruit of the tree. . . ." See 1 Nephi 8:7–11; 22–24.

43. The symmetry between Lehi's fruit tree and the fruit tree of Eden has been noted in Latter-day Saint scholarship. A striking example can be found in the fourth chapter of Terryl Givens's accessible introduction to the Book of Mormon. See Terryl Givens, *The Book of Mormon: A Very Short Introduction* (New York: Oxford University Press, 2009), 61.

   Further, that the tree of Lehi's vision stands in a field, and that Augustine is converted beneath a fig tree in a Milan garden, points the reader back toward the Garden of Eden—where they again recognise the presence of God. See the discussion above (where this reading is first suggested).

   Further still, the interpretation that God condescends to this world, articulated through the imagery of the tree, is one we find in Nephi's later dialogue with the "Spirit of the Lord." This same idea of condescension (to the suffering of the world through the virgin birth) is expressed later in the Book of Mormon when Alma preaches to the people of Gideon, instructing them to " . . . walk in his paths, which are straight." See 1 Nephi 11:16–26, Alma, 7:9–11. It should be noted that the use of the word "straight" rather than "strait" in Alma (in relation to paths) may be a typographical error. For a more detailed discussion on word and spelling changes (from the original manuscript of the Book of Mormon to present versions), see Noel Reynolds and Royal Skousen, "Was the Path Nephi Saw 'Strait and Narrow' or 'Straight and Narrow,'" no. 1487.

44. Here, when Lehi beckons to Sariah, Sam, and Nephi, they simply come to Lehi, and eat the fruit.

45. Compare 1 Nephi 8:9–10; with 19–20.

46. Beginning with verse 29, which reads: "And now I, Nephi, do not speak all the words of my father . . . ," there is a shift in narrator. Earlier verses see Lehi speak about his vision in the first person (in a variety of tenses). However, from verse 29 onwards, Nephi begins to speak in the first person and then refers to his father's experience in the third person: " . . . he saw other multitudes . . . he also saw other multitudes. . . . These are the words of my father. . . ." Whilst this may indicate that Nephi (at least in terms of the narrative) is copying an earlier version his father wrote, it also indicates greater complexity in an original version which, in turn, affords the modern exegete greater license when discerning implicit meaning.

47. In book 6 of his *Confessions*, Augustine credits Ambrose (who was part of the Alexandrian tradition) for transforming Augustine's approach to scripture, especially that of the Old Testament. Moving away from his former position, which was to be skeptical of scriptural claims, Augustine goes on to say that Ambrose:

"... took away the mystical veil and opened the spiritual sense of things which seemed, according to the letter, to inculcate what was unreasonable." See *Conf.* bk. 6, 4(6), 246–249.

48. On this, see Beryl Smalley, *The Study of the Bible in the Middle Ages* (Notre Dame, Indiana: University of Notre Dame Press, 1978), 1–36. Other relevant overviews include the more recent Duncan Robertson, *Lectio Divina: The Medieval Experience of Reading* (Collegeville, Minnesota: Liturgical Press, 2011), 38–71.

49. Both Smalley and Robertson write chapter sections on "Letter and Spirit." See Smalley, *Study of the Bible*, 1–26; Robertson, *Lectio Divina*, 38–43.

50. Robertson, *Lectio Divina*, 45-48. Here, Robertson demonstrates this in relation to Origen's *On First Principles*, which initiated a tradition of reading across several exegetes in western Christendom. See references above.

51. Hugh of St. Victor, *Didascalicon: A Medieval Guide to the Arts*, trans. Jerome Taylor (New York: Columbia University Press, 1991), bk. 6, ch. 3, 135–139.

52. In Hugh, the term *historia* incorporates both biblical history and the *literalis sensus* (the literal sense of words in order). In this, he adopts the exegetical terminology of Gregory the Great through the terms *historia, allegoria,* and *tropologia.* See Robertson, *Lectio Divina*, 215–216; 222.

    Whilst not always using the same terminology, Hugh's notion of "historia" is also found in Augustine, as both authors respectively refer to the importance of grammar when beginning to understand scripture, analogous to mastering the alphabet before learning to read. See Augustine, *On Christian Teaching*, preface, 7–11, 4–5; Hugh, *Didascalicon*, bk 6, ch. 3, 136.

53. Robertson, *Lectio Divina*, 41. It is here that Robertson acknowledges the confusion sometimes caused by the fact that the literal/historical sense can also convey figures, tropes, and metaphor—a term coined by Denys Turner as "metaphoricism."

    Also see Rowan Williams, "The Literal Sense of Scripture," *Modern Theology* 7, no. 2 (January 1991): 123–4. Here, Williams explores the thought of Thomas Aquinas to make the point that the obvious intention of the author can be seen as the "literal," a sense that extends beyond what can be considered an actual event or occurrence in time. To quote Williams: "As Thomas makes clear, the literal sense is not dependent on a belief that all scriptural propositions uncomplicatedly depict real states of affairs detail by detail; it can and does include metaphor within the literary movement that leads us into the movement of God within the time of human biography."

54. It may be more common for exegetes to use the term "spiritual sense" from the Latin *sensus spiritualis*. However, the idea of a "figurative" sense that incorporates the broader idea of the spiritual and thus avoids the complexity of defining the spiritual sense according to its subtypes may be useful for the purposes of this

chapter. It is also noteworthy that such use of the term *figura* is found in book 2 of Augustine's *De doctrina christiana* where he states that only when knowing the nature of names or things can "figurative expressions in scripture become quite clear." See Augustine, *On Christian Teaching*, bk. 2, 24(59), 44. Again, for the Latin terms, see Green's edition of both the Latin and the facing translation: Augustine, *De doctrina christiana*, bk. 2, 24(59), 82.

55. In his *The Literal Meaning of Genesis*, Augustine speaks about both the tree of knowledge of good and evil and the rivers of paradise maintaining both their literal reality and their deeper metaphorical (and figurative) significance. For instance, in relation to Adam partaking of the fruit and learning the difference between obedience and disobedience, Augustine writes: " . . . this too is to be taken not just as a metaphor but as a real tree. . . ." Later, with respect to the rivers of paradise, Augustine emphasises a similar relationship between the literal and the figurative: " . . . we should let ourselves be advised to take all the rest to begin with according to the strict literal sense and not to assume that it is being talked about figuratively, but that the things and events which are being related both exist and also stand figuratively for something else." See Augustine, "The Literal Meaning of Genesis," in *On Genesis*, trans. E. Hill (Hyde Park, New York: New City Press, 2013), bk. 8, 6(12)–7(14), 354–355.

56. Lehi's vision appears in 1 Nephi 8; and Nephi's figurative exposition of it begins in 1 Nephi 11. The ninth chapter, therefore, immediately follows Lehi's vision, and together with chapter 10 (on how the mysteries of God may be revealed to human readers) prefatorily guide the reader to the expositions beginning in chapter 11.

57. On this approach to reading, see the section titled "Reading Beyond Reading" in Robertson's monograph: Robertson, *Lectio Divina*, xix–xxi.

58. The wilderness-dwelling Lehi and the quest for a new promised land is first introduced in the second chapter of 1 Nephi. See 1 Nephi 2:1–20.

59. It is striking that Lehi's first recorded vision occurs within the walls of Jerusalem. See 1 Nephi 1:4–12. The vision Lehi receives occurs in " . . . his own house at Jerusalem." Later, the walls of Jerusalem are introduced when Nephi enters again, seeking Laban. See 1 Nephi 4:4.

60. It is significant that later in the Book of Mormon, Alma recommends this sort of reading of the narrative events of the small plates of Nephi to his son, Helman. For example, when speaking about the Liahona and Lehi's travels in the wilderness, Alma says: "And now my son, I would that ye should understand that these things are not without a shadow. . . . For just as surely as this director did bring our fathers, by following its course, to the promised land, [so too] shall the words of Christ, if we follow their course, carry us beyond this *vale of sorrow* into

a far better land of promise." See Alma 37:43–5. I should credit Joseph Spencer here, who brought this passage to my attention.

61. My approach here is inspired by the "Solar Ethics" of Don Cupitt that look not to the otherworldly but to the actual human world. See Don Cupitt, *Solar Ethics* (London: SCM Press, 1995), 16.

62. On the interest of patristic scholars in Augustine's pear theft, see footnote 3 above.

63. Abelard, *An Exposition on the Six-Day Work*, 112–113.

The Tree of Life: Cacophony, Risk, and Discernment

TERRYL GIVENS

1. See on this point as two examples, B. R. Rees: in the early fifth century, "a *new orthodoxy* sprung out of Augustine's head" (my emphasis). Brinley Rees, *Pelagius: Life and Letters* (Woodbridge, UK: Boydell, 1991), 25. Ali Bonner agrees that "Augustine and his allies installed as orthodoxy a much more novel Augustinian" gospel than anything Pelagius represented. Dominic Keech, "Review of Ali Bonner, *The Myth of Pelagianism*" (Oxford: Oxford University Press, 2018), *Journal of Theological Studies* (10 December 2019): 374.

2. Pelagius, "Confession of Faith," Patristics in English, http://www.seanmultimedia.com/Pie_Pelagius_Confession_Of_Faith.html.

3. Stuart Squires, *The Pelagian Controversy: An Introduction to the Enemies of Grace and the Conspiracy of Lost Souls* (Eugene, OR: Pickwick, 2019), 282.

4. Squires, *Pelagian Controversy*, 283.

5. Martin Luther, quoted in Roland Bainton, *Here I Stand: A Life of Martin Luther* (New York: Abingdon, 1950), 65.

6. Cited in Richard Marius, *Martin Luther: The Christian Between God and Death* (Cambridge, MA: Harvard University Press, 1999), 192–93.

7. Westminster Confession 18.1, 2, in Jaroslav Pelikan and Valerie Hotchkiss, *Creeds and Confessions of Faith in the Christian Tradition* (New Haven: Yale University Press, 2003), 2:627–28.

8. John Wesley, May 24, 1738, in *The Heart of Wesley's Journal* (New Canaan, Connecticut: Keats, 1979), 43.

9. David W. Grua et al., eds., *The Joseph Smith Papers, Documents, Volume 12: March–July 1843* (Salt Lake City: Church Historian's Press, 2021), 186.

10. Oliver Cowdery to W. W. Phelps, *Messenger & Advocate* 1, no. 3 (December 1834): 43.

11. Karen Lynn Davidson et al., eds. *Joseph Smith Papers: Histories, Volume 1* (Salt Lake City: Church Historian's Press, 2012), 11–13.

12. Adolf von Harnack, *History of Dogma*, trans. William M'Gilchrist (London: Williams & Norgate, 1899), 6:133.

13. In this chapter, references to verses with no specified chapter or book of scripture will apply strictly to 1 Nephi 8.

14. Graham Greene, *The Power and the Glory* (New York: Penguin, 2015), 69.

15. *The Shepherd of Hermas* 1, no. 1, trans. Joseph M.-F. Marique, *The Apostolic Fathers* (Washington, D.C.: Catholic University of America Press, 1947), 1:235.

16. Origen, *On First Principles: A Reader's Edition* 1.6.3, trans. John Behr (New York: Oxford University Press, 2019), 57.

17. Franklin D. Richards, "Words of the Prophets," 24. Several online sources reference this booklet, housed in the Church History Library.

18. *Joseph Smith Papers: Histories* 1:212.

19. "For us, the scriptures are not the ultimate source of knowledge. . . . The ultimate knowledge comes by revelation." Dallin H. Oaks, "Scripture Reading, Revelation, and Joseph Smith's Translation of the Bible," in *Plain and Precious Truths Restored: The Doctrinal and Historical Significance of the Joseph Smith Translation*, ed. Robert L. Millet and Robert J. Matthews (Salt Lake City: Bookcraft, 1995), 2. Elder Jeffrey R. Holland echoed: "The scriptures are not the ultimate source of knowledge for Latter-day Saints. They are manifestations of the ultimate source. The ultimate source of knowledge and authority for a Latter-day Saint is the living God. The communication of those gifts comes from God as living, vibrant, divine revelation." Jeffrey R. Holland, "My Words Never Cease," general conference, April 2008, https://www.churchofjesuschrist.org/study/general-conference/2008/04/my-words-never-cease?lang=eng. Joseph himself referred to "many things in the Bible which do not . . . accord with the revelation of the Holy Ghost to me." Andrew F. Ehat and Lyndon W. Cook, eds., *The Words of Joseph Smith* (Orem, UT: Grandin Book Company, 1991), 211.

20. "Apostles and Prophets," *Didache* 3.

21. Cited in Elaine Pagels, *Adam, Eve, and the Serpent* (New York: Vintage, 1989), 138.

22. "Prove," Webster's 1828 Dictionary, http://webstersdictionary1828.com/Dictionary/prove.

23. On this point, see the words of Reformers like Luther and Calvin alike, cited in Fiona Givens and Terryl Givens, *All Things New: Rethinking Sin, Salvation, and Everything in Between* (Meridian, ID: Faith Matters, 2020), 49–50.